PENGUIN BOOKS

The Penguin French Phrasebook

Jill Norman enjoys exploring language, speaks several
languages and has travelled widely. Jill also created the
Penguin Cookery Library in the 1960s and 1970s, bringing
many first-class authors to the list. She has written several
award-winning books on food and cookery and is a leading
authority on the use of herbs and spices. She is the literary
trustee of the Elizabeth David estate, and was Mrs David's
publisher for many years.

D0029421

THE PENGUIN
FRENCH
PHRASEBOOK

Fourth Edition

Jill Norman
Henri Orteu
Silva De Benedictis

PENGUIN BOOKS

PENGUIN BOOKS

Published by the Penguin Group
Penguin Books Ltd, 80 Strand, London WC2R 0RL, England
Penguin Group (USA) Inc. , 375 Hudson Street, New York, New York 10014, USA
Penguin Group (Canada), 90 Eglinton Avenue East, Suite 700, Toronto, Ontario, Canada M4P 2Y3
(a division of Pearson Penguin Canada Inc.)
Penguin Ireland, 25 St Stephen's Green, Dublin 2, Ireland (a division of Penguin Books Ltd)
Penguin Group (Australia), 707 Collins Street, Melbourne, Victoria 3008, Australia
(a division of Pearson Australia Group Pty Ltd)
Penguin Books India Pvt Ltd, 11 Community Centre, Panchsheel Park, New Delhi – 110 017, India
Penguin Group (NZ), 67 Apollo Drive, Rosedale, Auckland 0632, New Zealand
(a division of Pearson New Zealand Ltd)
Penguin Books (South Africa) (Pty) Ltd, Block D, Rosebank Office Park,
181 Jan Smuts Avenue, Parktown North, Gauteng 2193, South Africa

Penguin Books Ltd, Registered Offices: 80 Strand, London WC2R 0RL, England

www.penguin.com

First edition 1968
Second edition 1978
Third edition 1988
This revised and updated edition published 2013
010

Set in 9/12pt TheSans and TheSerif
Typeset by Jouve (UK), Milton Keynes
Printed in England by Clays Ltd, St Ives plc

ISBN: 978–0–141–03906–0

www.greenpenguin.co.uk

MIX
Paper from
responsible sources
FSC® C018179
www.fsc.org

Penguin Books is committed to a sustainable
future for our business, our readers and our planet.
This book is made from Forest Stewardship
Council™ certified paper.

CONTENTS

INTRODUCTION

This series of phrasebooks includes words and phrases essential to travellers of all kinds: the business traveller; the holidaymaker, whether travelling alone, with a group or the family; and the owner of a house, an apartment or a time-share. For easy use the phrases are arranged in sections which deal with specific situations and needs.

The book is designed to help those who never had the opportunity to learn French and it will be an invaluable refresher course for those whose knowledge has gone rusty.

Pronunciation is given for each phrase and for all words in the extensive vocabulary. See pp xi–xv for the pronunciation guide which should be read carefully before starting to use the book.

For those who would like to know a little more about the French language, a brief survey of the main points of its grammar is provided at the end of the book (pp. 262–274).

Some of the French phrases are marked with an **asterisk*** – these give an indication of the kind of reply you might get to your questions, and of questions you may be asked.

PRONUNCIATION

The pronunciation guide is intended for people with no knowledge of French. As far as possible the system is based on English pronunciation. This means that complete accuracy may sometimes be lost for the sake of simplicity, but the reader should be able to understand French pronunciation, and make himself understood, if he reads this section carefully.

Vowels
French vowels are much purer than English.

a	as 'a' in apple	symbol a	famille (fa-mee-y)
ai, e	as 'e' in pen	symbol e	mettre (metr) vinaigre (vee-negr)
è, er	as 'ai' in pair	symbol ai	père (pair) travers (tra-vair)
é, er, ez	as 'ay' in pay	symbol ay	élastique (ay-las-teek) marcher (mar-shay)
e, eu	this is like the vowel sound in 'the'	symbol eʳ	le, je (leʳ, zheʳ) mercredi (mair-kreʳ-dee) feu (feʳ)

eu +l, r	not an English sound, but it is a little like the sound in her or in burr without sounding the r	symbol œ	beurre (bœr) seul (sœl)
i	as 'ee' in meet NB i before e is usually pronounced 'y'	symbol ee	merci (mair-see) fermier (fair-myay)
o	as 'o' in olive	symbol o	poste (post) pomme (pom)
o, au, eau	as 'oh'	symbol o (h)	chaud (sho) eau (oh)
ou	as 'oo' in moon	symbol oo	ouvert (oo-vair) tout (too)
u	not an English sound; round the lips and push them forwards as though to say 'oo' and try to say 'ee'	symbol u^e	rue (ru^e) musée (mu^e-say)
oi	as 'wa'	symbol wa	voiture (vwa-tu^{e}r)
ui	as 'we'	symbol we(e)	pluie (plwee) oui (we)

Nasal sounds

These sounds should be made through the nose, but without pronouncing the 'n'.

an (m) en (m)	as 'an' in quantity	symbol ah^n	manger (mah^n-zhay) vent (vah ^{n})
on (m)	as 'on' in prong or 'aun' in laundry	symbol o^n	on (o^n) pont (po^n)
ain (m), in (m)	as 'an' in anger	symbol a^n	faim (fa^n) vin (va^n)
ien (m)		symbol ya^n	bien (bya^n)
un (m)	something like 'ur' in urn or burnt	symbol e^n	brun (bre^n) un (e^n)
ing	as in English	symbol **ing**	camping (kah^n-ping)

Consonants

ch	as 'sh' in ship	symbol **sh**	chercher (shair-shay)
j, g+e, i	as 's' in pleasure	symbol **zh**	garage (garazh)
g+a, o, u	as 'g' in good	'g' is sometimes followed by 'h' to make this clearer in the pronunciation guide	guide (gheed)

gn	as 'ny' in canyon	symbol **n-y**	peigne (peny)
h	not pronounced		hôtel (otel)
ill	pronounced as 'y'	symbol **ee-y**	fille (fee-y)
ail	pronounced as 'y'	symbol **a-y**	travail (tra-va-y)
euil	pronounced as 'y'	symbol **oe-y**	feuille (foe-y)
eil	pronounced as 'y'	symbol **e-y**	soleil (so-le-y)
qu	always pronounced 'k' not 'kw' as in English	symbol **k**	qualité (ka-lee-tay)
r	is rolled more than in English		
s	as 's' in slip	symbol **s**	sucre (su^e kr)
	as 's' in visit	symbol **z**	visite (vee-zeet)
	final 's' is not pronounced (unless the next word starts with a vowel or silent '**h**')		trois femmes (trwa fam) trois autos (trwa zo-toh) trois hommes (trwa zom)

The final consonant of a French word is not normally pronounced. However, if the next word begins with a vowel or silent 'h', the final consonant is then pronounced as the first sound of that word, e.g. les Anglais – layzah^n-gle.

French has no stress as in English. It has a musical inflexion which runs throughout a sentence rather than individual words. Syllables have more or less equal value (unlike in English), although the last pronounced syllable is sometimes very lightly stressed. Avoid anything resembling strong English stress, but you can give a little weight to the end of French words. (Compare English 'Canada', with the stress on the first syllable, with French 'Canada', ka-na-da, where stress is equal on all three syllables.)

The French Alphabet

A	a	**H**	ash	**O**	oh	**V**	vay
B	bay	**I**	ee	**P**	pay	**W**	doobl-vay
C	say	**J**	zhee	**Q**	ku^e	**X**	eex
D	day	**K**	ka	**R**	ehr	**Y**	ee-grek
E	e^r	**L**	el	**S**	es	**Z**	zed
F	ef	**M**	em	**T**	tay		
G	zhay	**N**	en	**U**	u^e		

ESSENTIALS

First Things

Key Phrases		
Yes	**Oui**	*Wee*
No	**Non**	*No^n*
OK	**D'accord**	*Da-kor*
Please	**S'il vous plaît**	*Seel-voo-ple*
Thank you	**Merci**	*Mair-see*
You're welcome (*in reply to thanks*)	**Je vous en prie/ De rien**	*Zhe' voo zah^n-pree/ de'-rya^n*
Yes, please	**Oui, merci**	*Wee mair-see*
No, thank you[1]	**(Non) merci**	*No^n mair-see*
Sorry	**Pardon**	*Par-do^n*

1. In reply to an offer of any kind **merci** means 'no thank you'. To accept, say **oui, merci** or **oui, s'il vous plaît**.

Greetings

Key Phrases

Good morning/good day/good afternoon	**Bonjour**	*Bon-zhoor*
Good evening	**Bonsoir**	*Bon-swar*
Good night	(*when going to bed*) **Bonne nuit** (*otherwise*) **Bonsoir**	*Bon nwee/bon-swar*

How are you?	**Comment allez-vous?**	*Ko-mahnta-lay-voo*
Fine, thank you	**Très bien, merci**	*Tre byan mair-see*
See you soon	**À bientôt**	*A byan-toh*
See you tomorrow	**À demain**	*A der-man*
Have a good journey	**Bon voyage**	*Bon vwa-yazh*
Have a good time	**Amusez-vous bien**	*A-mue-zay-voo byan*
Good luck/all the best	**Bonne chance**	*Bon shan s*

Polite Phrases

Key Phrases

Excuse me	**Excusez-moi**	*Ex-kue-zay mwa*
That's all right (*in reply to excuse me*)	**Il n'y a pas de mal/ Ce n'est rien**	*Eel nee ya pad-mal/se' nay ryan*
With pleasure	**Avec plaisir**	*A-vek play-zeer*

Not at all/don't mention it (after thanks)	Il n'y a pas de quoi/ je vous en prie	Eel nee ya pad kwa/ zhe' voo-zah^n pree
Is everything all right?	(Est-ce que) tout va bien?	(Es-ke') too va bya^n
It's all right	ça va	Sa va
Thanks for your help	Merci de votre aide	Mair-see de' vot-red

Don't worry	Ne vous inquiétez pas	Ne' voo za^n-kye-tay pa
It doesn't matter	Cela ne fait rien/ celan'a pas d' importance	Se'-la ne ' fay rya ^{n}/ se'-la na pa da^n- por-tah^{n}s
I beg your pardon? What?	Comment?	Ko-mah^n
Am I disturbing you?	Est-ce que je vous dérange?	Es-ke' zhe' voo day-rah^n zh
I'm sorry to have troubled you	Je suis désolé de vous avoir dérangé	Zhe' swee day-zoh-lay de' voo za-vwar day-rah^n-zhay
Good/that's fine	Bien/c'est parfait	Bya^n/say par-fe

Language Problems

Key Phrases

Do you speak English?	**Parlez-vous anglais?**	*Par-lay-voo ahⁿ -gle*
Does anyone here speak English?	**Est-ce que quelqu'un parle anglais ici?**	*Es-ke^r kel-keⁿ parl ahⁿ -gle ee-see*
I don't speak (much) French	**Je ne parle pas (bien) français**	*Zhe^r neⁿ parl pa (byaⁿ) frahⁿ -say*
I don't understand	**Je ne comprends pas**	*Zhe^r ne^r koⁿ -prahⁿ pa*
Would you say that again, please?	**Voulez-vous répéter, s'il vous plaît?**	*Voo-lay-voo ray-pay-tay, seel-voo-ple*
Please write it down	**Écrivez-le, s'il vous plaît**	*Ay-kree-vay-le^r, seel-voo-ple*

I'm English/American	**Je suis anglais(-e)/ américain(-e)**	*Zhe^r swee ahⁿ -gle (ahⁿ -glez)/a-may-ree-kaⁿ (ken)*
I speak a little French	**Je parle un peu le français**	*Zhe^r parl eⁿ pe^r le^r frahⁿ -say*
Do you understand (me)?	**Est-ce que vous (me) comprenez?**	*Es-ke^r voo me^r koⁿ -pre^r -nay*
Please speak slowly	**Parlez lentement, je vous prie**	*Par-lay lahⁿ -te^r -mahⁿ zhe^r voo pree*
What does that mean?	**Qu'est-ce que cela veut dire?**	*Kes-ke^r se^r -la ve^r deer*

Can you translate this for me?	**Pouvez-vous me traduire ceci?**	*Poo-vay-voo me^r tra-dweer se^r -see*
What do you call this in French?	**Comment appelez-vous ceci en français?**	*Ko-mahⁿ tape^r -lay-voo se^r -see ahⁿ frahⁿ -say*
I will look it up in my phrase book	**Je vais consulter mon manuel de conversation**	*Zhe^r ve koⁿ -su^e l-tay moⁿ ma-nu^e -el de^r koⁿ -vair-sa-syoⁿ*
Please show me the word in the book	**Montrez-moi le mot dans le livre**	*Moⁿ -tray mwa le^r mo dahⁿ leⁿ leevr*

Questions

Key Phrases		
Who?	**Qui?**	*Kee*
Where is/are ...?	**Où est/sont ...?**	*Oo-ay/soⁿ*
When?	**Quand?**	*Kahⁿ*
How?	**Comment?**	*Ko-mahⁿ*
How much/many?	**Combien?**	*Koⁿ -byaⁿ*
How much is/are ...?	**Combien coûte/coûtent ...?**	*Koⁿ -byaⁿ koot/koot*
Why?	**Pourquoi?**	*Poor-kwa*
Is there?	**Y a-t-il ...?**	*Ee-ya-teel*

How long?	**Combien de temps?**	*Ko^n -bya^n de' tah^n*
How far?	**C'est à quelle distance?**	*Se ta-kel dees-tah^n s*
What?	**Quoi?**	*Kwa*
What's that?	**Qu'est-ce que c'est?**	*Kes-ke'-say*
What do you want?	**Que voulez-vous?**	*Ke' voo-lay-voo*
What must I do?	**Que dois-je faire?**	*Ke' dwa-zhe' fair*
Have you ...?	**Avez-vous ...?**	*A-vay-voo*
Have you seen ...?	**Avez-vous vu ...?**	*A-vay-voo vu^e*
Where can I find ...?	**Où puis-je trouver ...?**	*Oo pwee-zhe' troo-vay*
May I have ...?	**Pourrais-je avoir ...?**	*Poo-rezh-a-vwar*
What is the matter?	**Qu'est-ce qu'il y a?**	*Kes-keel-ya*
Can you help me?	**Pouvez-vous m'aider?**	*Poo-vay-voo meh-day*
Can I help you?	***Puis-je vous aider?**	*Pwee-zhe' voo-ze-day*
Can you tell me/give me/show me?	**Pouvez-vous me dire/donner/montrer?**	*Poo-vay-voo me' deer/do-nay/mo^n -tray*

Useful Statements

Key Phrases

I want . . .	**Je veux . . .**	*Zhe' ve'*
I don't want . . .	**Je ne veux pas . . .**	*Zhe' ne' ve' pa*
I need . . .	**J'ai besoin de . . .**	*Zhay be' -zwaⁿ de'*
Here is/are . . .	**Voici . . .**	*Vwa-see*
I know	**Je sais**	*Zhe' se*
I don't know	**Je ne sais pas**	*Zhe' ne' se pa*
It's urgent	**C'est urgent**	*Say tue r -zhahⁿ*

It is . . .	**C'est . . .**	*Say*
It isn't . . .	**Ce n'est pas . . .**	*Se' nay pa*
I have . . .	**J'ai . . .**	*Zhay*
I don't have . . .	**Je n'ai pas de . . .**	*Zhe' nay pa de'*
I would like . . .	**Je voudrais**	*Zhe' voo-dre*
I like it	**Cela me plaît/ J'aime bien**	*Se' -la me' ple/ Zhem byaⁿ*
I don't like it	**Je n'aime pas ça**	*Zhe' nem pa sa*
It's cheap	**C'est bon marché**	*Say boⁿ mar-shay*
It's (too) expensive	**C'est (trop) cher**	*Say (troh) shair*
That's all	**C'est tout**	*Say too*
Ok that's fine	**Entendu/c'est parfait**	*Ahⁿ -tahⁿ -due/say par-fe*
There is/are . . .	**Il y a . . .**	*Eel-ee-ya*

I didn't know	**Je ne savais pas**	*Zhe' ne' sa-ve pa*
I think so	**Je crois que oui**	*Zhe' krwa ke' wee*
I'm hungry/thirsty	**J'ai faim/soif**	*Zhay fa^n/swaf*
I'm tired/in a hurry/ready	**Je suis fatigué/pressé/prêt**	*Zhe' swee fa-tee-gay/pray-say/pre*
Leave me alone	**Laissez-moi tranquille**	*Lay-say-mwa trah^n-keel*
Go away	**Allez-vous en**	*A-lay voo zah^n*
I'm lost	**Je (me) suis perdu**	*Zhe' (me') swee pair-du^e*
We're looking for . . .	**Nous cherchons . . .**	*Noo sher-sho^n*
Here it is	**Le/la voilà**	*Le'/la vwa-la*
There they are	**Les voilà**	*Lay vwa-la*
Just a minute	***Une minute/un instant**	*U^e n mee-nu^e t/e^n na^n-stah^n*
This way, please	***Par ici, s'il vous plaît**	*Par ee-see, seel-voo-ple*
Take a seat	***Asseyez-vous**	*A-say-yay voo*
Come in!	***Entrez!**	*Ah^n-tray*
It's important	**C'est important**	*Say ta^n-por-tah^n*
You are mistaken	**Vous vous trompez**	*Voo voo tro^n-pay*
You're right/wrong	**Vous avez raison/tort**	*Voo za-vay ray-zo^n/tor*

SIGNS AND PUBLIC NOTICES[1]

À louer	To let/for hire
À vendre	For sale
Ascenseur	Lift/elevator
Attention	Caution
Banque	Bank
Caisse	Cashier
Chambre à louer	Room to let
Chambres libres	Vacancies
Commissariat de police[2]	Police station
Complet	Full/no vacancies/no seats
Dames	Ladies
Danger	Danger
Défense d'entrer	Private/no entry
Défense d'entrer sous peine d'amende	Trespassers will be prosecuted
Défense de fumer	No smoking

1. See also SIGNS AT AIRPORTS AND STATIONS (p. 19) and ROAD SIGNS (p. 54).

2. See note, p. 54.

Eau non potable	(Water) not for drinking
Eau potable	Drinking water
Entrée	Entrance
Entrée interdite	No admission
Entrée libre	Admission free
Entrez sans frapper	Please enter
Fermé	Closed
Frappez	Knock
Gendarmerie[1]	Police station
Guide	Guide
Interprète	Interpreter
Issue de secours	Emergency exit
Libre	Vacant/free/unocccupied
Ne pas toucher	Do not touch
Occupé	Engaged/occupied
Ouvert de . . . à . . .	Open from . . . to . . .
Passage interdit	No entry
Piétons	Pedestrians
Places debout seulement	Standing room only
Point rencontre	Meeting point
La Poste/PTT	Post Office
Poussez	Push

1. See note, p. 144

Prière de ne pas ...	You are requested not to ...
Privé	Private
Renseignements	Information
Réservé	Reserved
Soldes	Sale
Sonnez	Ring
Sortie	Exit
Sortie de secours	Emergency exit
Tenez votre droite	Keep right
Tirez	Pull
Toilettes	Lavatory/toilets

Acronyms and Abbreviations

A	Autoroute	Motorway
AOC	Appellation d'origine contrôlée	Highest French wine classification
apr. J-C.	Après Jésus-Christ	AD
av. J-C.	Avant Jésus-Christ	BC
Bd	Boulevard	Boulevard
BP	Boîte postale	PO box
c.- à-d.	C'est-à-dire	i.e.
CB	Carte bancaire	Bank card
CCP	Compte courant postal	Giro account

Cedex	Courrier d'entreprise à distribution exceptionnelle	Postal code for corporate users
CHU	Centre hospitalier universitaire	Teaching hospital
CIP	Chambre de commerce internationale	International Chamber of Commerce
cpt.	Comptant	Cash
CRS	Compagnies républicaines de sécurité	Riot police
DOM	Département d'outre-mer	French overseas (administrative) department
EDF	Electricité de France	French electricity company
GDF	Gas de France	French gas company
h.	Heure	Hour
JMF	Jeunesses musicales de France	Association of young music lovers
M.	Métro	Underground, subway – see also **RATP**
m.	Minute, mètre	Minute, metre
MJC	Maison des jeunes et de la culture	Youth centre
ONU	Organisation des Nations Unies	United Nations Organization (UN)

ORL	Oto-rhino-laryngologie	Ear, nose and throat medicine
ORSEC	Organisation de la réponse de sécurité civile	Emergency measures
OVNI	Objet volant non identifié	UFO
P et T	Postes et télécommunications (formerly PTT)	Post Office
p ex	Par exemple	e.g.
PMU	Pari mutuel urbain	Tote
R.	Rue	Street
RATP	Régie autonome des transports parisiens	Paris transport authority
R.d.c.	Rez-de chaussée	Ground floor
RER	Réseau express régional	Fast suburban transport in Paris
RF	République française	French republic
RN	Route nationale	Trunk road
Rte	Route	Road
s/	Sur	On (in place names)
/s	Sous	Under (in place names)
SAMU	Service d'aide médicale urgente	Emergency medical services

SARL	Société à responsabilité limitée	Limited company
SI	Syndicat d'initiative	Tourist information office
Sida	Syndrome immunodéficitaire acquis	AIDS
SNCF	Société nationale des chemins de fer français	French railways
SPA	Société protectrice des animaux	Society for prevention of cruelty to animals
SS	Sécurité sociale	Social security
TCF	Touring club de France	French automobile association
TGV	Train à grande vitesse	High-speed train
TOM	Territoires d'outre-mer	French overseas territories
t.t.c.	toutes taxes comprises	All taxes included
TVA	Taxe sur la valeur ajoutée	VAT
UE	Union européenne	European Union (EU)
VDQS	Vin délimité de qualité supérieure	Second highest French wine classification
Vve	Veuve	Widow
ZUP	Zone à urbaniser en priorité	Development area

GETTING AROUND

Arrival

Key Phrases

I've lost my passport, I must have dropped it on the plane	**J'ai perdu mon passeport, j'ai dû le laisser tomber dans l'avion**	*Zhay pair-du^e moⁿ pas-por, zhay du^e le^r lay-say toⁿ-bay dahⁿ la-vyoⁿ*
My luggage has not arrived	**Mes bagages ne sont pas arrivés**	*May ba-gazh ne^r soⁿ pa za-ree-vay*
My luggage is damaged	**Mes bagages sont endommagés**	*May ba-gazh soⁿ tahⁿ-do-ma-zhay*
Is there an ATM/ currency exchange?	**Y a-t-il un distributeur de billets/un bureau de change?**	*Ee-ya-teel eⁿ dee-stree-bu^e-tœr de^r bee-yay/ eⁿ bu^e-roh de^r shahⁿ–zh*
Is there a bus/train into the town?	**Y a-t-il un autobus/ train pour aller en ville?**	*Ee-ya-teel eⁿ noh-toh-bu^e s/traⁿ poor a- lay ahⁿ veel*
How can I get to . . .?	**Comment puis-je me rendre à . . .?**	*Ko-mahⁿ pwee-zh me^r rahⁿ dr a*

Passports

Your passport, please	*Votre passeport, s'il vous plaît	Votr pas-por, seel-voo-ple
Are you together?	*Vous êtes ensemble?	Voo zet ah^n-sah^n bl
Are you with a group?	Vous êtes avec un groupe?	Voo zet a-vek e^n groop
I'm travelling alone	Je voyage seul(e)	Zhe' vwa-yazh sœl
I'm travelling with my wife/my husband/a friend	Je voyage avec ma femme/mon mari/un(e) ami(e)	Zhe' vwa-yazh a-vek ma fam/mo^n ma-ree/e^n (u^e) na-mee
I'm here on business	Je suis ici pour affaires	Zhe' swee ee-see poor a-fair
I'm here on holiday	Je viens passer mes vacances	Zhe' vya^n pa-say may va-kah^{n}s
What is your address in Paris/France?	*Quelle est votre adresse à Paris/en France?	Kel-ay votr a-dres a pa-ree/ah^n frah^n s
How long are you staying here?	*Combien de temps pensez-vous rester?	Ko^n -bya^n de' tah^n pah^n -say voo res-tay

Customs

Customs	*Douane	Dwan
Goods to declare	*Marchandise à déclarer	Mar-shah^n -deez a day-kla-ray
Nothing to declare	*Rien à déclarer	Rya^n a day-kla-ray

Which is your luggage?	*Quels sont vos bagages?	Kel so^n voh ba-gazh
Do you have any more luggage?	*Avez-vous d'autres bagages?	A-vay-voo dotre ba-gazh
This is (all) my luggage	Voici (tous) mes bagages	Vwa-see (too) may ba-gazh
Have you anything to declare?	*Avez-vous quelque chose à déclarer?	A-vay-voo kel-ke'-shoz a day-kla-ray
I have only my personal things in it	Il n'y a là que mes affaires personnelles	Eel-nee-ya la ke' may za-fair pair-so-nel
Open your bag, please	*Ouvrez votre sac, s'il vous plaît	Oo-vray votr sak, seel-voo-ple
Can I shut my case now?	Puis-je refermer ma valise maintenant?	Pwee-zh re'-fair-may ma va-leez ma^n –te' -nah^n
May I go through?	Puis-je passer?	Pwee-zh pa-say
It is for my own personal use	C'est pour mon usage personnel	Say poor mon ue-zazh pair-so-nel

Luggage

My luggage has not arrived	Mes bagages ne sont pas arrivés	May ba-gazh ne' so^n pa za-ree-vay
My luggage is damaged	Mes bagages sont endommagés	May ba-gazh so^n tah^n-do-ma-zhay
One suitcase is missing	Il manque une valise	Eel mah^n ku^e n va-leez
Are there any luggage trolleys?	Y a-t-il des chariots à bagages?	Ee-ya-teel day shar-yoh a ba-gazh

| Where is the left luggage office? | Où est la consigne? | *Oo ay la ko^n-seen-y* |
| Luggage lockers | Consigne automatique | *Ko^n-seen-y oh-toh-ma-teek* |

Moving on

Porter!	Porteur!	*Por-tœr*
Would you take these bags to	Portez ces bagages jusqu'à	*Por-tay say ba-gazh zhues-ka*
the bus	l'autobus	*loh-toh-bu^e s*
the car rental offices	l'agence de location de voitures	*la-zhah^n s de^r lo-ka-Syo^n de^r vwa-tu^e r*
a taxi	un taxi	*e^n tak-see*
What is the price for each piece of luggage?	C'est combien par bagage?	*Say ko^n-bya^n par ba-ga-zh*
I shall take this myself	Je porterai cela moi-même	*Zhe^r por-te^r-ray se^r-la mwa-mem*
That's not mine	Ce n'est pas à moi	*Se^r nay pa za mwa*
How much do I owe you?	Combien est-ce que je vous dois?	*Ko^n-bya^n es-ke^r zhe^r voo dwa*
Where is the information bureau	Où se trouve le bureau de renseignements?	*Oo se^r troov le^r bu^e-roh de^r rah^n-sen-y-mah^n*
Is there an ATM/currency exchange?	Y a-t-il un distributeur de billets/un bureau de change?	*Ee-ya-teel e^n dee-stree-bu^e-tœr de^r bee-yay/e^n bu^e-ro de^r shah^n-zh*

Where can I buy a bus/tube/train ticket?[1]	**Où puis-je acheter un ticket d'autobus/ de métro/de train?**	*Oo pwee-zh ash-tay e^n tee-kay doh-toh bu^e s/de^r may-tro/de^r tra^n*
Is there a bus/train into the town?	**Y a-t-il un autobus/ train pour aller en ville?**	*Ee-ya-teel e^n noh-toh-bu^e s/tra^n poor a- lay ah^n veel*
How can I get to ...?	**Commet puis-je me rendre à ...?**	*Ko-mah^n pwee-zh me^r rah^n dr a*

Signs at Airports and Stations

Arrivals	**Arrivées**
Booking office	**Guichet des billets**
Bus station	**Gare routière**
Buses	**Autobus**
Car rental	**Location de voitures**
Connections	**Correspondances**
Departures	**Départs**
Exchange	**Change**
Gate	**Porte**
Gentlemen	**Messieurs**
Hotel bookings	**Réservation de chambres d'hôtel**
Information	**Renseignements**
Ladies	**Dames**

1. See also BUS (p. 26), TRAIN (p. 30) and UNDERGROUND (p. 35).

Left luggage	**Consigne**
Deposits	**Dépôts**
Withdrawals	**Retraits**
Lift	**Ascenseur**
Lounge	**Salle d'embarquement**
Lost property	**Bureau des objets trouvés**
Luggage lockers	**Consigne automatique**
Main lines	**Grandes lignes**
Newsstand	**(Kiosque à) journaux**
No smoking	**Défense de fumer**
Other passports	**Autres passeports**
Passport control	**Contrôle des passeports**
Platform	**Quai**
Refreshments	**Restauration**
Reservations	**Réservations**
Smoking lounge	**Salon fumeurs**
Shuttle	**Navette**
Suburban lines	**Lignes de banlieue**
Taxis	**Taxis**
Terminal	**Aérogare**
Tickets	**Billets**
Toilets	**Toilettes/WC**
Tourist office	**Office du tourisme**

Transit desk	(Bureau de) transit
Underground	Métro (Métropolitain)
Waiting room	Salle d'attente

By Air

Key Phrases

What is the baggage allowance?	**Quelle est la franchise bagages?**	*Kel ay la frah^n-sheez ba-gazh?*
I'd like to change my reservation	**Je voudrais changer ma réservation**	*Zhe' voo-dre shah^n -zhay ma ray-zair-va-syo^n*
Can I check in online?	**Puis-je effectuer l'enregistrement en ligne?**	*Pwee-zh ay-fay-ktu^e -ay lah^n -re' -zhees-tre' -mah^n ah^n leen-y*
I have only hand luggage	**Je n'ai qu'un bagage à main**	*Zhe' nay ke^n ba-ga-zh a ma^n*
Flight ... to ... has been delayed/cancelled	***Le vol ... pour ... est retardé/annulé**	*Le' vol ... poor ... ay re' -tar-day/a-nu^e-lay*

| Where's the airline office? | **Oú se trouve l'agence de la compagnie aérienne?** | *Oo se' troov la-zhah^n s de' la ko^n -pan-yee a-ay-ryen* |
| I'd like two seats on the plane to ... | **Je voudrais réserver deux places dans l'avion à destination de ...** | *Zhe' voo-dre ray-zair-vay de' plas dah^nla-vyo^n a des-tee-na-syo^n de'* |

Is that the cheapest price?	Est-ce le prix le moins cher?	*Es le' pree le' mwa^n shair*
First class	Première classe	*Pre' -myair klas*
Business class	Classe affaires	*Klas a-fair*
Economy	Classe économique	*Klas ay-ko-no-meek*
How long is the flight?	Combien de temps le vol dure-t-il?	*Ko^n -bya^n de' tah^n le' vol du ^e r-teel*
I'd like an aisle/window seat	Je voudrais un siège côté couloir/fenêtre	*Zhe' voo-dre e^n see-aizh ko-tay kool-war/fe' -netr*
I'd like to order a vegetarian/special meal	Je voudrais commander un repas végétarien/sur mesure	*Zhe' voo-dre ko-mah^n -day e^n re' -pa vay- zhay-ta-rya^n/su^e r me' -zu^e r*
Is there a flight to ...?	Est-ce qu'il y a un vol à destination de ...?	*Es-keel ee-ya e^n vol a des-tee-na-syo^n de'*
When does it leave/arrive?	À quelle heure est le départ/l'arrivée?	*A kel-œr ay le' day-par/ la-ree-vay*
What is the flight number?	Quel est le numéro du vol?	*Kel ay le' nu^e -may-ro du^e vol*
When's the next plane?	Quand part le prochain avion?	*Kah^n par le' pro-sha^n na-vyo^n*
Please cancel my reservation to ...	Annulez ma réservation pour ..., s'il vous plaît	*A-nu^e -lay ma ray-zair-va-syo^n poor ... seel-voo-ple*
I have an open ticket	J'ai un billet open	*Zhay e^n bee-yay open*
Can I change my ticket?	Puis-je changer mon billet?	*Pwee-zh shah^n -zhay mo^n bee-yay*
Will it cost more?	Cela coûtera-t-il plus cher?	*Se' -la koo-te' -ra-teel plu^e shair*

Is there a bus between the town and the airport?	Y a-t-il un service d'autocars entre la ville et l'aéroport?	*Ee-ya-teel eⁿ sair-vees doh-toh-kar ahⁿ tr la veel ay la-ay-ro-por*
Which airport/terminal does the flight leave from?	De quel aéroport/aérogare le vol part-il?	*De' kel a-ay-ro-por/le' vol par-teel*
Where are the check-in desks for (Air France)?	Où sont les comptoirs d'enregistrement de (Air France)?	*Oo soⁿ lay koⁿ -twar dahⁿ -re' -zhees-tre' mahⁿ de' (Air Frahⁿ s)*
When must I check in?	Quand dois-je me présenter à l'enregistrement?	*Kahⁿ dwa-zh-me' pray-zahⁿ -tay a lahⁿ -re' -zhees-tre'-mahⁿ*
I've booked a wheelchair to take me to the plane	J'ai réservé un fauteuil roulant jusqu'à l'embarquement du vol	*Zhay ray-sair-vay eⁿ fo-tœ-y roo-lahⁿ zhu^e s-ka lahⁿ -bar-ke' -mahⁿ du^e vd*
Can I check in online?	Puis-je effectuer l'enregistrement en ligne?	*Pwee-zh ay-fay-ktu^e -ay lahⁿ -re' -zhees-tre' -mahⁿ ahⁿ leen-y*
I have only hand luggage	Je n'ai qu'un baggage à main	*Zhe' nay keⁿ ba-ga-zh a maⁿ*
You will have to pay for excess baggage	*Vous devrez payer l'excédent de bagages	*Voo de'-vray pe-yay lek-say-dahⁿ de' ba-ga-zh*
The plane leaves from gate	*L'avion part de la porte	*Lav-yoⁿ par de' la port*
I've lost my boarding card	J'ai perdu ma carte d'embarquement	*Zhay pair-du^e ma kart dahⁿ -bar-ke' - mahⁿ*

Flight ... to ... has been delayed/ cancelled	*Le vol ... pour ... est retardé/annulé	*Le' vol ... poor ... ay re' -tar-day/a-nue-lay

By Boat or Ferry

Key Phrases

Is there a boat/car ferry to ...?	Y a-t-il un bateau/ car ferry pour ...?	Ee-ya-teel e^n ba-toh/ kar fay-ree poor
When does the next boat leave?	Quand part le prochain bateau?	Kah^n par le' pro-sha^n ba-toh
I'd like a one way/ return ticket	Je voudrais un aller simple/aller-retour	Zhe' voo-dre e^n na-lay sa^n pl/a-lay-re' -toor

Where is the port?	Où est le port?	Oo ay le' por
How long does the crossing take?	Combien de temps la traversée dure-t-elle?	Ko^n-bya^n de' tah^n la tra-vair-say du^e r-tel
How often does the boat leave?	Tous les combien partent les bateaux?	Too lay ko^n -bya^n part lay ba-toh
Does the boat call at ...?	Est-ce que le bateau fait escale à ...?	Es-ke' le' ba-toh fay es-kal a
What does it cost	C'est combien	Say ko^n -bya^n
for a child?	pour un enfant?	poor e^n ah^n -fah^n
for a bicycle?	pour un vélo?	poor e^n vay-lo
for a motor cycle?	pour une moto?	poor u^e n mo-to
for a caravan?	pour une caravane?	poor u^e n ka-ra-van

Can I book a single berth cabin?	Puis-je réserver une cabine à une couchette?	Pwee-zh ray-zair-vay u^e n ka-been a u^e n koo-shet
How many berths are there in this cabin?	Combien de couchettes y a-t-il dans cette cabine?	Ko^n -bya^n de^r koo-shet ee-yu-teel dah^n set ka-been
When must we go on board?	À quelle heure devons-nous embarquer?	A kel-œr de^r -vo^n noo ah^n -bar-kay
How do we get on to the deck?	Par où monte-t-on sur le pont?	Par oo mo^n t-to^n su^e r le^r po^n
When do we dock?	À quelle heure accostons-nous?	A kel-œr a-kos-to^n noo
How long do we stay in port?	Combien de temps l'escale dure-t-elle?	Ko^n -bya^n de^r tah^n les-kal du^e r-tel
Where are the toilets?	Où sont les toilettes?	Oo so^n lay twa-let
I feel seasick	J'ai le mal de mer	Zhay le^r mal de^r mair
lifeboat	le cannot de sauvetage	ka-no de^r sov-tazh
lifevest	le gilet de sauvetage	zhee-lay de^r sov-tazh

By Bus or Coach

Key Phrases

Where can I buy a bus ticket?	Où puis-je acheter un ticket d'autobus?	Oo pwee-zh ash-tay e^n tee-kay doh-toh-bu^e s
Do I pay the driver?	J'achète le billet auprès du conducteur?	Zha-shait le^r bee-yay o-prai du^e ko^n -du^e k-tœr
When's the next bus?	À quelle heure est le prochain autobus?	A kel-oer ay le^r pro-sha^n noh-toh-bu^{e}s
Where can I get a bus to ...?	Où puis-je prendre un autobus pour ...?	Oo pwee-zh prah^n dr e^n oh-toh-bu^e s poor
Where do I get off?	Où dois-je descendre?	Oo dwa-zh de-sah^n dr

Where's the bus station/coach station?	Où est la station d'autobus/la gare routière?	Oo ay la sta-syo^n doh-toh-bu^e s/la gar roo-tyair
Bus stop	Arrêt d'autobus	A-ray doh-toh-bu^e s
Compulsory stop	Arrêt fixe	A-ray feeks
Request stop	Arrêt facultatif	A-ray fa-ku^e l-ta-teef
Is there a daily/weekly ticket?	Y a-t-il un ticket journalier/hebdomadaire?	Ee-ya-teel e^n tee-kay zhoor-na-lyay/eb-do-ma-dair?
I'd like to reserve a seat at the front of the coach	Je voudrais réserver un siège à l'avant de l'autocar	Zhe^r voo-dre ray-zair-vay e^n see-aizh a la-vah^n de^r loh-toh-kar
What is the fare?	Quel est le prix du billet?	Kel ay le^r pree du^e bee-yay

When does the coach leave?	À quelle heure part l'autocar?	A kel-œr par loh-toh-kar
When does the coach get to...?	À quelle heure est-ce que l'autocar arrive à...?	A kel-œr es-ke' loh-toh-kar a-reev a
What stops does it make?	Où est-ce qu'il s'arrête?	Wes-keel sa-ret
How long is the journey?	Combien de temps le voyage/le trajet dure-t-il?	Ko^n-bya^n de' tah^n le' vwa-yazh/le' trazhay du^e r-teel
How often does the bus to...run?	Il y a un autobus pour...tous les combien?	Eel-ya e^n oh-toh-bu^e s poor...too lay ko^n-bya^n
What time is the last bus?	À quelle heure est le dernier autobus?	A kel-œr ay le' dair-nyay oh-toh-bu^e s
Does this bus go	Est-ce que cet autobus va	Es-ke' set oh-toh-bu^e s va
to the beach?	à la plage?	a la plazh
to the station?	à la gare?	a la gar
to the town centre?	au centre-ville?	oh sah^n tr de' la veel
Do you go near...?	Allez-vous du côté de...?	A-lay-voo du^e ko-tay de'
Is this the right stop for...?	Est-ce le bon arrêt pour...?	Es le' bo^n a-re poor
Which bus goes to...?	Quel autobus va à (au)...?	Kel oh-toh-bu^e s va a/oh
I want to go to...	Je voudrais aller à (au)...?	Zhe' voo-dre a-lay a/oh

I want to get off at . . .	**Je veux descendre à . . .**	*Zhe^r ve^r de-sah^n dr a*
The bus to . . . stops over there	***L'autobus pour . . . s'arrête là-bas**	*Loh-toh-bu^e s poor . . . sa-ret la-ba*
You must take a number . . .	***Il faut prendre le . . .**	*Eel foh prah^n dr le^r*
(You) get off at the next stop	***(Vous) descendez au prochain arrêt**	*(Voo) de-sah^n -day oh pro-sha^n na-re*
The buses run every ten minutes/every hour	***L'autobus passe toutes les dix minutes/toutes les heures**	*Loh-toh-bu^e s pas toot lay dee mee-nu^e t/ toot lay zoer*

By Taxi

Key Phrases

Please get me a taxi	**Voulez-vous m'appeler un taxi, s'il vous plaît**	*Voo-lay-voo ma-pe^r -lay e^n tak-see, seel-voo ple*
Where can I find a taxi?	**Où puis-je trouver un taxi?**	*Oo pwee-zh troo-vay e^n tak-see*
Please wait for me	**Attendez-moi, s'il vous plaît**	*A-tah^n -day mwa, seel-voo-ple*
Stop here	**Arrêtez-vous ici**	*A-re-tay-voo ee-see*

I'd like to book a taxi for tomorrow at . . .	**Je voudrais réserver un taxi pour demain à . . .**	*Zhe' voo-dre ray-zair-vay e^n tak-see poor de' -ma^n a*
Are you free?	**Êtes-vous libre?**	*Et voo leebr*
Please turn on the meter	**Allumez le taximètre, s'il vous plaît**	*A-lu^e -may le' tak-see-maitr, seel-voo-ple*
Please take me	**Conduisez-moi, s'il vous plaît,**	*Kon^n -dwee-zay mwa, seel-voo-ple,*
to this address	**à cette adresse**	*a set a-dres*
to the city centre	**au centre-ville**	*oh sahntr-veel*
to the . . . hotel	**à l'hôtel . . .**	*à lo-tel*
to the station	**à la gare**	*a la gar*
Can you hurry? I'm late	**Pouvez-vous aller vite? Je suis en retard**	*Poo-vay voo a-lay veet zhe' swee ah^n re' -tar*
Is it far?	**C'est loin?**	*Say lwa^n*
How far is it to . . .?	**Il y a combien d'ici à . . .?**	*Eel-ya ko^n -bya^n dee-see a*
Turn right/left at the next corner	**Tournez à droite/ à gauche au prochain tournant**	*Toor-nay a drwat/ a gosh oh pro-sha^n toor-nah^n*
Straight on	**Tout droit**	*Too drwa*
How much do you charge by the hour/ for the day?	**Combien coûte l'heure de location/ la journée de location?**	*Ko^n -bya^n koot lœr de' lo-ka-syo^n/la zhoor-nay de' lo-ka-syo^n*

| How much will you charge to take me to ...? | **Quel est le prix de la course pour aller à ...?** | *Kel-ay le' pree de' la koors poor a-lay a* |
| How much is it? | **Combien vous dois-je?** | *Koⁿ -byaⁿ voo dwa-zh* |

By Train[1]

Key Phrases

Where's the railway station?	**Où est la gare?**	*Oo-ay la gar*
What's the cheapest fare to ...?	**Combien coûte le billet le moins cher pour ...?**	*Koⁿ -byaⁿ koot le' bee-yay le' mwaⁿ shair poor*
Is there a day return?	**Y a-t-il un billet aller-retour dans la journée?**	*Ee-ya-teel eⁿ bee-yay a-lay-re' -toor dahⁿ la zhoor-nay*
Where do I change?	**Où dois-je changer?**	*Oo dwa-zh shahⁿ -zhay*
What station is this?	**Quelle est cette gare?**	*Kel ay set gar*

1. The main types of train in France are: **TGV** (*train à grande vitesse*) – high-speed train – supplement payable; **Thalys** – international high-speed train going to Brussels, Amsterdam and Cologne; **rapide** – express train – supplement payable; **express** – stops only at main stations; **omnibus** – stops at every station; **Transilien** – train going through the Parisian suburbs and the Ile de France; **TER** *(transport express régional)* train going through one region or connecting different regions; **intercités** – intercity, medium-distance passenger train.

Where is the ticket office?	Où est le guichet de vente des billets?	*Oo ay le' ghee-shay de' vah'' t day bee-yay*
Have you a timetable, please?	Avez-vous un horaire, s'il vous plaît?	*A-vay-voo e'' no-rair, seel-voo-ple*
How much is it first class to ...?	Combien coûte un billet de première pour ...?	*Ko'' -bya'' koot e'' bee-yay de' pre' -myair poor*
A second class single to ...	Un aller simple en deuxième classe pour ...	*E'' na-lay sa'' pl ah'' de' -zyem klas poor*
Three singles to ...	Trois allers simples pour ...	*Trwa za-lay sa'' pl poor*
A return to ...	Un aller-retour pour ...	*E'' na-lay ay re' -toor poor*
When are you coming back?	*Quand revenez-vous?	*Kah'' re' -ve' -nay-voo*
There is a supplement for the TGV	*Il y a un supplément pour le TGV	*Eel-ya e'' su^e -play-mah'' poor le' tay-zhay-vay*
What is the child fare?	Quel est le tarif enfants?	*Kel ay le' ta-reef ah'' -fah''*
How old is he/she?	*Quel âge a-t-il/ a-t-elle?	*Kel azh a-teel/a-tel*
How long is this ticket valid?	Combien de temps ce billet est-il valable?	*Ko'' -bya'' de' ta'' se' bee-yay ay-teel va-labl*
Do I need to reserve a seat?	Faut-il que je réserve un siège?	*Fo-teel ke' zhe' ray-zairv e'' see-aizh*
I want	Je voudrais	*Zhe' voo-dre*

an aisle seat	un siège côté couloir	e^n see-aizh ko-tay kool-war
a couchette	une couchette	u^e n koo-shet
a sleeper	un wagon-lit	e^n va-go^n lee
a window seat	un siège côté fenêtre	e^n see-aizh ko-tay fe^r -netr
When is the next train to...?	À quelle heure part le prochain train pour...?	A kel-œr par le^r pro-sha^n tra^n poor
Is it an express or a local train?	Est-ce un train express ou un omnibus?	Es e^n tra^n ek-spres oo e^n nom-nee-bu^e s
Is there an earlier/ later train?	Y a-t-il un train plus tôt/plus tard?	Ee-ya-teel e^n tra^n plu^e toh/ plu^e tar
When does the train get to...?	À quelle heure arrive le train à...?	A kel-œr a-reev le^r tra^n a
Does the train stop at...?	Est-ce que le train s'arrête à...?	Es-ke^r le^r tra^n sa-ret a
Is there a restaurant car on the train?	Ce train a-t-il un wagon-restaurant?	Se^r tra^n a-teel e^n va-go^n res-to-rah^n
I'd like to make a motorail reservation to...	Je voudrais faire une réservation pour le train auto-couchettes à destination de...	Zhe^r voo-dre fair u^e n ray-zair-va-syo^n poor le^r tra^n oh-toh-koo-shet a des-tee-na-syo^n de^r
Where is the motorail loading platform?	Où se trouve le quai de chargement du train auto-couchettes?	Oo se^r troov le^r ke de^r shar-zhe^r -mah^n du^e tra^n oh-toh-koo-shet

Changing

Is there a through train to ...?	**Y a-t-il un train direct pour ...?**	*Ee-ya-teel eⁿ traⁿ dee-rekt poor*
Do I have to change?	**Dois-je changer de train?**	*Dwa-zh shahⁿ-zhay deʳ traⁿ*
Where do I change?	**Où dois-je changer?**	*Oo dwa-zh shahⁿ-zhay*
Is this where I change for ...?	**Est-ce ici la correspondance pour ...?**	*Es ee-see la kores-poⁿ-dahⁿ s poor ...?*
When is there a connection to ...?	**Quand y a-t-il une correspondance pour ...?**	*Kahⁿ ee-ya-teel uᵉ n kores-poⁿ-dahⁿ s poor*
When does the train from ... get in?	**À quelle heure arrive le train de ...?**	*A kel-œr a-reev leʳ traⁿ deʳ*
Is the train late?	**Est-ce que le train a du retard?**	*Es-keʳ leʳ traⁿ a duᵉ reʳ-tar*
From which platform does the train to ... leave?	**De quel quai part le train pour ...?**	*Deʳ kel ke par leʳ traⁿ poor*
Change at ... and take the local train	***Changez à ... et prenez le train local**	*Shahⁿ-zhay a ... ay preʳ-nay leʳ traⁿ lo-kal*

Departure

When does the train leave?	**À quelle heure part le train?**	*A kel-œr par leʳ traⁿ*
Is this the train for ...?	**Est-ce bien le train pour ...?**	*Es-byaⁿ leʳ traⁿ poor*
There will be a delay of ...	***Il y a un retard de ...**	*Eel-ya eⁿ reʳ-tar deʳ*

On the train

dining car	**la voiture restaurant**	*vwa-tu^e r res-to-rah^n*
ticket inspector	**le contrôleur**	*ko^n -tro-lœr*
We have reserved seats	**Nous avons des places réservées**	*Noo-za-vo^n day plas ray-zair-vay*
Is this seat free?	**Est-ce que cette place est libre?**	*Es-ke^r set plas ay leebr*
This seat is taken	***Cette place est occupée**	*Set plas ay to-ku^e -pay*
When is the buffet car open?	**Quand ouvre la voiture-buffet?**	*Kah^n oovr la vwa-tu^e r bu^n -fay*
Where is the sleeping car?	**Où est la voiture-lit/ le wagon-lit?**	*Oo ay la vwa-tu^e r lee/ le^r va-go^n lee*
Which is my sleeper?	**Lequel est mon wagon-lit?**	*Le^r -kel ay mo^n va-go^n lee*
Could you wake me at . . . please?	**Pourriez-vous me réveiller à . . . heures, s'il vous plaît?**	*Poor-yay-voo me^r ray-vay-yay a . . . œr, seel-voo-ple*
The heating is too high/low	**Il y a trop/pas assez de chauffage**	*Eel-ya tro/pa-za-say de^r shoh-fazh*
I can't open/close the window	**Je ne peux pas ouvrir/ fermer la fenêtre**	*Zhe^r ne^r pe^r pa oo-vreer/ fair-may la fe^r -netr*
What station is this?	**Quelle est cette gare?**	*Kel ay set gar*
How long do we stop here?	**Combien de temps le train s'arrête-t-il ici?**	*Ko^n -bya^n de^r tah^n le^r tra^n sa-ret-teel ee-see*

By Underground

Key Phrases

Where is the nearest underground station?	**Où se trouve la station de métro la plus proche?**	*Oo se' troov la sta-syo^n de' may tro la plu^e prosh*
Does this train go to...?	**Est-ce que ce train va à...?**	*Es-ke' se' tra^n va a*
Have you a map of the underground?	**Avez-vous un plan du métro?**	*A-vay-voo e^n plah^n du^e may-tro*

A book of tickets, please[1]	**Un carnet de tickets, s'il vous plaît**	*E^n kar-nay de' tee-kay, seel-voo-ple*
Can I use it on the bus too?	**Puis-je l'utiliser aussi pour prendre l'autobus?**	*Pwee-zh lu^e-tee-lee-zay oh-see poor prah^n dr loh-toh-bu^e s*
Is there a daily/ weekly ticket?[2]	**Y a-t-il un ticket journalier/ hebdomadaire?**	*Ee-ya-teel e^n tee-kay zhoor-na-lyay/ eb-do-ma-dair*
Which line goes to...?	**Quelle ligne va à...?**	*Kel leen-y va a*

1. This is only available for bus or tube journeys. It is much cheaper to buy a **carnet** than single tickets for each journey.
2. **Forfait mobilis** = daily ticket, unlimited travel by all public transport modes except boats in the Île de France region **Pass navigo** = weekly ticket, unlimited travel by all public transport modes except boats in the Île de France region.

Where do I change for ...?	**Où dois-je changer pour ...?**	*Oo dwa-zh shahⁿ -zhay poor*
Is the next station ...?	**C'est ... la prochaine station?**	*Say ... la pro-shen sta-syoⁿ*
What station is this?	**Quelle est cette station?**	*Kel ay set sta-syoⁿ*

By Car[1]

Key Phrases

Have you a road map, please?	**Avez-vous une carte routière, s'il vous plaît?**	*A-vay-voo u^e n kart roo-tyair, seel-voo-ple*
Where is the nearest car park/garage?	**Où est le parking/ le garage le plus proche?**	*Oo-ay le' par-king/ le' ga-razh le' plu^e prosh*
May I see your driving licence and passport?	***Votre permis de conduire et votre passeport, s'il vous plaît**	*Votr pair-mee de' koⁿ -dweer ay votr pas-por, seel-voo-ple*

(How long) can I park here?	**(Combien de temps) peut-on stationner ici?**	*(Koⁿ -byaⁿ de' tahⁿ) pe' toⁿ sta-syo-nay ee-see*
Have you any change for the meter, please?	**Avez-vous de la monnaie pour le parc-mètre, s'il vous plaît?**	*A-vay-voo de' la mo-nay poor le' park-metr, seel-voo-ple*

1. See also DIRECTIONS (p. 57) and ROAD SIGNS (p. 54).

How far is the next petrol station?	À combien d'ici est la prochaine station d'essence?	A koⁿ-byaⁿ dee-see ay la pro-shaⁿ sta-syoⁿ de-sahⁿ s
May I see your logbook, please?	*Votre carte grise, s'il vous plaît	Votr kart greez, seel-voo-ple
Is this your car?	*C'est votre voiture?	Say votr vwa-tu^e r
You were speeding	*Vous avez commis un excès de vitesse	Voo-za-vay ko-mee eⁿ ekse de^r vee-tes
pedestrian precinct	Zone piétonnière	zon pyay-to-nyair
speed limit	Limitation de vitesse, vitesse limitée	Lee-mee-la-syoⁿ de^r vee-tes, vee-tes lee-mee-tay

Car Rental

Where can I rent a car?	Où pourrais-je louer une voiture?	Oo-poo-rezh loo-ay u^e n vwa-tu^e r
I want to hire a car/a car and a driver	Je voudrais louer une voiture/ une voiture avec chauffeur	Zhe^r voo-dre loo-ay u^e n vwa-tu^e r/u^e n vwa-tu^e r a-vek sho fœr
I want	Je voudrais	Zhe^r voo-dre
an automatic	une voiture à boîte automatique	u^e n vwa-tu^e r a bwat oh-toh-ma-teek
a convertible	une décapotable	u^e n day-ka-poh-tabl
a large car	une grande voiture	u^e n grahⁿ d vwa-tu^e r
a manual	une voiture à boîte manuelle	u^e n vwa-tu^e r a bwat ma-nu^e-ail
a small car	une petite voiture	u^e n pe^r-teet vwa-tu^e r

I'd like car with a sun roof/air conditioning	**Je voudrais une voiture avec un toit ouvrant/l'air conditonné**	*Zhe' voo-dre u^e n vwa-tu^e r a-vek eⁿ twa oo-vrahⁿ/ lair koⁿ -dee- syo-nay*
Does it have a GPS system/CD player?	**Y a-t-il un GPS/un lecteur CD?**	*Ee-ya-teel eⁿ zhay-pay-es/ eⁿ lay-ktœr de' say-day*
We've reserved a camper van	**Nous avons réservé un camping-car**	*Noo za-voⁿ ray-zair-vay eⁿ kahⁿ -ping-kar*
Can we rent a baby/ child seat?	**Peut-on louer un siège auto bébé/enfant?**	*Pe' -toⁿ loo-ay eⁿ see-aizh oh-toh bay-bay/ahⁿ -fahⁿ*
What kind of fuel does it take?	**Quel est le type de carburant à utiliser pour ce véhicule?**	*Kel ay le' teep de' kar-bu^e -rahⁿ a u^e -tee-lee-zay poor se' vay-ee-k u^e l*
Is there a special weekend rate?	**Y a-t-il un tarif spécial weekend?**	*Ee-ya-teel eⁿ ta-reef spay-syal weekend*
Is there a midweek rate?	**Y a-t-il un tarif spécial milieu de semaine?**	*Ee-ya-teel eⁿ ta-reef spay-syal meel-yœ de' se' -men*
I need it for two days/a week	**J'en ai besoin pour deux jours/une semaine**	*Zhahⁿ nay be' -zwaⁿ poor de' zhoor/u^e n se' -men*
How much is it by the day/week?	**Combien coûte la location à la journée/ à la semaine?**	*Koⁿ -byaⁿ koot la lo-ka-syoⁿ a la zhoor-nay/a la se' -men*
Does that include unlimited mileage?	**Est-ce que le prix inclut le kilométrage illimité?**	*Es-ke' le' pree aⁿ -klu^e le' kee-lo-may-trazh ee-lee-mee-tay*
The charge per kilometer is . . .	***Le tarif du kilomètre est de . . .**	*Le' ta-reef du^e kee-lo-metr ay de'*
Do you want comprehensive insurance?	***Voulez-vous une assurance tous risques?**	*Vou-lay-voo u^e n a-su^e -rahⁿ s too reesk*

I will pay by credit card	Je paierai avec ma carte de crédit	Zhe' pe-re a-vek ma kart de' kray-dee
How much is the deposit?	Quel est le montant de la caution?	Kel-ay-le' mo'' -tah'' de' la koh-syo''
You have to pay the first . . .euros	*Vous devez payer un dépôt de . . .euros	Voo de' -vay pe-yuy e'' day-poh de' . . .e' -roh
May I see your driving licence and passport?	*Votre permis de conduire et votre passeport, s'il vous plaît	Votr pair-mee de' ko'' -dweer ay votr pas-por seel-voo-ple
Can I return the car in . . .?	Puis-je rendre la voiture à . . .?	Pwee-zh rah'' dre la vwa-tu'' r a
Could you show me how to work the controls/lights?	Pourriez-vous me montrer comment fonctionnent les commandes/ fonctionne l'éclairage?	Poor-yay-voo me' mo'' -tray ko-man'' fo'' k-syon lay ko-mah'' d/fo'' k-syon lay-kle-razh
The car is scratched/ dented here	La voiture est rayée/ cabossée ici	La vwa-tu'' r ay re-yay/ ka-bo-say ee-see

At a Garage or Petrol Station

Fill it up, please	Le plein, s'il vous plaît	Le' pla'', seel-voo-ple
How much is petrol a litre?	Combien vaut le litre d'essence?	Ko'' -bya'' voh le' leetr de-sah'' s
diesel/standard petrol	gasoil/essence ordinaire	ga-zo-el/sah'' s or-dee-nair
It's a diesel engine	C'est un moteur diesel	Say te'' mo-tœr dee-ay-zel

Please check the oil and water/the battery	**Vérifiez l'huile et l'eau/la batterie, s'il vous plaît**	*Ve-ree-fyay lweel ay loh/la bat-ree, seel-voo-ple*
The oil needs changing	**Il faut faire la vidange d'huile**	*Eel foh fair la vee-dahⁿ zh dweel*
Could you check the brake/transmission fluid?	**Pouvez-vous vérifier le liquide des freins/le niveau de la boîte?**	*Poo-vay-voo ve-ree-fyay le^r lee-keed day fraⁿ/le^r nee-vo de^r la bwat*
Check the tyre pressure, please	**Vérifiez la pression des pneus, s'il vous plaît**	*Ve-ree-fyay la pre-syoⁿ day pne^r, seel-voo-ple*
Would you clean the windscreen, please?	**Pouvez-vous nettoyer le pare-brise, s'il vous plaît?**	*Poo-vay-voo ne-twa-yay le^r par-breez, seel-voo-ple*
I'd like my car serviced	**Je voudrais faire réviser ma voiture**	*Zhe^r voo-dre fair ray-vee-zay ma vwatu^e r*
Please wash the car	**Pouvez-vous laver la voiture, s'il vous plaît?**	*Poo-vay-voo la-vay la vwa-tu^e r, seel-voo-ple*
Can I garage the car here?	**Est-ce que je peux garer la voiture ici?**	*Es-ke^r zhe^r pe^r ga-ray la vwa-tu^e r ee-see*
What time does the garage close?	**À quelle heure ferme le garage?**	*A kel-œr fairm le^r ga-razh*
Where are the toilets?	**Où sont les toilettes?**	*Oo soⁿ lay twa-let*
Please pay at the cash desk	***Veuillez régler à la caisse, s'il vous plaît**	*Vœ-yay ray-glay a la kes, seel-voo-ple*

Problems and repairs

I've locked the keys in the car	**J'ai perdu ma clé**	*Zhay pair-du^e ma klay*
The lock is broken/jammed	**La serrure est cassée/bloquée**	*La se-ru^e r ay ka-say/ blo-kay*
My car won't start	**Ma voiture ne démarre pas**	*Ma vwa-tu^e r ne^r day-mar pa*
My car has broken down	**Ma voiture est en panne**	*Ma vwa-tu^e r ay tahⁿ pan*
Could you give me a lift to a garage?	**Pourriez-vous me déposer au garage?**	*Poor-yay-voo me^r day-poh-zay oh ga-razh*
May I use your phone?	**Puis-je utiliser votre téléphone?**	*Pwee-zh u^e -tee-lee-zay votr tay-lay-fon*
Where is there a ... agent?	**Où y a-t-il une agence ...?**	*Oo-ee-ya-teel u^e n a-zhahⁿ*
Have you a breakdown service?	**Avez-vous un service de dépannage?**	*A-vay-voo eⁿ sair-vees de^r day-pa-nazh*
Is there a mechanic?	**Y a-t-il un mécanicien?**	*Ee-ya-teel-eⁿ may-ka-nee-syaⁿ*
Can you send someone to look at it/tow it?	**Pouvez-vous envoyer quelqu'un pour l'examiner/pour la remorquer?**	*Poo-vay-voo ahⁿ -vwa-yay kel-keⁿ poor lek-za-mee-nay/poor la re^r -mor-kay*
Where are you?	***Où êtes-vous?**	*Oo et-voo*
Where is your car?	***Où est votre voiture?**	*Oo ay votr vwa-tu^e r*

I'm on the road from ... to ... near kilometer post ...	Je suis sur la route de ... à ... près de la borne kilométrique ...	Zhe' swee su' r la root de' ... a ... pre de' la born kee-lo-me-treek
How long will you be?	Combien de temps vous faudra-t-il?	Ko'' -bya'' de' tah'' voo fo-dra-teel
This tyre is flat; can you repair it?	Ce pneu est à plat; pouvez-vous le réparer?	Se' pne' ay-ta pla; poo-vay-voo le' ray-pa-ray
The exhaust is broken	Le tuyau d'échappement est cassé	Le' twee-yoh day-shap-mah'' ay ka-say
The windscreen wipers do not work	Les essuie-glaces ne fonctionnent pas	Lay ze-swee glas ne' fo'' k-syon pa
The valve/radiator is leaking	La valve/le radiateur perd	La valv/le' ra-dya-tœr pair
The battery is flat, it needs charging	Ma batterie est déchargée, il faut la recharger	Ma bat-ree ay day-shar-zhay eel fo la re'-shar-zhay
It's not running properly	Elle ne marche pas bien	El ne' mar-sh pa bya''
The engine is overheating	Le moteur chauffe	Le' mo-tœr shof
The engine is firing badly	Le moteur tourne mal	Le' mo-tœr toorn mal
Can you change this faulty plug?	Pouvez-vous remplacer cette bougie défectueuse?	Poo-vay-voo rah'' -pla-say set boo-zhee day-fek-tu' -œz
There's a petrol/ oil leak	Il y a une fuite d'essence/d'huile	Eel-ya u' n fweet de-sah'' s/dweel

There's a smell of petrol/burnt rubber	Il y a une odeur d'essence/de caoutchouc brûlé	*Eel-ya u^e n-o-d$œr$ de-sah^n s/de^r ka-oo-tshoo bru^e -lay*
There's a rattle/squeak	Il y a un bruit/quelque chose qui grince	*Eel-ya e^n brwee/kelk-shoz kee gra^n s*
Something is wrong with the ...	Le/la ...ne marche pas bien	*Le^r/la ...ne^r mar-sh pa bya^n*
I've got electrical/mechanical trouble	J'ai des ennuis électriques/mécaniques	*Zhay day zah^n -nwee ay-lek-treek/may-ka-neek*
The carburettor needs adjusting	Le carburateur a besoin d'un réglage	*Le^r kar-bu^e -ra-t$œr$ a be^r -zwa^n de^n re-glazh*
Can you repair it?	Pouvez-vous réparer cela?	*Poo-vay-voo ray-pa-ray se^r -la*
How long will it take to repair?	Combien de temps prendra la réparation?	*Ko^n -bya^n de^r tah^n prah^n -dra la ray-pa-ra-syo^n*
What will it cost?	Combien est-ce que cela coûtera?	*Ko^n -bya^n es-ke'se-la koo-te^r -ra*
When can I pick the car up?	Quand puis-je venir chercher ma voiture?	*Kah^n pwee-zh ve^r -neer shair-shay ma vwa-tu^e r*
I need it as soon as possible/in three hours/in the morning	Je la voudrais le plus tôt possible/dans trois heures/demain matin	*Zhe^r la voo-dre le^r plu^e toh po-seebl/dah^n trwa z$œr$/de^r -ma^n ma-ta^n*
It will take two days	*Cela prendra deux jours	*Se^r -la prah^n -dra de^r zhoor*

We can repair it temporarily	*Nous pouvons faire une réparation provisoire	*Noo poo-vo^n fair u^e n ray-pa-ra-syo^n pro-vee-zwar*
We haven't the right spares	*Nous n'avons pas les pièces de rechange nécessaires	*Noo na-vo^n pa lay pyes de^r re^r -shah^n zh nay-say-sair*
We have to send for the spares	*Nous devons faire venir les pièces de rechange	*Noo de^r -vo^n fair ve^r -neer lay pyes de^r re^r -sha^n zh*
You will need a new . . .	*Il vous faudra un nouveau (une nouvelle) . . .	*Eel voo fo-dra e^n noo-voh (u^e n noo-vel)*
Could I have an itemized bill, please?	**Pourrais-je avoir une facture détaillée, s'il vous plaît?**	*Poo-rezh a-vwar u^e n faktu^e r day-ta-yay, seel-voo-ple*

Parts of a car and other useful words

accelerate (to)	**accélérer**	*ak-say-lay-ray*
accelerator	**l'accélérateur** *m*	*ak-say-lay-ra-tœr*
aerial	**l'antenne** *f*	*ah^n -ten*
air pump	**la pompe à air**	*po^n pa air*
alarm	**l'alarme auto** *f*	*a-larm oh-toh*
alternator	**l'alternateur** *m*	*al-tair-na-tœr*
anti-freeze	**l'antigel** *m*	*ah^n -tee-zhel*
automatic transmission	**la boîte de vitesses automatique**	*bwat de^r vee-tes oh-toh-ma-teek*
axle	**l'essieu** *m*	*es-ye^r*

battery	**la batterie**	*bat-ree*
bonnet	**le capot**	*ka-poh*
boot/trunk	**le coffre**	*kofr*
brake	**le frein**	*fra^n*
brake lights	**le feu stop**	*fe^r stop*
brake lining	**la garniture des freins**	*gar-nee-tu^e r day fra^n*
brake pads	**les plaquettes de frein**	*pla-ket de^r fra^n*
breakdown	**la panne**	*pan*
bulb	**l'ampoule** *f*	*ah^n -pool*
bumper	**le pare-choc**	*par-shok*
carburettor	**le carburateur**	*kar-bu^e -ra-tœr*
CD player	**le lecteur CD**	*lay-ktœr de^r say-day*
clutch	**l'embrayage** *m*	*ah^n -bre-yazh*
cooling system	**le système de refroidissement**	*sees-tem de^r re^r -frwa-dees-mah^n*
crank-shaft	**le vilebrequin**	*veel-bre^r -ka^n*
cylinder	**le cylindre**	*see-la^n dr*
differential gear	**le différentiel**	*dee-fay-rah^n -syel*
dip stick	**la jauge d'huile**	*zhozh dweel*
distilled water	**l'eau distillée** *f*	*oh dee-stee-lay*
distributor	**le distributeur**	*dee-stree-bu^e -tœr*
door	**la portière**	*por-tyair*

door handle	**la poignée**	*pwan-yay*
drive (to)	**conduire**	*ko^n-dweer*
driver	**le chauffeur**	*sho-fœr*
dynamo	**la dynamo**	*dee-na-mo*
engine	**le moteur**	*mo-tœr*
exhaust	**l'échappement** *m*	*ay-shap-mah^n*
fan	**le ventilateur**	*vah^n-tee-la-tœr*
fanbelt	**la courroie de ventilateur**	*koo-rwa de^r vah^n-tee-la-tœr*
(oil) filter	**le filtre (à huile)**	*feeltr (a weel)*
flat tyre	**le pneu à plat**	*pne^r a pla*
foglamp	**le phare antibrouillard**	*far ah^n-tee-broo-yar*
fuse-box	**la boîte à fusible**	*bwat a fu^e-zeebl*
gasket	**le joint**	*zhwa^n*
gear-box	**la boîte de vitesses**	*bwat de^r vee-tes*
gear-lever	**le levier du changement de vitesse**	*le^r-vyay du^e shah^n zh-mah^n de^r vee-tes*
gears	**les vitesses** *f*	*vee-tes*
grease (to)	**graisser**	*gre-say*
handbrake	**le frein à main**	*fra^n a ma^n*
headlights	**les phares** *m*	*far*
heater	**le chauffage**	*shoh-fazh*

horn	le klaxon	klak-so^n
hose	la durite	du^e-reet
ignition	l'allumage *m*	a-lu^e-mazh
ignition key	la clé de contact	klay de^r ko^n-takt
indicator	le clignotant	kleen-yoh-tah^n
jack	le cric	kreek
lights (headlights)	les phares *m*	far
lock/catch	la serrure	se-ru^e r
mirror	le rétroviseur	ray-troh-vee-zœr
number plate	la plaque d'immatriculation	plak d'ima-tree-cu^e-la-syo^n
nut	le boulon	boo-lo^n
oil	l'huile *f*	weel
parking lights	les feux de stationnement	fœ de^r sta-syon-mah^n
pedal	la pédale	pay-dal
petrol	l'essence *f*	e-sah^n s
petrol can	le bidon d'essence	bee-do^n de-sa^n s
piston	le piston	pee-sto^n
points	les vis platinées *f*	vees-pla-tee-nay
(fuel) pump	la pompe (à essence)	po^n p (a e-sah^n s)
puncture	la crevaison	kre^r-vay-zo^n
radiator	le radiateur	ra-dya-tœr

rear axle	le pont arrière	*po^n ar-yair*
rear lights	les lanternes arrière	*lah^n -tairn ar-yair*
rear view mirror	le rétroviseur	*ray-tro-vee-zœr*
reverse	la marche arrière	*mar-sh ar-yair*
reverse (to)	faire marche arrière	*fair mar-sh ar-yair*
reversing lights	les phares de recul	*far de^r re^r -ku^e l*
roof	le toit	*twa*
screwdriver	le tournevis	*toor-ne^r -vees*
seat	le siège	*see-aizh*
seat belt	la ceinture de sécurité	*sa^n -tu^e r de^r say-ku^e -ree-tay*
shock absorber	l'amortisseur *m*	*a-mor-tee-sœr*
silencer	le silencieux	*see-lah^n -see-e^r*
(plug) spanner	la clé (à bougie)	*klay (a boo-zhee)*
spares	les pièces de rechange *f*	*pee-ess de^r re^r -shah^n zh*
spark plug	la bougie	*boo-zhee*
speed	la vitesse	*vee-tes*
speedometer	le compteur de vitesse	*ko^n -tœr de^r vee-tes*
spring	le ressort	*re^r -sor*
stall (to)	caler	*ka-lay*

steering	**la direction**	*dee-rek-syo^n*
steering wheel	**le volant**	*vo-lah^n*
sunroof	**le toit ouvrant**	*twa oo-vrah^n*
suspension	**la suspension**	*su^{e}s-pah^n-syo^n*
tank	**le réservoir**	*ray-zair-vwar*
tappets	**les culbuteurs** *m*	*ku^{e}l-bu^e-tœr*
transmission	**la transmission**	*trah^{n}s-mee-syo^n*
tyre	**le pneu**	*pne^r*
tyre pressure	**la pression des pneus**	*pre-syo^n day pne^r*
valve	**la soupape**	*soo-pap*
warning light	**le feu de détresse**	*fe^r de^r day-trays*
wheel – back	**la roue arrière**	*roo ar-yair*
wheel – front	**la roue avant**	*roo a-vah^n*
wheel – spare	**la roue de secours**	*roo de^r se^r-koor*
window	**la vitre/la glace**	*veetr/glas*
windscreen	**le pare-brise**	*par-breez*
windscreen washers	**le lave-glace**	*lav-glas*
windscreen wipers	**l'essuie-glace** *m*	*es-wee-glas*

By Bike or Moped[1]

Key Phrases

Where can I hire	**Où puis-je louer**	*Oo pwee-zh loo-ay*
a moped	**un vélomoteur?**	*e^n vay-lo-mo-tœr*
a motorbike	**une moto?**	*u^e n mo-to*
a mountain bike	**un VTT (un vélo tout terrain)?**	*e^n vay-tay-tay (e^n vay-lo too te-ra^n)*
a bicycle	**une bicyclette/ un vélo?**	*u^e n bee-see-klet/ e^n vay-lo*
Is it obligatory to wear a helmet?	**Le casque est-il obligatoire?**	*Le kas-ke^r ay-teel o-blee-ga-twar*
Do you repair bicycles?	**Est-ce que vous réparez les bicyclettes?**	*Es-ke^r voo ray-pa-ray lay bee-see-klet*

What does it cost per day/per week	**C'est combien pour la journée/pour la semaine?**	*Say ko^n -bya^n poor la zhoor-nay/ poor la se^r -men*
I'd like a lock, please	**Je voudrais un cadenas, s'il vous plaît**	*Zhe^r voo-dre e^n ka-de^r -na, seel-voo-ple*
The saddle is too high/too low	**La selle est trop haute/trop basse**	*La sel ay troh ot/troh bas*

1. see also DIRECTIONS (p. 58) and ROAD SIGNS (p. 54).

Where is the cycle shop?	**Où est le magasin de bicyclettes/vélos?**	*Oo ay le' ma-ga-zan de' bee-see-klet/vay-lo*
The brake isn't working	**Le frein ne marche pas**	*Le' fran ne' mar-sh pa*
Could you tighten/ loosen the brake cable?	**Pourriez-vous serrer/ desserrer le câble du frein?**	*Poor-yay-voo say-ray/ day-say-ray le' kabl du^e fran*
The tyre is punctured	**Le pneu est crevé**	*Le' pne' ay kre' -vay*
The gears need adjusting	**Le changement de vitesses a besoin d'être réglé**	*Le' shahn zh-mahn de' vee-tes a be' -zwan detr ray-glay*
Could you straighten the wheel?	**Pourriez-vous redresser la roue?**	*Poor-yay-voo re' -dre-say la roo*
The handlebars are loose	**Le guidon est desserré**	*Le' ghee-don ay day-say-ray*
Could you lend me a spanner/a tyre lever?	**Pourriez-vous me prêter une clé/un démonte-pneu?**	*Poor-yay-voo me' pre-tay u^e n klay/en day-mon t pne'*
Can I take my bike on the boat/train?	**Puis-Je monter dans le bateau/train avec mon vélo?**	*Pwee-zh mon -lay dahn le' ba-toh/tran a-vek mon vay-lo?*

Parts of a bicycle and other useful words

basket	**le panier à vélo**	*pan-yay a vay-lo*
bell	**la sonnette**	*so-net*
brake – front	**le frein avant**	*fran a-vahn*
brake – rear	**le frein arrière**	*fran ar-yair*

brake cable	le câble de frein	*kabl de' fra^n*
brake lever	le frein à main	*fra^n a ma^n*
bulb	l'ampoule *f*	*ah^n -pool*
chain	la chaîne	*shen*
chain guard	le garde-chaîne	*gar-de' shen*
child's seat	le siège vélo pour enfant	*see-aizh vay-loo poor ah^n -fah^n*
dynamo	la dynamo	*dee-na-mo*
fork	la fourche	*foorsh*
frame	le cadre	*kadr*
gear cable	le cable de vitesses	*kabl de' vee-tes*
gear lever	le levier de chàngement de vitesses	*le' vyay de' shah^n zh-mah^n de' vee-tes*
gears	le changement de vitesses	*shah^n zh-mah^n de' vee-tes*
handlebar	le guidon	*ghee-do^n*
helmet	le casque	*kask*
high visibility jacket	le gilet fluorescent de visibilité à vélo	*zhee-lay flu^e o-ray-sah^n de' vee-zee-bee-lee-tay a vay-lo*
inner tube	la chambre à air	*shah^n br a air*
light – front	le phare	*far*
light – rear	le feu rouge	*fe' roozh*

mudguard	le garde-boue	*gard-boo*
panniers	les sacoches	*sa-kosh*
pedal	la pédale	*pay-dal*
pump	la pompe	*poⁿ p*
puncture	la crevaison	*kre^r -vay-zoⁿ*
puncture repair kit	le kit de réparation de pneus de vélo	*keet de^r ray-pa-ra-syoⁿ de^r pne^r de^r vay-lo*
reflector	le catadioptre/ le cataphote	*ka-ta-dyoptr/ka-ta-fot*
rim	la jante	*zhahⁿ t*
saddle	la selle	*sel*
saddlebag	la sacoche (de selle)	*sa-kosh (de^r sel)*
spoke	le rayon	*ray-yoⁿ*
suspension	la suspension	*su^e -spahⁿ -syoⁿ*
tyre	le pneu	*pne^r*
valve	la valve	*valv*
wheel	la roue	*roo*

Road Signs[1]

Allumez vos lanternes	Lights on
Allumez vos phares	Headlights on
Attention	Caution
Attention travaux	Road works ahead
Boulevard périphérique	Ring road
Cédez le passage	Give way
Chaussée déformée	Uneven surface
Chute de pierres	Falling stones
Circulation ralentie	Slow traffic
Couloir réservé aux autobus	Bus lane
Danger	Danger
Défense de (doubler)	(Overtaking) prohibited
Descente dangereuse/rapide	Steep hill
Déviation	Diversion
Disque (de stationnement) obligatoire	Parking disc required
Douane	Customs
Feux (de circulation)	Traffic lights

1. It is important to note that, unless there are road signs to the contrary, vehicles coming from the right have priority at road junctions.

Fin de la zone de stationnement interdit	End of no-parking zone
Gravillons	Loose chippings
Impasse	No through road
Inondation	Flooding
Passage à niveau	Level crossing
Passage protégé	Priority over traffic from the right
Péage	Toll
Poids lourds	Lorries
Priorité à droite	Give way to traffic from the right
Prudence	Caution
Réservé aux piétons	Pedestrians only
Roulez lentement	Slow
Route/Rue barrée	Road blocked
Route étroite	Narrow road
Rue sans issue	Dead end
Sens interdit	No entry
Sens unique	One way (street)
Serrez à droite	Keep in the right-hand lane
Sortie (de camions)	Exit (for lorries)
Stationnement autorisé	Parking allowed
Stationnement interdit	No parking
Stationnement réglementé	Restricted parking

Tenez votre droite	Keep right
Toutes directions	Through traffic
Verglas	Icy surface
Virages	Bends; winding road
Vitesse limite	Maximum speed
Zone bleue	Restricted parking

DIRECTIONS

Key Phrases

Where is . . .?	Où est . . .?	*Oo-ay*
How do I get to . . .?	**Comment fait-on pour aller à . . .?**	*Ko-mah^n fay-to^n poor a-lay a*
How many kilometres?	**Combien de kilomètres?**	*Koh^n -bya^n de^r kee-lo-metr*
Please show me on the map	**Montrez-moi l'endroit sur la carte, s'il vous plaît**	*Mo^n -tray mwa lah^n -drwa su^e r la kart seel-voo-ple*
You are going the wrong way	***Vous allez dans la mauvaise direction**	*Voo za-lay dah^n la mo-vez dee-rek-syon^n*

Excuse me; could you tell me the way to	**Pardon, Monsieur/ Madame/ Mademoiselle; pouvez-vous m'indiquer le chemin pour aller**	*Par-do^n me^r -sye^r/ ma-dam/mad-mwa-zel; poo-vay-voo ma^n -dee-kay le^r she^r -ma^n poor a-lay*
the post office?	**au bureau de poste?**	*oh bu^e -ro de^r post*
the station?	**à la gare?**	*a la gar*
the town centre?	**au centre-ville?**	*oh sah^n tr-veel*

I'm looking for	Je cherche	*Zhe' shairsh*
an ATM	un distributeur de billets	*e^n dee-stree-bu^e -tœr de' bee-yay*
a chemist	une pharmacie	*u^e n far-ma-see*
an Internet café	un cybercafé	*e^n see-ber-ka-fay*
It isn't far	*Ce n'est pas loin	*Se' nay pa lwa^n*
It's on the square/opposite the . . . hotel/at the end of this street	*C'est sur la place/en face de l'hôtel . . ./au bout de la rue	*Say su^e r la plas/ah^n fas de' lo-tel. . . ./ oh boo de' la ru^e*
There is one in the pedestrian street	*Il y en a un(une) dans la rue piétonne	*Eel ee-yah^n na e^n (une) dah^n la ru^e pyay-ton*
Is it far?	C'est loin?	*Say lwa^n*
How do we get on to the motorway to . . .?	Comment parvient-on à l'autoroute qui va à . . .?	*Ko-mah^n par-vya^n -to^n a loh-toh-root kee va a*
Which is the best road to . . .?	Quelle est la meilleure route pour aller à . . .?	*Kel-ay la me-yœr root poor a-lay a*
Is this the right road for . . .?	Est-ce la bonne direction pour . . .?	*Es la bon dee-rek-syo^n poor*
Is there a scenic route to . . .?	Y a-t-il un itinéraire touristique pour aller à . . .?	*Ee-ya-teel e^n ee-tee-nay-rair too-ree-steek poor a-lay a*
Where does this road lead to?	Où est-ce que cette route mène?	*Wes-ke' set root men*
Is it a good road?	Est-ce que la route est bonne?	*Es-ke' la root ay bon*

Is it a motorway?	**Est-ce que c'est une autoroute?**	*Es-ke' say-tu^e n oh-toh-root*
Is there a toll?	**Y a-t-il un péage?**	*Ee-ya-teel eⁿ pay-azh*
Is the tunnel/pass open?	**Est-ce que le tunnel/ le col est ouvert?**	*Es-ke' le' tu^e -nel/le' kol ay too-vair*
Is the road to ... clear?	**Est ce que la route de ... est dégagée?**	*Es-ke' la root de' ... ay day-ga-zhay*
How far is the next village?	**Le prochain village est à combien d'ici?**	*Le' pro-shaⁿ vee-lazh ay-ta koⁿ -byaⁿ dee-see*
How far is the next petrol station?	**La prochaine station d'essence est à combien d'ici?**	*La pro-shen sta-syoⁿ de-sahⁿ s ay-ta koⁿ -byaⁿ dee-see*
Is there any danger of avalanches/ snowdrifts?	**Risque-t-il d'y avoir des avalanches/des congères?**	*Rees-ke' -teel dee-avwar day-za-va-lahⁿ sh/ day koⁿ -zhair*
Will we get to ... by evening?	**Pourrons-nous arriver à ... dans la soirée?**	*Poo-roⁿ -noo a-ree-vay a ... dahⁿ la swa-ray*
How long will it take by car/by bicycle/on foot?	**Combien de temps faut-il pour y aller en voiture/à erovélo/à pied?**	*Koⁿ -byaⁿ de' tahⁿ fo-leel poor ee a-lay ahⁿ vwa-tu^e r/a ah/vay-lo/a pyay*
Where are we now?	**Où sommes-nous maintenant?**	*Oo som-noo maⁿ -te' -nahⁿ*
What is the name of this place?	**Quel est le nom de cet endroit?**	*Kel-ay le' noⁿ de' set ahⁿ -drwa*
I'm lost	**Je (me) suis perdu(e)**	*Zhe' (me') swee pair-du^e*

Please show me on the map	Montrez-moi l'endroit sur la carte, s'il vous plaît	Mo^n -tray mwa lah^n -drwa su^e r la kart seel-voo-ple
It's that way	*C'est de ce côté/ C'est par là	Say de^r se^r ko-tay/ say par la
Follow signs for ...	*Pour aller à ... suivez les panneaux indicateurs	Poor a-lay a ... swee-vay lay pa-noh a^n -dee-ka-tœr
Follow this road for five kilometres	*Suivez cette route sur cinq kilomètres	Swee-vay set root su^e r sa^n k kee-lo-metr
Keep straight on	*Allez tout droit	A-lay too drwa
Turn right at the crossroads/ roundabout	*Tournez à droite au croisement/rond-point	Toor-nay a drwat oh krwa-ze^r -mah^n/ro^n -pwa^n
Take the second road on the left	*Prenez la deuxième route à gauche	Pre^r -nay la de^r -zyem root a gosh
Turn right at the traffic-lights	*Tournez à droite aux feux	Toor-nay a drwat oh fœ
Turn left after the bridge	*Tournez à gauche après le pont	Toor-nay a gosh a-pre le^r po^n
Take the next left/ right	*Prenez la prochaine à gauche/droite	Pre^r -nay la pro-shen a gosh/drwat
The best road is the N7[1]	*La meilleure route est la N7	La me-yœr root ay la en set

1. N7 = route nationale 7. All trunk roads are indicated by N followed by a number. D21 = route départementale 21. Secondary roads are indicated by D followed by a number. Motorways are indicated by A followed by a number. A1 = autoroute 1 (Paris–Lille).

Take the D21 to . . . and ask again	*Prenez la D21 jusqu'à . . . et demandez à quelqu'un	Pre' -nay la day vaⁿ tay eⁿ zhu^e s-ka . . . ay de' -mahⁿ -day a kel-keⁿ
Take junction 12/the exit for . . .	*Prenez la sortie 12 (douze)/la sortie pour . . .	Pre' -nay la sor-tee 12 (dooz)/la sor-tee poor . . .
You are going the wrong way	*Vous allez dans la mauvaise direction	Voo za-lay dahⁿ la mo-vez dee-rek-syonⁿ
one-way system	sens unique	sahⁿ s u^e -neek
north	nord	nor
south	sud	su^e d
east	est	est
west	ouest	oo-est

ACCOMMODATION

B&B	**Chambre d'hôte**	*Shah[n] br doht*
Campsite	**Terrain de camping**	*Te-ra[n] -de[r] kah[n] -ping*
Cottage	**Gîte**	*Zheet*
Country inn	**Auberge**	*Oh-bairzh*
Guesthouse	**Pension**	*Pah[n] -syo[n]*
Youth hostel	**Auberge de jeunesse**	*Oh-bairzh de[r] zhe[r] -nes*
Rooms to let/ vacancies	**Chambres (à louer)**	*Shah[n] br a loo-ay*
No vacancies	**Complet**	*Ko[n] -play*
No camping	**Camping interdit**	*Kah[n] -ping a[n] -tair-dee*
Can you show me on the map where the hotel is?	**Pourriez-vous m'indiquer sur le plan où se trouve l'hôtel?**	*Poor-yay-voo ma[n] -dee-kay su[r] r le[r] plah[n] oo se[r] troov lo-tel*
Is it	**Est-ce**	*Es*
in the centre?	**dans le centre-ville?**	*dah[n] le[r] sah[n] tr-veel*
near a bus stop?	**près d'un arrêt d'autobus?**	*pre de[n] na-ray doh-toh-bu[e] s*
on a train/ underground line?	**en train/en métro?**	*ah[n] may-tro/ah[n] tra[n]*

Check In

Key Phrases

Have you a room for the night?	**Avez-vous une chambre pour une nuit?**	*A-vay-voo u^e n shah^n br poor u^e nwee*
Does the hotel have wi-fi?	**A l'hôtel, y a-t-il la WiFi (la connexion internet sans fil)?**	*A lo-tel ee-ya-teel la wee-fee (la ko-nay-ksyo^n a^n -tair-nayt sah^n feel)*
I've reserved a room; my name is . . .	**J'ai réservé une chambre; je m'appelle . . .**	*Zhay ray-sair-vay u^e n shah^n br; zhe^r ma-pel*
Is there a lift/ elevator?	**Y a-t-il un ascenseur?**	*Ee-ya-teel e^n na-sah^n -sœr*
How much is the room per night?	**Quel est le prix de la chambre pour une nuit?**	*Kel-ay le^r pree de^r la shah^n br poor u^e n nwee*

Can you recommend	**Pouvez-vous m'indiquer**	*Poo-vay-voo ma^n -dee-kay*
another good hotel?	**un autre bon hôtel?**	*e^n notr bo^n no-tel*
an inexpensive hotel?	**un hôtel bon marché?**	*e^n o-tel bo^n mar-shay*
a moderately priced hotel?	**un hôtel à prix modéré?**	*e^n o-tel a pree mo-day-ray*
Is there an internet connection in the rooms?	**Y a-t-il une connexion internet dans les chambres?**	*Ee-ya-teel u^e n ko-nay-ksyo^n a^n -tair-nayt dah^n lay shah^n br*

Yes, it's free/it costs €…per hour	*Oui, c'est gratuit/ça coûte…€ par heure	*Wee, say gra-twee/ sa koot.…e'-roh par œr*
Does the hotel have a business centre?	Y a-t-il un centre d'affaires à l'hôtel?	*Ee-ya-teel e^n sah^n tr da-fair a lo-tel*
Is there a spa/ fitness centre?	Y a-t-il un spa/ une salle de sport?	*Ee-ya-teel e^n spa/ u^en sal de' spor*
Does the hotel have a swimming pool/ private beach?	L'hôtel a-t-il une piscine/une plage privée?	*Lo-tel a-teel u^e n pee-seen/u^e n plazh pree-vay*
I'd like a single room with a shower	Je voudrais une chambre avec douche pour une personne	*Zhe' voo-dre u^e n shah^n br a-vek doosh poor u^e n pair-son*
We'd like	Nous voudrions	*Noo voo-dree-o^n*
a room with a double bed and a bathroom	une chambre avec un grand lit et salle de bain	*u^e n shah^n br a-vek e^n grah^n lee ay sal de' ba^n*
a family room	une chambre familiale	*u^e n shah^n br fa-mee-lyal*
adjoining rooms	des chambres adjacentes	*day shah^n br ad-zha-sah^nt*
Have you a room with twin beds/a double bed?	Avez-vous une chambre à deux lits/ un grand lit?	*A-vay-voo u^e n shah^n br a de' lee/e^n grah^n lee*
Is the room air-conditioned?	Est-ce que la chambre est climatisée?	*Es-ke' la shah^n br ay klee-ma-tee-zay*
How long will you be staying?	*Combien de temps comptez-vous rester?	*Ko^n -bya^n de' tah^n ko^n -tay-voo res-tay*

Is it for one night only?	*C'est pour une nuit seulement?	Say poor u^e n nwee sœl-mah^n
I want a room	Je voudrais une chambre	Zhe^r voo-dre u^e n shah^n br
for two or three days	pour deux ou trois jours	poor de^r oo trwa zhoor
for a week	pour une semaine	poor u^e n se^r -men
until Friday	jusqu'à vendredi	zhu^e -ska vah^n -dre^r -dee
What floor is the room on?	À quel étage se trouve la chambre?	A kel ay-tazh se^r troov la shah^n br
Are there facilities for the disabled?	Y a-t-il des aménagements pour les handicapés?	Ee-ya-teel day za-may-nazh-mah^n poor lay ah^n -dee-ka-pay
Have you a room on the ground floor?	Avez-vous une chambre au rez-de-chaussée?	A-vay-voo u^e n shah^n br oh ray de^r sho-say
May I see the room?	Pourrais-je voir la chambre?	Poo-rezh vwar la shah^n br
I'll take this room	Je prends cette chambre	Zhe^r prah^n set shah^n br
I don't like this room	Je n'aime pas cette chambre	Zhe^r nem pa set shah^n br
Have you another one?	En avez-vous une autre?	Ah^n -na-vay-voo u^e n otr
I want a quiet/a bigger room	Je veux une chambre calme/plus grande	Zhe^r ve^r u^e n shah^n br kalm/u^e n shah^n br plu^e grah^n d

There's too much noise	Il y a trop de bruit	*Eel-ee-ya troh de' brwee*
I'd like a room with a balcony	**Je voudrais une chambre avec balcon**	*Zhe' voo-dre u^e n shah^n br a-vek bal-ko^n*
Have you a room looking on to the street/the sea?	**Avez-vous une chambre qui donne sur la rue/sur la mer?**	*A-vay-voo u^e n shah^n br kee don su^e r la ru^e/su^e r la mair*
Have you a room near the swimming pool?	**Avez-vous une chambre près de la piscine?**	*A-vay-voo u^{e}n shah^n br pre de' la pee-seen*
We've only a twin-bedded room	***Nous n'avons qu'une chambre à deux lits**	*Noo-na-vo^n ku^e n shah^n br a de' lee*
This is the only room vacant	***C'est la seule chambre libre**	*Say la sœl shah^n br leebr*
We shall have another room tomorrow	***Nous aurons une autre chambre demain**	*Noo-zo-ro^n u^e n otr shah^n br de' -ma^n*
The room is only available tonight	***Cette chambre n'est libre que ce soir seulement**	*Set shah^n br nay leebr ke' se' swar sœlmah^n*
How much is the room per night?	**Quel est le prix de la chambre pour une nuit?**	*Kel-ay le' pree de' la shah^n br poor u^e n nwee*
Have you nothing cheaper?	**Vous n'avez rien de moins cher?**	*Voo na-vay rya^n de' mwa^n shair*
What do we pay for the children?	**Combien devons-nous payer pour les enfants?**	*Ko^n -bya^n de' -vo^n noo pe-yay poor lay zah^n -fah^n*

Could you put a cot/ an extra bed in the room?	**Pouvez-vous mettre un lit d'enfant/un lit supplémentaire dans la chambre?**	*Poo-vay-voo metr e^n lee dah^n -fah^n/e^n lee su^e -play-mah^n -tair dah^n la shah^n br*
Are service and tax included?	**Est-ce que le service et la taxe sont compris?**	*Es-ke' le' sair-vees ay la taks so^n ko^n -pree*
Is breakfast included?	**Est-ce que le petit déjeuner est compris?**	*Es-ker' le' pe' -tee day-zhe' -nay ay ko^n -pree*
How much is full board?	**Quel est le prix de la chambre avec pension complète?**	*Kel-ay le' pree de' la shah^n br a-vek pah^n -syo^n ko^n -plet*
How much is the room without meals?	**Quel est le prix de la chambre sans repas?**	*Kel-ay le' pree de' la shah^n br sah^n re' -pa*
I'd like a room with breakfast	**Je voudrais une chambre avec petit déjeuner**	*Zhe' voo-dre u^e n shah^n br a-vek pe' -tee day-zhe' -nay*
Do you have a weekly rate?	**Avez-vous un tarif hebdomadaire?**	*A-vay-voo e^n ta-reef eb-doh-ma-dair*
What is the weekly rate?	**Quel est le prix à la semaine?**	*Kel ay le' pree a la se' -men*
It's too expensive	**C'est trop cher**	*Say troh shair*
Would you fill in the registration form, please?	***Voulez-vous remplir la fiche (de police), s'il vous plaît?**	*Voo-lay-voo rah^n -pleer la feesh (de' po-lees), seel-voo-ple*
Nom/prénom	Surname/first name	
Lieu de domicile	Address	

Date/lieu de naissance	Date and place of birth	
Numéro de passeport	Passport number	
Could I have your passport, please?	***Puis-je avoir votre passeport?**	*Pwee-zh a-vwar votr pas-por*
What is your car registration number?	***Quel est le numéro d'immatriculation de votre voiture?**	*Kel ay le^r nu^e -may-ro dee-ma-tree -ku^e -la-syo^n de^r votr vwa-tu^e r*

Check Out

I have to leave tomorrow	**Je dois partir demain**	*Zhe^r dwa par-teer de^r -ma^n*
How would you like to pay?	***Comment voulez-vous payer?**	*Ko-mah^n voo-lay voo pe-yay*

I'll pay by credit card	**Je payerai avec ma carte de crédit**	*Zhe pe-yer-ay a-vek ma kart de' kray-dee*
I shall be coming back on ..., can I book a room for that date?	**Je reviendrai le ..., pouvez-vous me réserver une chambre pour cette date?**	*Zhe' re' -vya^n -dray le' ..., poo-vay-voo me' ray-zair-vay u^e n shah^n br poor set dat*
Could you have my luggage brought down?	**Pouvez-vous faire descendre mes bagages?**	*Poo-vay-voo fair de-sah^n dr may ba-gazh*
Please order a taxi for me at 11 a.m.	**Commandez-moi un taxi pour onze heures, s'il vous plaît**	*Ko-mah^n -day mwa e^n tak-see poor o^n zœr, seel-voo-ple*
Thank you for a pleasant stay	**Je vous remercie de votre aimable accueil**	*Zhe' voo re' -mair-see de votr e-mabl a-kœ-y*

Problems and Complaints

The air conditioning/ the television doesn't work	**La climatisation/ la télévision ne fonctionne pas**	*La klee-ma-tee-za-syo^n/la tay-lay-vee-zho^n ne' fo^n k-syon pa*
There are no towels in my room	**Il n'y a pas de serviettes dans ma chambre**	*Eel-nee-ya pa de' sair-vyet dah^n ma shah^n br*
There's no soap	**Il n'y a pas de savon**	*Eel-nee-ya pa de' sa-vo^n*

There's no (hot) water	Il n'y a pas d'eau (chaude)	*Eel-nee-ya pa doh (shod)*
There's no plug in my washbasin	**Mon lavabo n'a pas de bonde**	*Mo^n la-va-bo na pa de^r bo^{n}d*
There's no toilet paper in the lavatory	Il n'y a pas de papier hygiénique aux toilettes	*Eel-nee-ya pa de^r pa-pyay ee-zhee-ay-neek oh twa-let*
The lavatory won't flush	**La chasse d'eau ne fonctionne pas**	*La shas doh ne^r fo^n k-syon pa*
The toilet is blocked	**Les toilettes sout bouchées**	*Le twa-let so^n boo-shay*
The shower doesn't work/is flooded	**La douche ne fonctionne pas/ est inondée**	*La doosh ne^r fo^n k-syon pa/ay-tee-no^n -day*
The bidet leaks	**Le bidet fuit**	*Le^r bee-day fwee*
The light doesn't work	**La lumière ne marche pas**	*La lu^e m-yair ne^r mar-sh pa*
The lamp is broken	**La lampe est cassée**	*La lah^n p ay ka-say*
The blind is stuck	**Le store est bloqué**	*Le^r stor ay blo-kay*
The curtains won't close	**Les rideaux ne ferment pas**	*Lay ree-doh ne^r fairm pa*

Camping

Key Phrases

Is there drinking water?	**Ya-t-il de l'eau potable?**	*Ee-ya-teel de' loh po-tabl*
electricity?	**de l'électricité?**	*de' lay-lek-tree-see-tay*
Is there a campsite nearby?	**Y a-t-il un (terrain de) camping près d'ici?**	*Ee-ya-teel e^n (te-ra^n de') kah^n -ping pre dee-see*
May we camp	**Pouvons-nous camper**	*Poo-vo^n -noo kah^n -pay*
on the beach?	**à la plage?**	*a la plazh*
in your field?	**dans votre champ?**	*dah^n votr shah^n*
here?	**ici?**	*ee-see*

Where should we put our tent/caravan?	**Où devons-nous placer notre tente/caravane?**	*Oo de' -vo^n -noo pla-say notr tah^n t/ka-ra-van*
Can I park the car next to the tent?	**Puis-je garer la voiture à côté de la tente?**	*Pwee-zh ga-ray la vwa-tu^e r a ko-tay de' la tah^n t*
Can we hire a tent?	**Pouvons-nous louer une tente?**	*Poo-vo^n -noo loo-ay u^e n tah^n t*
Are there	**Y a-t-il**	*Ee-ya-teel*
showers?	**des douches?**	*day doosh*
toilets?	**des toilettes?**	*day twa-let*

What does it cost	Quel est le tarif	Kel-ay le' ta-reef
per night?	journalier?	zhoor-na-lyay
per person?	par personne?	par pair-son
per week?	hebdomadaire?	eb-do-ma-dair
Is there	Y a-t-il	Ee-ya-teel
a launderette?	une laverie automatique?	u' n la-ve' -ree oh-toh-ma-teek
a playground?	un terrain de jeux?	e^n te-ra^n de' zhe'
a restaurant?	un restaurant?	e^n res-to-rah^n
a shop?	un magasin?	e^n ma-ga-za^n
a swimming pool?	une piscine?	u^e n pee-seen
Can I buy ice?	Puis-je acheter de la glace?	Pwee-zh ah-tay de' la glas
Where can I buy butane gas?	Où puis-je acheter du gaz butane?	Oo pwee-zh ash-tay du^e gaz bu^e-tan
Where do I put the rubbish?	Où puis-je vider les ordures?	Oo pwee-zh vee-day lay zor-du^e r
Should we sort the rubbish (for recycling)?	Doit-on trier les ordures (pour le recyclage)?	Dwa to^n tree-ay lay zor-du^e r (poor le' ray-see-klazh)
Where can I wash up/wash clothes?	Où puis-je faire la vaisselle/laver du linge?	Oo pwee-zh fair la vay-sel/la-vay du^e la^n zh
Is there somewhere to dry clothes?	Y a-t-il un endroit pour faire sécher le linge?	Ee-ya-teel e^n nah^n -drwa poor fair say-shay le' la^n zh

My camping gas has run out	Je n'ai plus de gaz butane	Zhe' nay plu^e de' gaz bu^e-tan
May we light a fire?	Peut-on faire du feu?	Pe' -to^n fair du^e fe'
Please prepare the bill, we are leaving today	Veuillez préparer la note, nous partons aujourd'hui	Voe-yay pray-pa-ray la not noo par-to^n oh-zhoor-dwee
How long do you want to stay?	*Combien de temps comptez-vous rester?	Ko^n -bya^n de' tah^n ko^n -tay-voo res-tay
I'm afraid the campsite is full	*Je regrette, le camping est complet	Zhe' re' -gret le' kah^n -ping ay ko^n -play

Hostels

Is there a youth hostel here?	Y a-t-il une auberge de jeunesse ici?	Ee-ya-teel u^e n o-bairzh de' zhe' -nes ee-see
How long is the walk to the youth hostel?	Combien de temps faut-il pour aller à pied à l'auberge de jeunesse?	Ko^n -bya^n de' tah^n fo-till poor a-lay a pyay a lobairzh de' zhe' -nes
Have you a room/bed for the night?	Avez-vous une chambre/un lit pour la nuit?	A-vay-voo u^e n shah^n br/ e^n lee poor la nwee
How many days can we stay here?	Combien de jours pouvons-nous rester ici?	Ko^n -bya^n de' zhoor poo-vo^n -noo res-tay ee-see
Here is my membership card	Voici ma carte de membre	Vwa-see ma kart de' mah^n br

Do you serve meals?	**Servez-vous des repas?**	*Sair-vay-voo day re' -pa*
Can I use the kitchen?	**Puis-je utiliser la cuisine?**	*Pwee-zh u^e -tee-lee-zay la kwee-zeen*
Is there somewhere cheap to eat nearby?	**Peut-on manger pour pas cher près d'ici?**	*Pe' -ton mahn -zhay poor pa shair pre dee-see*
I want to rent sheets/a sleeping bag	**Je voudrais louer des draps/un sac de couchage**	*Zhe' voo-dre loo-ay day dra/en sak de' koo-shazh*
Does the hostel have an Internet connection?	**L'auberge de jeunesse a une connexion Internet?**	*Lo-bairzh de' zhœ-nes a u^e n ko-nay-ksyon an -tair-nayt*

Hotels

In your room

chambermaid	**la femme de chambre**	*fam de' shahn br*
room service	**service dans les chambres**	*sair-vees dahn lay shahn br*
I'd like breakfast in my room, please	**Je voudrais prendre le petit déjeuner dans ma chambre, s'il vous plaît**	*Zhe' voo-dre prahn dr le' pe' -tee day-zhe' -nay dahn ma shahn br seel-voo-ple*
I'd like some ice cubes	**Je voudrais des glaçons**	*Zhe' voo-dre day gla-son*
Can I have more hangers, please?	**Puis-je avoir d'autres cintres, s'il vous plaît?**	*Pwee-zh a-vwar dotr san tr, seel-voo-ple*

Is there a socket for an electric razor?	**Est-ce qu'il y a une prise pour rasoir électrique?**	*Es-keel-ya u^e n preez poor ra-zwar ay-lek-treek*
Where is the bathroom?	**Où est la salle de bain?**	*Oo-ay la sal de^r baⁿ*
Is there a shower?	**Y a-t-il une douche?**	*Ee-ya-teel u^en doosh*
May I have another blanket/another pillow?	**Pourrais-je avoir une autre couverture/un autre oreiller?**	*Poo-rezh a-vwar u^e n otr koo-vair-tu^e r/eⁿ notr o-re-yay*
These sheets aren't clean	**Ces draps ne sont pas propres**	*Say dra ne^r soⁿ pa propr*
I can't open my window; please open it	**Je ne peux pas ouvrir ma fenêtre; voulez-vous l'ouvrir, s'il vous plaît**	*Zhe^r ne^r pe^r pa oo-vreer ma fe^r -netr; voo-lay-voo loo-vreer, seel-voo-ple*
It's too hot/cold	**Il fait trop chaud/ froid**	*Eel fay troh shoh/frwa*
Can the heating be turned up/down?	**Pouvez-vous chauffer davantage/ baisser le chauffage?**	*Poo-vay-voo shoh-fay da-vahⁿ -tazh/be-say le^r shoh-fazh*
Come in	**Entrez**	*Ahⁿ -tray*
Put it on the table, please	**Mettez cela sur la table, s'il vous plaît**	*Me-tay se^r -la su^e r la tabl, seel-voo-ple*
How long will the laundry take?	**Combien de temps faut-il pour le blanchissage/pour faire laver le linge?**	*Koⁿ -byaⁿ de^r tahⁿ fo-teel poor le^r blahⁿ -shee-sazh/ poor fair la-vay le^r laⁿ zh*
Have you a needle and thread/an iron and ironing board?	**Avez-vous du fil et une aiguille/une table et un fer à repasser?**	*A-vay-voo du^e feel ay u^e n ay-gwee-y/u^en ta-bl ay eⁿ fair a re^r -pa-say*

I'd like these shoes cleaned	Je voudrais faire cirer cette paire de chaussures	*Zhe' voo-dre fair see-ray set pair de' sho-su^e r*
I'd like this dress cleaned	Je voudrais faire nettoyer cette robe	*Zhe' voo-dre fair ne-twa-yay set rob*
I'd like this suit pressed	Je voudrais faire repasser ce costume	*Zhe' voo-dre fair re' -pa-say se' kos-tu^e m*
When will it be ready?	Quand est-ce que ce sera prêt?	*Kahⁿ es-ke' se' se' -ra pre*
It will be ready tomorrow	*Ce sera prêt demain	*Se' se' -ra pre de' -maⁿ*

Other services

hall porter	le garçon d'hôtel	*gar-soⁿ do-tel*
manager	le gérant/le directeur (zhay-rahⁿt)	*zhay-rahⁿ(zhay-rahⁿt)/dee-rek-tœr dee-rek-trees*
page	le groom/le chasseur	*groom/sha-sœr*
porter	le concierge/le portier	*koⁿ -syairzh/por-tyay*
telephonist	le/la téléphoniste	*tay-lay-fo-neest*
A second key, please	Une deuxième clé, s'il vous plaît	*U^e n de' -zyem klay, seel-voo-ple*
I've lost my keya	J'ai perdu ma clé	*Zhay pair-du^e ma klay*
Have you a map of the town/ an entertainment guide?	Avez-vous un plan de la ville/un guide des spectacles?	*A-vay-voo eⁿ plahⁿ de' la veel/eⁿ gheed day spek-takl*

Can I leave this in the safe?	Puis-je déposer ceci dans votre coffre-fort?	Pwee-zh day-poh-zay se' -see dah^n votr kofr-for
Are there any letters/ any messages for me?	Y a-t-il du courrier/ un message pour moi?	Ee-ya-teel du^e koor-yay/ e^n me-sazh poor mwa
What is the international dialling code?	Quel est l'indicatif pour les appels à l'international?	Kel ay a^n -dee-ka-teef poor lay za-pel a la^n -tair-na-syo-nal
Could you send this fax for me, please?	Pourriez-vous envoyer ce fax, s'il vous plaît?	Poor-yay-voo ah^n -vwa-yay se' fax, seel-voo-ple
Is there a computer for guests to use?	Y a-t-il un ordinateur réservé à l'usage des clients?	Ee-ya-teel e^n or-dee-na-tœr ray-sayr-vay a lu^e -zazh day klee-ah^n
How much does it cost?	C'est combien, s'il vous plaît?	Say ko^n -bya^n seel-voo-ple
Do I need a password?	Faut-il un mot de passe?	Fo-teel e^n mo de' pas?
There's a lady/ gentleman to see you	*Une dame/un monsieur vous demande	U^e n dam/e^n me' -sye' voo de' -mah^n d
Please ask her/him to come up	Faites la/le monter, s'il vous plaît	Fet-la/le' mo^n -tay, seel-voo-ple
I'm coming down	Je descends	Zhe' day-sah^n
Have you	Avez-vous	A-vay-voo
any envelopes?	des enveloppes?	day zah^n -vlop
any stamps?	des timbres?	day ta^n br
any writing paper?	du papier à lettre?	du^e pa-pyay a letr

Please send the chambermaid/the waiter	Envoyez-moi la femme de chambre/le garçon, s'il vous plaît	*Ahⁿ -vwa-yay mwa la fam de' shahⁿ -br/le' gar-soⁿ, seel-voo-ple*
I need a guide/interpreter	J'ai besoin d'un guide/d'un interprète	*Zhay be' -zwaⁿ deⁿ gheed/deⁿ naⁿ -tair-pret*
Does the hotel have a babysitting service?	Est-ce qu'il y a un service de garde d'enfants à l'hôtel?	*Es-keel-ya eⁿ sair-vees de' gard dahⁿ -fahⁿ a lo-tel*
Where are the toilets?	Où sont les toilettes?	*Oo soⁿ lay twa-let*
Where is the cloakroom/the dining room?	Où est le vestiaire/la salle à manger?	*Oo ay le' ves-tyair/la sal a mahⁿ -zhay*
What time is	À quelle heure est	*A kel-œr ay*
breakfast?	le petit déjeuner?	*le' pe' -tee day-zhe' -nay*
lunch?	le déjeuner?	*le' day-zhe' -nay*
dinner?	le dîner?	*le' dee-nay*
Is there a garage?	Est-ce qu'il y a un garage?	*Es-keel-ya eⁿ ga-razh*
Where can I park the car?	Où puis-je garer ma voiture?	*Oo pwee-zh ga-ray ma vwa-tuᵉ r*
Is the hotel open all night?	Est-ce que l'hôtel reste ouvert toute la nuit?	*Es-ke' lo-tel rest oo-vair toot la nwee*
What time does it close?	À quelle heure ferme-t-il?	*A kel-œr fairm-teel*
Please wake me at . . .	Veuillez me réveiller à . . .	*Vœ-yay me' ray-vay-yay a . . .*

APARTMENTS AND VILLAS

Key Phrases

Please show us around	**Pourriez-vous nous faire visiter les lieux, s'il vous plaît?**	*Poor-yay-voo noo fair vee-zee-tay lay lye', seel-voo-ple*
How does the heating/hot water work?	**Comment fonctionne le chauffage/ le système d'eau chaude?**	*Ko-mah[n] fo[n] k-syon le' shoh-fazh/le' sees-tem doh shod*
Please show me how this works	**Pourriez-vous me montrer comment ça marche?**	*Poor-yay-voo me' mo[n] -tray ko-mah[n] sa mar-sh*
Which days does the maid come?	**Quels jours vient la femme de ménage?**	*Kel zhoor vya[n] la fam de' may-nazh*
When is the rubbish collected?	**Quand est-ce qu'on ramasse les ordures?**	*Kah[n] es-ko[n] ra-mas lay zor-du[e] r*
Please give me another set of keys	**Pourriez-vous me donner un autre jeu de clés?**	*Poor-yay-voo me' do-nay e[n] notr zhe' de' klay*

We have rented an apartment/villa	**Nous avons loué un appartement/ une villa**	*Noo za-vo[n] loo-ay e[n] na-par-te' -mah[n]/ u[e] n vee-la*
Here is our reservation	**Voici notre réservation**	*Vwa-see notr ray-zair-va-syo[n]*

Is the cost of	Est-ce que le prix de	Es-ke' le' pree de'
electricity	l'électricité	lay-lek-tree-see-tay
the gas cylinder	la bouteille de gaz	la boo-te-y de' gaz
the maid included?	la femme de ménage est compris?	la fam de' may-nazh ay ko^n -pree
Where is the	Où se trouve	Oo se' troov
electricity mains switch?	l'interrupteur général d'électricité/le disjoncteur?	la^n -tay-ru' p-tœr zhay-nay-ral day-lek-tree-see-tay/ le' dees-zho^n k-tœr
light switch?	l'interrupteur/le commutateur?	la^n -tay-ru' p-tœr/ le' ko-mu' -ta-tœr
power point?	la prise de courant?	la preez de' koo-rah^n
water mains stopcock?	le robinet principal de distribution d'eau?	le' ro-bee-nay pra^n -see-pal de' dees-tree-bu' -syo^n doh
Where is the fuse box?	Où sont les fusibles?	Oo so^n lay fu' -zeebl
Is there a spare gas cylinder?	Y a-t-il une bouteille de gaz de rechange?	Ee-ya-teel u' n boo-te-y de' gaz de' re' -shah^n zh
Are gas cylinders delivered?	Est-ce qu'on livre les bouteilles de gaz?	Es-ko^n leevr lay boo-te-y de' gaz
For how long does the maid come?	Pour combien d'heures vient la femme de ménage?	Poor ko^n-bya^n dœr vya^n la fam de' may-nazh

Should we sort the rubbish for recycling?	**Faut-il trier les ordures pour le recyclage?**	*Fo-teel tree-ay lay zor-du^e r poor le$'$ ray-see-klazh*
The rubbish hasn't been collected	**Les poubelles n'ont pas été ramassées**	*Lay poo-bel no^n pa zay-lay ra-ma-say*
Where can we buy logs for the fire?	**Où pouvons-nous acheter du bois de chauffage?**	*Oo poo-vo^n -noo ash-tay du^e bwa de$'$ shoh-fazh*
Is there a barbecue?	**Y a-t-il un barbecue?**	*Ee-ya-teel e^n bar-be$'$ -ku^e*
Does someone come to service the swimming pool?	**Y a-t-il quelqu'un pour l'entretien de la piscine?**	*Ee-ya-teel kel-ke^n poor lah^n -tre$'$ -tya^n de$'$ la pee-seen*
Is there an inventory?	**Y a-t-il un inventaire?**	*Ee-ya-teel e^n a^n -vah^n -tayr*
This was broken when we arrived	**Ceci était déjà cassé quand nous sommes arrivés**	*Se$'$ -see ay-tay de$'$ -zha ka-say kah^n noo som a-ree-vay*
We have replaced the broken ...	**Nous avons remplacé le/la ... cassé(e)**	*Noo za-vo^n rah^n -pla-say le$'$/la ... ka-say*
Here is the bill	***Voici la facture/ la note**	*Vwa-see la fak-tu^e r/ la not*
Please return my deposit against damage	**Pouvez-vous me rembourser la caution/le cautionnement**	*Poo-vay-voo me$'$ rah^n -boor-say la koh-syo^n/le$'$ koh-syon-mah^n*

Cleaning and Maintenance[1]

Where is a DIY centre/hardware shop?	Où se trouve un magasin de bricolage/une quincaillerie?	*Oo se' troov e{n} ma-ga-za{n} de' bree-ko-lazh/u{e} n ka{n} -ka-ye' -ree*
Where can I get butane gas?	Où puis-je trouver une bouteille de gaz butane?	*Oo pwee-zh troo-vay u{e} n boo-te-y de' gaz bu{e}-tan*
all-purpose cleaner	le produit nettoyant tous usages	*le' pro-dwee nay-twa-ya{n} too zu{e}-sazh*
bleach	l'eau de javel *f*	*oh de' zha-vel*
bracket	la console/le tasseau	*ko{n} -sol/ta-so*
broom	le balai	*ba-lay*
brush	la brosse	*bros*
bucket	le seau	*so*
charcoal	le charbon de bois	*shar-bo{n} de' bwa*
clothes line	la corde à linge	*kord a la{n} zh*
clothes pegs	les pinces à linge *fpl*	*pa{n} s a la{n} zh*
detergent	le détergent	*day-tair-zhah{n}*
dustbin	la poubelle	*poo-bel*
dustpan	la pelle (à poussière)	*pel (a poos-yair)*
fire extinguisher	l'extincteur *m*	*eks-ta{n} k-tœr*
hammer	le marteau	*mar-toh*
mop	le balai à franges	*ba-lay a frah{n} zh*
nails	les clous *m*	*kloo*

---

1. See also SHOPS AND SERVICES (p. 183).

paint	la peinture	*paⁿ -tuᵉ r*
paintbrush	le pinceau	*paⁿ -soh*
plastic	le plastique	*plas-teek*
pliers	les pinces *f*	*paⁿ s*
rubbish sack	le sac à poubelle	*sak a poo-bel*
saw	la scie	*see*
screwdriver	le tournevis	*toor-neʳ -vees*
screws	les vis *f*	*vees*
spanner	la clé/(*adjustable*) la clé à molette	*klay/klay a mo-let*
stainless steel	l'acier inoxydable *m*	*a-syay ee-no-xee-dabl*
tile	le carreau/(*roof*) la tuile	*ka-roh/tweel*
vacuum cleaner	l'aspirateur *m*	*as-pee-ra-tœr*
washing powder	la lessive (en poudre)	*lay-seev (ahⁿ poodr)*
washing-up liquid	le liquide-vaisselle	*lee-keed vay-sel*
wire	le fil de fer/(*electricity*) le fil électrique	*feel deʳ fair/feel ay-lek-treek*
wood	le bois	*bwa*

Furniture and Fittings

armchair	le fauteuil	*fo-tœ-y*
barbecue	le barbecue	*ba-beʳ -kuᵉ*
bath	la baignoire	*ben-ywar*

bed	**le lit**	*lee*
blanket	**la couverture**	*koo-vair-tu^e r*
bolt (for door)	**le verrou**	*ve-roo*
chair	**la chaise**	*shez*
clock	**la pendule/(***large***)** **l'horloge** *f*	*pahⁿ -du^e l/or-lozh*
cooker	**la cuisinière**	*kwee-zeen-yair*
cupboard	**le placard/l'armoire** *f*	*pla-kar/ar-mwar*
curtains	**les rideaux**	*ree-doh*
cushions	**les coussins**	*koo-saⁿ*
deckchair	**la chaise longue**	*shez loⁿ g*
dishwasher	**le lave-vaisselle**	*lav vay-sel*
doorbell	**la sonnette**	*so-net*
doorknob	**la poignée (de porte)**	*pwan-yay (de^r port)*
hinge	**le gond/la charnière**	*goⁿ/shar-nyair*
immersion heater	**le chauffe-eau électrique**	*shof-oh ay-lek-treek*
iron	**le fer à repasser**	*fair a re^r -pa-say*
lamp	**la lampe**	*lahⁿ p*
lampshade	**l'abat-jour** *m*	*a-ba-zhoor*
light bulb	**l'ampoule** *f*	*ahⁿ -pool*
lock	**la serrure**	*se-ru^e r*
mattress	**le matelas**	*ma-te^r -la*
mirror	**le miroir/la glace**	*mee-rwar/glas*

padlock	le cadenas	ka-de' -na
pillow	l'oreiller *m*	o-re-yay
pipe	le tuyau	twee-yoh
plug (bath)	la bonde	bo^n d
plug (electric)	la prise de courant	preez de' koo-rah^n
radio	la radio	ra-dyo
refrigerator	le réfrigérateur	ray-free-zhay-ra-toer
sheet	le drap	dra
shelf	l'étagère *f*/le rayon	ay-ta-zhair/re-yo^n
shower	la douche	doosh
sink	l'évier *m*	ay-vyay
sofa	le canapé/le sofa	kap-na-pay/so-fa
stool	le tabouret	ta-boo-ray
sun-lounger	le transat	trah^n -zat
table	la table	tabl
tap	le robinet	ro-bee-nay
television	la télévision	tay-lay-vee-zyo^n
toilet	les toilettes *f*	twa-let
towel	la serviette	sair-vyet
washbasin	le lavabo	la-va-bo
washing machine	la machine à laver	ma-sheen a la-vay
window latch	le loquet de la fenêtre	lo-kay de' la fe' -netr
window sill	le rebord de la fenêtre	re' -bor de' la fe' -netr

Kitchen Equipment

bottle opener	**le décapsuleur**	*day-kap-su^e-lœr*
bowl	**la cuvette**/(*for food*) **la jatte**/(*small*) **le bol**/(*salad*) **le saladier**	*ku^e-vet/zhat/bol/sa-la-dyay*
can opener	**l'ouvre-boîte** *m*	*oovr-bwat*
candles	**les bougies** *f*	*boo-zhee*
chopping board	**la planche à hacher**	*plah^n sh a a-shay*
coffee pot	**la cafetière**	*kaf-tyair*
colander	**la passoire**	*pa-swar*
coolbag	**le sac isotherme**	*sak ee-zo-tairm*
corkscrew	**le tire-bouchon**	*teer-boo-sho^n*
cup	**la tasse**	*tas*
fork	**la fourchette**	*foor-shet*
frying pan	**la poêle (à frire)**	*pwal (a freer)*
glass	**le verre**	*vair*
grill	**le grill**	*greel*
ice tray	**le bac à glaçons**	*bak a gla-so^n*
kettle	**la bouilloire**	*boo-ywar*
knife	**le couteau**	*koo-toh*
matches	**les allumettes** *f*	*a-lu^e-met*
microwave	**le micro-onde**	*mee-kro o^n d*
pan with lid	**la casserole avec couvercle**	*kas-rol a-vek koo-vairkl*

plate	l'assiette *f*	*as-yet*
scissors	les ciseaux *m*	*see-zoh*
sieve	le tamis	*ta-mee*
spoon	la cuiller	*kwee-yair*
teatowel	le torchon	*tor-sho^n*
toaster	le grille-pain	*gree-y pa^n*
torch	la lampe de poche/ la lampe-torche	*lah^n p de^r posh/lah^n p torsh*

Parts of a House and Grounds

balcony	le balcon/la loggia	*bal-ko^n/lodzh-ya*
bathroom	la salle de bain	*sal de^r ba^n*
bedroom	la chambre (à coucher)	*shah^n br (a koo-shay)*
ceiling	le plafond	*pla-fo^n*
chimney	la cheminée	*she^r-mee-nay*
corridor	le couloir	*koo-lwar*
door	la porte	*port*
fence	la barrière/la clôture	*bar-yair/klo-tu^e r*
fireplace	la cheminée	*she^r-mee-nay*
floor	le sol/(*wooden*) le plancher	*sol/plah^n-shay*
garage	le garage	*ga-razh*
garden	le jardin	*zhar-da^n*

gate	le portail/(*iron*) la grille	*por-ta-y/gree-y*
hall	le hall	*ol*
kitchen	la cuisine	*kwee-zeen*
living room	le salon/la salle de séjour	*sa-lo^n/sal de^r say-zhoor*
patio	le patio	*pat-yo*
roof	le toit	*twa*
shutters	les volets	*vo-lay*
stairs	l'escalier	*les-ka-lyay*
swimming pool	la piscine	*pee-seen*
terrace	la terrasse	*te-ras*
wall	le mur	*mu^e r*
window	la fenêtre	*fe^r -netr*

Problems

The drain is blocked	Les canalisations sanitaires sont bouchées	*Lay ka-na-lee-za-syo^n sa-nee-tair so^n boo-shay*
The pipe/sink is blocked	Le tuyau/l'évier est bouché	*Le^r twee-yoh/lay-vyay ay boo-shay*
The toilet doesn't flush	La chasse d'eau ne fonctionne pas	*La shas doh ne^r fo^n k-syon pa*
There's no water	Il n'y a pas d'eau	*Eel-nee-ya pa doh*

We can't turn the water off	**Nous ne pouvons pas fermer l'eau**	*Noo ne' poo-vo^n pa fair-may loh*
We can't turn the shower on	**Nous ne pouvons pas faire couler la douche**	*Noo ne' poo-vo^n pa fair koo-lay la doosh*
There is a leak (water, gas)/a broken window	**Il y a une fuite (d'eau, de gaz)/une fenêtre cassée**	*Eel-ya u^e n fweet (doh, de' gaz)/u^e n fe' -netr ka-say*
The shutters won't close	**Les volets ne ferment pas**	*Lay vo-lay ne' fairm pa*
The window won't open	**La fenêtre ne s'ouvre pas**	*La fe' -netr ne' soovr pa*
The electricity has gone off	**Il n'y a plus d'électricité**	*Eel-nee-ya plu^e day-lek-tree-see-tay*
The heating . . .	**Le chauffage . . .**	*Le' shoh-fazh*
The cooker . . .	**La cuisinière . . .**	*La kwee-zeen-yair*
The refrigerator . . .	**Le réfrigérateur . . .**	*Le' ray-free-zhay-ra-tœr*
The water heater doesn't work	**Le chauffe-eau ne marche pas**	*Le' shof oh ne' mar-sh pa*
The lock is stuck	**La serrure est coincée**	*La se-ru^e r ay kwa^n -say*
This is broken	**C'est cassé**	*Say ka-say*
This needs repairing	**Cela a besoin d'être réparé**	*Se' -la a be' -zwa^n detr ray-pa-ray*
The apartment/villa has been burgled	**L'appartement/ la villa a été cambriolé(e)**	*La-par-te' -mah^n/la vee-la a ay-tay kah^n -bree-o-lay*

COMMUNICATIONS

Key Phrases

Is there an Internet café near here?	**Y a-t-il un cybercafé près d'ici?**	*Ee-ya-teel eⁿ see-ber-ka-fay pre dee-see*
Do I need a password?	**Faut-il un mot de passe?**	*Fo-teel eⁿ mo de^r pas*
Can I print this?	**Puis-je imprimer ceci?**	*Pwee-zh aⁿ -pree-may se^r -see*
What is your email address?	**Quelle est votre adresse mél?**	*Kel ay vo-tr a-dres mayl*
I want to get a local SIM card for this phone	**Je voudrais acheter une carte SIM locale pour ce téléphone**	*Zhe^r voo-dre ash-tay u^en kart seem lo-kal poor se^r tay-lay-fon*
Where is the nearest post office?	**Où est le bureau de poste le plus proche?**	*Oo ay le^r bu^e -roh de^r post le^r plu^e prosh*

Email and Internet

Does this café have wi-fi?	**Est-ce que ce café a la WiFi (la connexion Internet sans fil)?**	*Es-ke^r ce^r ka-fay a la Wee-Fee (la ko-nay-ksyoⁿ aⁿ -tair-nayt sahⁿ feel)*
Is there a connection fee?	**Y a-t-il des frais de connexion?**	*Ee-ya-teel day fray de^r ko-nay-ksyoⁿ*

Can I access the Internet?	**Puis-je avoir accès à l'Internet?**	*Pwee-zh a-vwar ak-say al a[n] -tair-nayt*
Can I check my emails?	**Puis-je consulter mes méls?**	*Pwee-zh ko[n] -su[e] l-tay may mayl*
Can I use my computer?	**Puis-je utiliser mon ordinateur?**	*Pwee-zh u[e] -tee-lee-zay mo[n] or-dee-na-tœr*
How much does it cost for an hour/ half an hour?	**Combien coûte une heure/demi-heure de connexion?**	*Ko[n] -bya[n] koot u[e] n œr/de[r] -mee œr de[r] ko-nay-ksyo[n]*
How do I turn on the computer?	**Comment on allume l'ordinateur?**	*Ko-mah[n] o[n] a-lu[e] -me[r] lor-dee-na-tœr*
How do I log on/ log off?	**Comment je me connecte/ me déconnecte?**	*Ko-mah[n] zhe[r] me[r] ko-naykt/me[r] day-ko-naykt*
I can't log on	**Je n'arrive pas à me connecter**	*Zhe[r] na-reev pa a me[r] ko-nay-ktay*
The computer doesn't respond	**L'ordinateur ne répond pas**	*Lor-dee-na-tœr ne[r] ray-po[n] pa*
The computer has frozen	**L'ordinateur se bloque**	*Lor-dee-na-tœr se[r] blok*
Can you change this to an English keyboard?	**Est-ce possible d'installer un clavier anglais?**	*Es po-seebl da[n] s-ta-lay e[n] kla-vee-ay ah[n] -gle*
Where is the @/at sign on the keyboard?	**Où est l'arobase sur le clavier?**	*Oo ay la-ro-baz su[e] r le[r] kla-vee*
I need an adapter	**J'ai besoin d'un adaptateur**	*Zhay be[r] -zwa[n] de[n] -nadap-ta-tœr*
My email address is …	**Mon adresse mél est …**	*Mo[n] na-dres mayl ay*

How do you spell it?	**Épelez s'il vous plaît**	*Ay-per -lay, seel-voo-ple*
all one word	**en un seul mot**	*ahn en sœl mo*
all lower case	**tout en minuscules**	*too ten mee-nee-skue l*
at/@	**arobase**	*a-ro-baz*
dot	**point**	*pwan*
hyphen	**trait d'union**	*tray du-nee-on*
Did you get my email?	**Avez-vous reçu mon mél?**	*A-vay voo rer -sue mon mayl*
Email me, please	**Envoyez-moi un mél, s'il vous plaît**	*Ahn -vwa-yay mwa en mayl, seel-voo-ple*
Do you have a website?	**Avez-vous un site web?**	*A-vay voo en seet web*

Faxing, Copying and Telegrams

Do you have a fax?	**Avez-vous un fax?**	*A-vay voo en fax*
What is your fax number?	**Quel est votre numéro de fax?**	*Kel ay votr nue -may-ro der fax*
I want to send a fax	**Je voudrais envoyer un fax**	*Zher voo-dre ahn -vwa-yay en fax*
Can I receive faxes here?	**Puis-je recevoir des fax ici?**	*Pwee-zher rer-ser -vwar day fax ee-see*
How much does it cost per page?	**Quel est le prix par page?**	*Kel ay ler pree par pazh*
Please resend your fax	**Envoyez à nouveau votre fax, s'il vous plaît**	*Ahn -vwa-yay a noo-voh votr fax, seel-voo-ple*

Can I make photocopies here?	**Puis-je faire des photocopies ici?**	*Pwee-zh fair day fo-to-ko-pee ee-see*
Could you scan this for me?	**Pourriez-vous me scanner ceci, s'il vous plaît?**	*Poor-yay-voo me' ska-nay se' -see, seel-voo-ple*
I want to send a (reply-paid) telegram	**Je voudrais envoyer un télégramme (réponse payée)**	*Zhe' voo-dre ah^n -vwa-yay e^n tay-lay-gram (ray-po^n s pe-yay)*
How much does it cost per word?	**C'est combien le mot?**	*Say ko^n -bya^n le' mo*
Do I need to fill in a form?	**Dois-je remplir un formulaire?**	*Dwa-zh rah^n -pleer e^n for-mu^e -lair*
Write the message here and your own name and address	***Écrivez le texte ici et mettez votre nom et votre adresse**	*Ay-kree-vay le' tekst ee-see ay me-tay votr no^n ay votr a-dres*

Post[1]

Where's the main post office?	**Où est le bureau de poste principal?**	*Oo ay le' bu^e -ro de' post pra^n -see-pal*
Where's the nearest post office?	**Où est le bureau de poste le plus proche?**	*Oo ay le' bu^e -ro de' post le' plu^e prosh*
What time does the post office open/ close?	**À quelle heure ouvre/ferme le bureau de poste?**	*A kel-œr oovr/fairm le' bu^e -roh de' post*
Where's the post box?	**Où est la boîte aux lettres?**	*Oo ay la bwa-toh-letr*

1. In France stamps are on sale in **bar-tabacs** and some newsagents as well as in post offices.

Is there a stamp machine?	Y a-t-il une machine à timbres?	*Ee-ya-teel u^e n ma-sheen a ta^n br*
Which counter do I go to for stamps/ poste restante?	À quel guichet faut-il s'adresser pour les timbres/la poste restante?	*A kel ghee-shay fo-teel sa-dre-say poor lay ta^n br/ la post res-tah^n t*
How much is a postcard to Britain?	À combien faut-il affranchir une carte postale pour la Grande-Bretagne?	*A ko^n -bya^n fo-teel a-frah^n -sheer u^e n kart pos-tal poor la grah^n d-bre^r -tan-y*
How much is an airmail letter to the USA?	À combien faut-il affranchir une lettre avion pour les États-Unis?	*A ko^n -bya^n fo-teel a-fra^n -sheer u^e n letr av-yo^n poor lay-ze-ta-zu^e nee*
How much is it to send a letter surface mail to the USA?	À combien faut-il affranchir une lettre pour les États-Unis par la voie ordinaire?	*A ko^n -bya^n fo-teel a-frah^n -sheer u^e n letr poor lay-ze-ta-zu^e nee par la vwa or-dee-nair*
It's for France	C'est pour la France	*Say poor la frah^n s*
Give me three ... euro stamps, please	Donnez-moi trois timbres à ... euros, s'il vous plaît	*Do-nay mwa trwa ta^n br a ... e^r -roh, seel-voo-ple*
I want to send this letter special delivery	Je voudrais envoyer cette lettre en exprès	*Zhe^r voo-dre ah^n -vwa-yay set letr ah^n exprays*
I want to register this letter	Je voudrais recommander cette lettre	*Zhe^r voo-dre re^r -ko-mah^n -day set letr*
I want to send a parcel	Je voudrais envoyer un colis	*Zhe^r voo-dre ah^n -vwa-yay e^n ko-lee*

Are there any letters for me?	**Y a-t-il du courrier pour moi?**	*Ee-ya-teel du^e koor-yay poor mwa*
What is your name?	***Comment vous appelez-vous?**	*Ko-mah^n voo za-pe^r -lay-voo*
Have you any means of identification?	***Avez-vous une pièce d'identité?**	*A-vay-voo u^e n pyes dee-dah^n -tee-tay*

Telephones, Mobiles and SMS

Do you have a mobile (cell phone)?	**Avez-vous un portable?**	*Avay-voo e^n por-tabl*
What is your mobile (cell) number?	**Quel est votre numéro de portable?**	*Kel ay votr nu^e -may-ro de^r por-tabl*
My mobile (cell) isn't working here	**Mon portable ne fonctionne pas ici**	*Mo^n por-tabl ne^r fo^n k-syon pa zee-see*
I want to get a local SIM card for this phone	**Je voudrais acheter une carte SIM locale pour ce téléphone**	*Zhe^r voo-dre ash-tay u^e n kart seem lo-kal poor se^r tay-lay-fon*
Could you give me his/her mobile (cell) number?	**Pourriez-vous me donner son numéro de portable?**	*Poor-yay-voo me^r do-nay so^n nu^e -may-ro de por-tabl*
I'll send you a text/SMS	**Je vous enverrai un texto/SMS**	*Zhe voo zah^n -vay-ray e^n teks-to/es em es*

Where's the nearest phone box?[1]	Où est la cabine téléphonique la plus proche?	Oo ay la ka-been tay-lay-fo-neek la plu[e] prosh
I would like a phonecard, please	Je voudrais une télécarte, s'il vous plaît	Zhe[r] voo-dre u[e] n tay-lay-kart, seel-voo-ple
I want to make a phone call	Je voudrais passer un coup de téléphone	Zhe[r] voo-dre pa-say e[n] koo de[r] tay-lay-fon
May I use your phone?	Puis-je utiliser votre téléphone?	Pwee-zh u[e] -tee-lee-zay votr tay-lay-fon
Please give me an outside line	Donnez-moi une ligne extérieure, s'il vous plaît	Do-nay mwa u[e] n leen-y ek-ste-ree-oer seel-voo-ple
Do you have a telephone directory for ...?	Avez-vous un annuaire téléphonique pour ...?	A-vay-voo e[n] na-nu[e] -air tay-lay-fon-eek poor
Could you give me the number for international directory enquiries?	Pourriez-vous me donner le numéro pour les renseignements internationaux?	Poor-yay-voo me[r] do-nay le[r] nu[e] -may-ro poor lay rah[n] -sen-ye[r] -mah[n] a[n] -tair-na-syo-no
What is	Quel est	Kel ay
the area code for ...?	l'indicatif départemental/ régional pour ...?	la[n] -dee-ka-teef day-par-te[r] -mah[n] -tal/ ray-zhyo-nal poor

1. Telephone boxes are found in post offices and in public places (e.g. stations, streets, town squares). Most operate with phonecards which can be bought from post offices, and from **bar-tabacs** and some newspaper kiosks. Main post offices have special telephone booths where you can make calls via the operator, whom you pay after the call.

the country code for...?	l'indicatif pour ...	laⁿ-dee-ka-teef poor
the international access code	l'indicatif pour l'international?	laⁿ-dee-ka-teef poor laⁿ-tair-na-syo-nal
Can I dial an international number direct?	Puis-je composer un numéro international directement?	Pwee-zh koⁿ-po-say eⁿ nu^e-may-ro aⁿ-tair-na-syo-nal dee-rayk-te^r-mahⁿ
What do I dial to get the international operator?	Quel numéro dois-je faire pour avoir l'international?	Kel nu^e-may-ro dwa-zh fair poor a-vwar laⁿ-tair-na-syo-nal
I want to telephone Australia	Je voudrais téléphoner en Australie	Zhe^r voo-dre tay-lay-fo-nay ahⁿ no-stra-lee
Please get me ...	Donnez-moi le ...	Do-nay mwa le^r
I was cut off, can you reconnect me?	J'ai été coupé, pouvez-vous me redonner la communication?	Zhay ay-tay koo-pay, poo-vay-voo me^r re^r-do-nay la ko-mu^e-nee-ka-syoⁿ
The number is out of order	*Le numéro est en dérangement	Le^r nu^e-may-ro ay-tahⁿ day-rahⁿ zh-mahⁿ
The line is engaged	*La ligne est occupée	La lee-nye ay to-ku^e-pay
There's no reply	*Il n'y a pas de réponse/le numéro ne répond pas	Eel-nya-pa de^r ray-poⁿ s/le nu^e-may-ro ne^r ray-poⁿ pa
Hang up	*Raccrochez	Ra-kro-shay
You have the wrong number	*Vous vous êtes trompé de numéro	Voo voo-zet troⁿ-pay de^r nu^e-may-ro

On the phone

Hello	Allô	A-lo
I want extension forty-three	Je voudrais le poste quarante-trois	Zhe' voo-dre le' post ka-rah'' t-trwa
May I speak to . . .?	Pourrais-je parler à . . .?	Poo-rezh par-lay a
Speaking	*Lui-même (man)/ elle-même (woman)	Lwee-mem/el-mem
Who's speaking?	*Qui est à l'appareil, s'il vous plaît?	Kee ay-ta-la-pa-re-y, seel-voo-ple
Hold the line, please	*Ne quittez pas	Ne' kee-tay-pa
He's not here	*Il n'est pas là	El nay pa la
She's at . . .	*Elle est à . . .	El ay ta
When will she be back?	Quand sera-t elle de retour?	Kah'' se' -ra-tel de' re' -toor
Will you take a message?	Voulez-vous prendre un message?	Voo-lay-voo prah'' dr e'' me-sazh
Tell him that . . . phoned	Dites-lui que . . . a téléphoné	Deet-lwee ke' . . . a tay-lay-fo-nay
I'll ring again later	Je rappellerai plus tard	Zhe' ra-pel-ray plu' tar
Please ask him to phone me	Demandez-lui de me rappeler, s'il vous plaît	De' -mah'' -day-lwee de' me' ra-pe' -lay, seel-voo-ple
Could you repeat that, please	Pourriez-vous répéter, s'il vous plaît?	Poor-yay-voo ray-pay-tay, seel-voo-ple

Please speak slowly	**Parlez lentement, s'il vous plaît**	*Par-lay lahn -ter -mahn , seel-voo-ple*
I can't hear you well	**Je vous entends très mal**	*Zher voo zahn -tahn tray mal*
What's your number?[1]	***Quel est votre numéro?**	*Kel ay votr nue -may-ro*
My number is ...	**Mon numéro est ...**	*Mon nue -may-ro ay*

1. For numbers see p. 258. In French phone numbers are given in pairs: e.g. 44 12 30 is **quarante-quatre, douze, trente**.

DISABLED TRAVELLERS

Key Phrases

Is there a disabled parking area?	**Y a-t-il un parking pour les personnes à mobilité réduite?**	*Ee-ya-teel e^n par-king poor lay pair-son a mo-bee-lee-tay ray-dweet*
Are there facilities for the disabled?	**Y a-t-il des infrastructures pour les personnes à mobilité réduite?**	*Ee-ya-teel day za^n-fra-stru^e-ktu^e r poor lay pair-son a mo-bee-lee-tay ray-dweet*
I'd like to reserve a wheelchair (from the check-in desk to the plane), please	**Je voudrais réserver un fauteuil roulant (du comptoir d'enregistrement jusqu'à l'embarquement du vol), s'il vous plaît**	*Zhe^r voo-dre ray-zair-vay e^n fo-tœ-y roo-lah^n (du ko^n-twar dah^n-re^r-zhees-tre^r mah^n zhu^e s-ka lah^n-bar-ke^r-mah^n du^e vol), seel-voo-ple*
I need a bedroom on the ground floor/ near the lift	**J'ai besoin d'une chambre au rez-de-chaussée/près de l'ascenseur**	*Zhay be^r-zwa^n du^e n shah^n br oh ray de shoh-say pre de^r la-sah^n-sœr*
Do the buses take wheelchairs?	**Est-ce que les fauteuils roulants sont admis dans l'autobus?**	*Es-ke^r lay fo-tœ-y roo-lah^n so^n tad-mee dah^n loh-toh-bu^e s*

Access

Can we borrow/hire a wheelchair/mobility scooter?	**Peut-on emprunter/ louer un fauteuil roulant/un scooter électrique pour les personnes à mobilité réduite?**	*Pe' -ton ahn -pren -tay/ loo-ay en fo-tœ-y roo-lahn poor lay pair-son a mo-bee-lee-tay ray-dweet*
Is it possible to visit the old town in a wheelchair?	**Est-ce possible de visiter la vieille ville en fauteuil roulant?**	*Es po-seebl de' vee-zee-tay la vye-y veel ahn fo-tœ-y roo-lahn*
Is there wheelchair access to the gallery/ theatre/concert hall?	**Y a-t-il un accès pour fauteuils roulants au musée/théâtre/à la salle de concert?**	*Ee-ya-teel en ak-say poor fo-tœ-y roo-lah oh mue -zay/tay-atr/a la sal de' kon -sair*
Are the paths in the garden/park suitable for wheelchairs?	**Y a-t-il des allées pour fauteuils roulants dans le jardin/parc?**	*Ee-ya-teel day za-lay poor fo-tœ-y roo-lahn dahn le' zhar-dan/park*
Is there a wheelchair ramp?	**Y a-t-il une rampe pour fauteuils roulants?**	*Ee-ya-teel ue n rahn p poor fo-tœ-y roo-lahn*
Are there seats reserved for the disabled?	**Y a-t-il des sièges réservés aux personnes à mobilité réduite?**	*Ee-ya-teel day see-aizh ray-zay-rvay oh pair-son a mo-bee-lee-tay ray-dweet*
Is there a table with a place for a wheelchair?	**Y a-t-il une table avec un espace pour un fauteuil roulant?**	*Ee-ya-teel ue n ta-bl a-vek en es-pas poor fo-tœ-y roo-lahn*
Are mobility scooters allowed inside?	**Les scooters électriques sont-ils admis?**	*Lay skoo-tœr ay-lek-treek son teel ad-mee*

Where is the lift?	**Où est l'ascenseur?**	*Oo ay la-sahn -sœr*
Are there disabled toilets?	**Y a-t-il des toilettes pour les personnes à mobilité réduite?**	*Ee-ya-teel day twa-let poor lay pair-son a mo-bee-lee-tay ray-dweet*
Is there a reduction for the disabled?	**Y a-t-il une réduction pour les personnes à mobilité réduite?**	*Ee-ya-teel ue n ray-due k-syon poor lay pair-son a mo-bee-lee-tay ray-dweet*
Are guide dogs allowed?	**Les chiens d'aveugles sont-ils admis?**	*Lay shyan da-vœgl son teel ad-mee*
I can't walk far	**Je ne peux pas marcher très loin**	*Zhe ne pe' pa mar-shay tray lwan*
I can't climb stairs	**Je ne peux pas monter d'escalier**	*Zhe ne pe' pa mon -tay des-ka-lyay*
I need a bedroom on the ground floor/ near the lift	**J'ai besoin d'une chambre au rez-de-chaussée/près de l'ascenseur**	*Zhay be' -zwan due n shahn br oh ray de shoh-say/pre de' la-sahn -sœr*
Is the bathroom equipped for the disabled?	**La salle de bain est-elle équipée pour les personnes à mobilité réduite?**	*La sal de' ban ay-tel ay-kee-pay poor lay pair-son a mo-bee-lee-tay ray-dweet*

Assistance

| Could you please hold the door open? | **Pourriez-vous me tenir la porte, s'il vous plaît?** | *Poor-yay-voo me' te' -neer la port, seel-voo-ple* |
| Can you help me? | **Pourriez-vous m'aider?** | *Poor-yay-voo meh-day* |

I am rather deaf, please speak louder	**Je suis malentendant(e), merci de parler plus fort**	*Zhe' swee ma-lahⁿ -tahⁿ -dahⁿ (-dahⁿt), mair-see de' par-lay plu^e for*
Could you help me cross the road, please?	**Pourriez-vous m'aider à traverser la rue, s'il vous plaît?**	*Poor-yay-voo meh-day a tra-vair-say la ru^e, seel-voo-ple*

Travel

Do the buses take wheelchairs?	**Est-ce que les fauteuils roulants sont admis dans l'autobus?**	*Es-ke' lay fo-tœ-y roo-lahⁿ sohⁿ tad-mee dahⁿ loh-toh-bu^e s*
Can I take a mobility scooter on the train/plane?	**Puis-je emmener un scooter électrique dans le train/l'avion?**	*Pwee-zh oh-me-nay e^h skoo tœr ay-lek-treek dahⁿ le traⁿ/lav-yoⁿ*
Could you order a taxi that will take a wheelchair, please?	**Pourriez-vous réserver un taxi aménagé pour les personnes en fauteuil roulant, s'il vous plaît?**	*Poor-yay-voo ray-zair-vay eⁿ tak-see a-may-na-zhay poor lay fo-tœ-y roo-lahⁿ, seel-voo-ple*

EATING OUT

Key Phrases

Can you suggest	**Connaissez-vous**	*Ko-nay-say-voo*
a cheap restaurant?	**un restaurant bon marché?**	*en res-to-rahn bon mar-shay*
a good restaurant?	**un bon restaurant?**	*en bon res-to-rahn*
a vegetarian restaurant?	**un restaurant végétarien?**	*en res-to-rahn vay-zhay-ta-ryan*
I've reserved a table; my name is . . .	**J'ai réservé une table; je m'appelle . . .**	*Zhay ray-sair-vay ue n tabl; zher ma-pel*
May I see the menu/ the wine list, please?	**Pourrais-je voir le menu/la carte des vins, s'il vous plaît**	*Poo-rezh vwar ler mer -nue/la kart day van, seel-voo-ple*
Is there a set menu?	**Y a-t-il un menu à prix fixe?**	*Ee-ya-teel en mer -nue a pree feeks*
What is your dish of the day?	**Quel est le plat du jour?**	*Kel ay ler pla due zhoor*
The bill, please	**L'addition, s'il vous plaît**	*La-dee-syon, seel-voo-ple*
Does it include service?	**Est-ce que le service est compris?**	*Es-ker ler sair-vees ay kon -pree*
It was very good	**C'était très bon**	*Say-tay tre bon*

I'd like to book a table for four at 1 p.m.	**Je voudrais réserver une table pour quatre pour une heure**	*Zhe' voo-dre ray-zair-vay u^e n tabl poor katr poor u^e n œr*
We did not make a reservation	**Nous n'avons pas réservé de table**	*Noo na-voⁿ pa ray-zair-vay de' tabl*
There are three of us	**Nous sommes trois**	*Noo som trwa*
We'd like a table where there is room for a wheelchair	**Nous voudrions une table avec un espace pour un fauteuil roulant**	*Noo voo-dree-yaⁿ u^e n tabl a-vek eⁿ es-pas poor eⁿ fo-tœ-y roo-lahⁿ*
Do you have a high chair?	**Avez-vous une chaise haute?**	*A-vay-voo u^e n shez ot*
Is there a table	**Y a-t-il une table**	*Ee-ya-teel u' n tabl*
in a corner?	**dans un coin?**	*dahⁿ zeⁿ kwaⁿ*
on the terrace?	**à la terrasse?**	*a la te-rás*
by the window?	**près de la fenêtre?**	*pre de' la fe' -netr*
This way, please	***Par ici, s'il vous plaît**	*Par ee-see, seel-voo-ple*
We shall have a table free in half an hour	***Il y aura une table libre dans une demi-heure**	*Eel-yo-ra u^e n tabl leebr dahⁿ zu^e n de' -mee-œr*
You will have to wait about . . . minutes	***Vous devez attendre environ . . . minutes**	*Voo de' -vay a-tahⁿ dr ahⁿ -vee-roⁿ . . . mee-nu^e t*
We don't serve lunch until noon	***On ne sert pas le déjeuner avant midi**	*Oⁿ ne' sair pa le' day-zhe' -nay a-vahⁿ mee-dee*

We don't serve dinner until 8 p.m.	*On ne sert pas le dîner avant huit heures	O^n ne^r sair pa le^r dee-nay a-vah^n weet œr
We stop serving at eleven o'clock	*On ne sert plus après onze heures	O^n ne^r sair plu^e a-pre o^n zœr
Last orders are taken at . . .	*On prend les dernières commandes à . . .	O^n prah^n lay dair-nyair ko-mah^n d a
Sorry, the kitchen is closed	*Désolé, la cuisine est fermée	Day-zo-lay la kwee-zeen ay fair-may
Where are the toilets?	Où sont les toilettes?	Oo so^n lay twa-let
They are downstairs	*Elles sont en bas	El so^n ah^n ba
We are in a hurry	Nous sommes pressés	Noo som pray-say
Do you serve snacks?	Est-ce que vous servez des casse-croûtes?	Es-ke^r voo sair-vay day kas-kroot
I am a vegetarian	Je suis végétarien(ne)	Zhe^r swee vay-zhay-ta-rya^n (-ry en)
I am allergic	Je suis allergique	Zhe^r swee za-layr-zheek
to dairy products	aux produits laitiers	oh pro-dwee lay-tee-ay
to nuts	aux noix	oh nwa
to wheat	au blé	oh blay

Ordering

Cover charge	**Pain et couvert**	*Pa^n ay koo-ver*
All taxes included	**TTC (toutes taxes comprises)**	*Tay tay say (toot taks ko^n-preez*
Service charge	**Supplément pour le service**	*Su^e-play-mah^n poor le^r sair-vees*
Service and VAT (not) included	**Service et TVA (non) compris**	*Sair-vees ay tay-vay-a (no^n) ko^n-pree*
Waiter/waitress (*to address*)	**Monsieur/madame/ mademoiselle**	*Me^r-sye^r/ma-dam/mad-mwa-zel*
Excuse me (*to call the waiter*)	**S'il vous plaît**	*Seel voo ple*
May I see the menu/ the wine list, please?	**Pourrais-je voir le menu/la carte des vins, s'il vous plaît?**	*Poo-rezh vwar le^r me^r-nu^e/la kart day va^n, seel-voo-ple*
Is there a set menu?	**Y a-t-il un menu à prix fixe?**	*Ee-ya-teel e^n me^r-nu^e a pree feeks*
I'll have the 25 euro menu, please	**Je prend le menu à 25 euros, s'il vous plaît**	*Zhe^r prah^n le^r me^r-nu^e a va^n-sa^n k e^r-roh, seel voo ple*
I want something light	**Je voudrais quelque chose de léger**	*Zhe^r voo-dre kel-ke^r-shoz de^r lay-zhay*
Do you have children's helpings?	**Avez-vous de petites portions pour les enfants?**	*A-vay-voo de^r pe^r-teet por-syo^n poor lay-zah^n-fah^n*
What is your dish of the day?	**Quel est le plat du jour?**	*Kel ay le^r pla du^e zhoor*

What do you recommend?	Qu'est-ce que vous recommandez?	Kes-ke' voo re' -ko-mah" -day
Can you tell me what this is?	Pouvez-vous me dire ce que c'est?	Poo-vay-voo me' deer se' ke' say
What is the speciality of the restaurant?	Quelle est la spécialité de ce restaurant?	Kel-ay la spay-sya-lee-tay de' se' res-to-rah"
What local dishes should we try?	Quels plats régionaux nous recommandez-vous?	Kel pla ray-zhyo-noh noo re' -ko-mah" -day-voo?
Do you have any vegetarian dishes?	Est-ce que vous faites des plats végétariens?	Es-ke' -voo fet day pla vay-zhay-ta-rya"
I'd like . . .	Je voudrais . . .	Zhe' voo-dre
today's special menu	le menu d'aujourd'hui	le' me' -nu^e doh-zhoor-dwee
as the first course	en entrée	ah" ah" -tray
main course	le plat principal	pla pra" -see-pal
side dish	le plat d'accompagnement	pla da-ko" -pan-y-mah"
dessert	le dessert	de-ser
May I have peas instead of beans?	Pourrais-je avoir des petits pois à la place des haricots?	Poo-rezh a-vwar day pe' -tee pwa a la plas day a-ree-koh
Is it hot or cold?	Est-ce chaud ou froid?	Es shoh oo frwa
Without oil/sauce, please	Sans huile/sauce, s'il vous plaît	Sah" zweel/sohs, seel-voo-ple

Some more bread, please	**Un peu plus de pain, s'il vous plaît**	*E^n pe^r plu^e de^r pa^n seel-voo-ple*
Salt and pepper/ napkins, please	**Le sel et le poivre/ les serviettes, s'il vous plaît**	*Le sayl ay le pwavr/ lay sair-vyet, seel-voo-ple*
Would you like to try...?	***Voulez-vous goûter...?**	*Voo-lay-voo goo-tay*
There's no more...	***Il n'y a plus de...**	*Eel-nee-ya plu^e de^r*
How would you like it cooked?	***Vous désirez quelle cuisson?**	*Voo day-zee-ray kel kwee-so^n*
Rare/medium/well done	**Saignant/à point/ bien cuit**	*Sayn-y-ah^n/a pwa^n/ bya^n kwee*
Would you like a dessert?	***Prenez-vous un dessert?**	*Pre^r -nay voo e^n de-sert*
Something to drink?	***Vous désirez boire quelque chose?**	*Voo day-zee-ray bwar kel-ke^r -shoz*
The wine list, please	**La carte des vins, s'il vous plaît**	*La kart day va^n, seel-voo-ple*
A (half) bottle of the local wine, please	**Une (demi-) bouteille de vin du pays, s'il vous plaît**	*U^e n (de^r -mee) boo-te-y de^r va^n du^e pay-ee, seel-voo-ple*

Paying

| The bill, please | **L'addition, s'il vous plaît** | *La-dee-syo^n, seel-voo-ple* |
| Does it include service? | **Est-ce que le service est compris?** | *Es-ke^r le^r sair-vees ay ko^n -pree* |

Please check the bill; I don't think it's correct	**Voulez-vous vérifier l'addition; je crois qu'il y a une erreur**	*Voo-lay-voo vay-ree-fyay la-dee-syo^n; zhe^r krwa keel ya u^e n e-rœr*
What is this amount for?	**À quoi correspond cette somme?**	*A kwa ko-res-po^n set som*
I didn't have soup	**Je n'ai pas pris de soupe**	*Zhe^r nay pa pree de^r soop*
I had an entrecôte, not a tournedos	**J'ai pris une entrecôte, pas un tournedos**	*Zhay pree u^e n ah^n -tre^r -kot pa e^n toor-ne^r -do*
May we have separate bills?	**Pouvez-vous faire l'addition séparément?**	*Poo-vay-voo fair la-dee-syo^n say-pa-ray-mah^n*
Do you take credit cards?	**Acceptez-vous les cartes de crédit?**	*Ak-sep-tay-voo lay kart de^r kray-dee*
Keep the change	**Gardez la monnaie**	*Gar-day la mo-nay*

Compliments

It was very good	**C'était très bon**	*Say-tay tre bo^n*
We enjoyed it, thank you	**Nous avons beaucoup apprécié, merci**	*Noo za-vo^n boh-koo a-pray-syay, mair-see*
The food was delicious	**Le repas était délicieux**	*Le^r re^r -pa ay-tay day-lee-sye^r*
We particularly liked . . .	**Nous avons tout particulièrement apprécié . . .**	*Noo za-vo too par-tee-ku^e -lyair-mah^n a-pray-syay*

Complaints

We've been waiting a long time for our drinks	**Nous attendons nos boissons depuis longtemps**	*Noo za-tahⁿ -dahⁿ no bwa-soⁿ de-pwee loⁿ-tahⁿ de-pwee*
Why is the food taking so long?	**Pourquoi est-ce que le service est si lent?**	*Poor-kwa es-ke^r le^r sair-vees ay see lahⁿ*
This isn't what I ordered, I want …	**Ce n'est pas ce que j'ai commandé, je veux …**	*Se^r nay pa se^r ke^r zhay ko-mahⁿ -day zhe^r ve^r*
This is bad	**Ce n'est pas bon**	*Se^r nay pa boⁿ*
This isn't fresh	**Ceci n'est pas frais**	*Se^r -see nay pa fre*
This is uncooked	**Ce n'est pas cuit**	*Se^r nay pa kwee*
This is overcooked	**C'est trop cuit**	*Say troh kwee*
The bread is stale	**Ce pain est rassis**	*Se^r paⁿ ay ra-see*
This is too cold/salty	**C'est trop froid/salé**	*Say troh frwa/sa-lay*
This plate/spoon/ knife/glass/is not clean	**Cette assiette/ cuillère/ce couteau/ verre n'est pas propre**	*Set a-syet/kwee-yair/ se^r koo-toh/vair nay pa propr*
I'd like to see the headwaiter	**Je voudrais voir le maître d'hôtel**	*Zhe^r voo-dre vwar le^r metr do-tel*
I'm sorry, I will bring you another	***Je suis désolé, je vous en apporte un autre**	*Zhe^r swee day-zo-lay, zhe^r voo zahⁿ na-port eⁿ otr*

Breakfast and Tea[1]

café	le café	ka-fay
tea room	le salon de thé	sa-lon der tay
breakfast	le petit déjeuner	per -tee day-zher -nay
A large white coffee/a black coffee, please	Un grand café crème/un café (noir), s'il vous plaît	En grahn ka-fay krem/ un ka-fay (nwar), seel-voo-ple
I'd like a decaf	Je voudrais un déca (décaféiné)	Zher voo-dre en day-ka (day-ka-fay-ee-nay)
I'd like tea/chocolate, please	Du thé/chocolat, s'il vous plaît	Due tay/sho-ko-la, seel-voo-ple
I'd like a herbal tea	Je voudrais une tisane	Zher voo-dre ue n tee-zan
May we have some sugar, please?	Pourriez-vous nous donner du sucre, s'il vous plaît?	Poor-yay-voo noo do-nay due sue kr, seel-voo-ple
Do you have	Avez-vous	A-vay-voo
cereal?	des céréales f?	day say-ray-al
croissants?	des croissants m?	day krwa-sahn
hot/cold milk?	du lait chaud/froid?	due le shoh/frwa
a roll/bread/toast and butter?	un petit pain/du pain/du pain grillé avec du beurre?	un per -tee pan/due pan/due pan gree-yay a-vek due bœr
sweeteners?	des sucrettes/du sucre de régime?	day sue -kret/due sue kr der ray-zheem
yoghurt	le yaourt	ya-oor

1. Le petit déjeuner (complet) usually consists of coffee, tea or chocolate, rolls, croissants, butter and jam. If breakfast isn't included in the price of your hotel room, go to a local café. Salons de thé offer pastries and cakes, ice creams and sometimes light lunches.

More butter, please	**Un peu plus de beurre, s'il vous plaît**	*E^n pe^r plu^e de^r bœr, seel-voo-ple*
Do you have some jam/marmalade/ honey?	**Avez-vous de la confiture/de la marmelade/du miel?**	*A-vay-voo de^r la ko^n -fee-tu^e r/de^r la mar-me^r-lad/ du^e myel*
I'd like	**Je voudrais**	*Zhe^r voo-dre*
a soft-boiled egg	**un œuf à la coque**	*e^n nœf a la kok*
a hard-boiled egg	**un œuf dur**	*e^n nœf du^e r*
fried eggs	**des œufs au plat**	*day ze^r oh pla*
scrambled eggs	**des œufs brouillés**	*day ze^r broo-yay*
fresh fruit	**des fruits frais**	*day frwee fre*
What fruit juices do you have?	**Quelles sortes de jus de fruit avez-vous?**	*Kel sort de^r zhu^e de^r frwee a-vay-voo*
Orange/grapefruit/ tomato juice	***Le jus d'orange/ de pamplemousse/ de tomate**	*Zhu^e do-rah^n zh/de^r pah^n -ple^r -moos/de^r to-mat*
Help yourself at the buffet	***Servez-vous au buffet**	*Sair-vay-voo oh bu^e -fay*
We'd like a selection of pastries	**Nous voudrions une sélection de pâtisseries**	*Noo voo-dree-yo^n u^e n say-layk-syo^n de^r pa-tee-se^r -ree*
Do you have ice creams and sorbets?	**Avez-vous des glaces et des sorbets?**	*A-vay voo day glas ay day sor-bay*
What flavours would you like?	***Quels parfums vous prenez?**	*Kel par-fe^n voo pre^r -nay*
We have chocolate, vanilla, strawberry, pistachio and lemon	***Nous avons chocolat, vanille, fraise, pistache et citron**	*Noo zav-o^n sho-ko-la, va-nee-y, fraiz, pees-tash ay see-tro^n pees-tash ay see-tro^n*

pastry	**la pâtisserie**	*pa-tee-se'-ree*
cake	**le gâteau**	*ga-toh*
hot chocolate	**le chocolat chaud**	*sho-ko-la shoh*
ice cream	**la glace**	*glas*
iced coffee	**le café glacé**	*ka-fay gla-say*
China tea	**le thé de Chine**	*tay de' sheen*
iced tea	**le thé glacé**	*tay gla-say*
Indian tea	**le thé indien**	*tay a^n -dya^n*
tea with lemon	**le thé (au) citron**	*tay (oh) see-tro^n*
tea with milk	**le thé au lait**	*tay oh le*
black tea	**le thé nature**	*tay na-tu^e r*
camomile tea	**la camomille**	*ka-mo-mee-y*
herbal tea	**la tisane**	*tee-zan*
mint tea	**le thé à la menthe**	*tay a la mah^n t*
verbena tea	**la verveine**	*vayr-vayn*

Drinks[1]

What will you have to drink?	***Que désirez-vous comme boisson?**	*Ke' day-zee-ray-voo kom bwa-so^n*
Do you serve the wine by the glass?	**Est-ce que vous servez du vin au verre?**	*Es-ke' voo sair-vay du^e va^n oh vair*
Do you serve cocktails?	**Est-ce que vous servez des cocktails?**	*Es-ke' voo sair-vay day kok-tel*

1. For the names of beverages, see p. 141.

I'd like a soft drink with ice/fresh lemonade	Je voudrais une boisson sans alcool avec de la glace/ un citron pressé	Zhe' voo-dre u^e n bwa-so^n sah^n zal-kol a-vek de' la glas/e^{n}see-tro^n pre-say
What smoothies do you have?	Quels types de smoothies avez-vous?	Kel teep de' smoo-teez a-vay-voo
carafe/glass	la carafe/le verre	ka-raf/vair
bottle/half bottle	la bouteille/ demi-bouteille	boo-te-y/de' -mee boo-te-y
large/small beer	un sérieux/un demi	e^n sayr-ye'/e^n de' -mee
lager/(brown) ale	la bière blonde/ brune	byair blo^n d/bru^e n
Do you have draught beer?	Avez-vous de la bière à la pression?	A-vay-voo de' la byair a la pre-syo^n
Two more beers, please	Encore deux demis, s'il vous plaît	Ah^n -kor de' de' -mee, seel-voo-ple
apple juice	le jus de pomme	zhu^e de' pom
fruit juice	le jus de fruit	zhu^e de' frwee
orange juice	le jus d'orange	zhu^e do-rah^n zh
milk	le lait	le
mineral water (with/ without gas)	l'eau minérale (gazeuse/ non gazeuse)	oh mee-nay-ral (ga-zœz, no^n ga-zœz)
tap water	l'eau du robinet	oh du^e roh-bee-nay
neat	pur	pu^e r
on the rocks	avec de la glace	a-vek de' la glas
with water/soda water	avec de l'eau/du soda	a-vek de' loh/du^e so-da

ice cubes	**les glaçons** *m*	*lay gla-son*
Cheers!	**À votre santé!**	*A votr sah -tay*
I'd like another glass of water, please	**Je voudrais encore un verre d'eau, s'il vous plaît**	*Zher voo-dre ah -kor en vair doh, seel-voo-ple*
The same again, please	**La même chose, s'il vous plaît**	*La mem shoz, seel-voo-ple*

Quick Meals and Snacks

What is there to eat?	**Qu'avez-vous à manger?**	*Ka-vay-voo a mah -zhay*
We are in a hurry, what can you suggest that won't take long?	**Nous sommes pressés, pouvez-vous nous recommander un plat rapide?**	*Noo som pray-say, poo-vay-voo noo rer -ko-mah -day en pla ra-peed?*
I only want a snack	**Je ne prendrai qu'un casse-croûte**	*Zhe ne prah -dray ken kas-kroot*
Is it to eat here or to take away?	***À manger sur place ou à emporter?**	*A mah -zhay sue r plas oo a ah -por-tay*
It's to take away	**C'est pour emporter**	*Say poor ah -por-tay*
What sandwiches do you have?	**Quels sandwichs avez-vous?**	*Kel sah -dweech a-vay-voo*
A cheese . . .	**Un sandwich au fromage**	*En sah -dweech oh fro-mazh*
cooked ham . . .	**au jambon cuit**	*oh zhah -bon kwee*
cured ham . . .	**au jambon cru**	*oh zhah -bon krue*

pâté ...	**au pâté**	*oh pa-tay*
salami ...	**au saucisson**	*oh so-see-son*
toasted ham and cheese ...	**un croque-monsieur**	*en kro-ker mer -syer*
tuna sandwich	**au thon**	*oh ton*
I'd like a sandwich with/without butter	**Je voudrais un sandwich au beurre/ sans beurre**	*Zher voo-dre en sahn -dweech oh bœr/ sahn bœr*
I'm sorry, we've run out of ...	***Je suis désolé, nous n'avons plus de ...**	*Zher swee day-zo-lay, noo na-von plue der*
What are those things over there?	**Qu'est-ce que c'est que ça là-bas?**	*Kes-ker say ker sa la-ba*
What are they made of?	**Avec quoi est-ce fait?**	*A-vek kwa es fe*
What is in them?	**Qu'est-ce qu'il y a dedans?**	*Kes-keel-ya der -dahn*
I'll have one of those, please	**Je prendrai un de ceux-là**	*Zhe prahn -dre en der ser -la*
I'll have a ... pancake, please	**Je prendrai une crêpe au ..., s'il vous plaît**	*Zher prahn -dre ue n krayp oh ..., seel-voo-ple*
biscuits	**les biscuits** *m*	*bees-kwee*
bread	**le pain**	*pan*
bread roll	**le petit pain**	*per -tee pan*
some chips	**des frites**	*freet*
chocolate bar	**la tablette de chocolat**	*ta-blet der sho-ko-la*
cold meats	**l'assiette anglaise**	*as-yet ahn -glez*

eggs	les œufs *m*	*ze^r*
a cheese omelette	**une omelette au fromage**	*u^e n o-me^r -layt oh fro-mazh*
a plain omelette	**une omelette nature**	*u^e n o-me^r -layt na-tu^e r*
ham	**le jambon**	*zhahⁿ -boⁿ*
hamburger	**le hamburger**	*ahⁿ -bu^e r-gair*
pancake	**la crêpe**	*krep*
buckwheat pancake	**la galette**	*ga-let*
salad	**la salade**	*sa-lad*
sausage	**la saucisse**	*so-sees*
sausage roll	**le friand**	*free-ahⁿ*
snack	**le casse-croûte**	*kas-kroot*
waffles	**des gaufres** *f*	*goh-fr*

Restaurant Vocabulary

bill	**l'addition** *f*	*a-dee-syoⁿ*
bowl	**le bol**	*bol*
bread	**le pain**	*paⁿ*
butter	**le beurre**	*bœr*
course/dish	**le plat**	*pla*
cream	**la crème**	*krem*
cup	**la tasse**	*tas*
dessert	**le dessert/ l'entremets**	*de-ser/ahⁿ -tre-may*

dish of the day	**le plat du jour**	*pla du^e zh*
first course/starter	**l'entrée**	*ah^n -tray*
fork	**la fourchette**	*foor-shet*
glass	**le verre**	*vair*
headwaiter	**le maître d'hôtel**	*metr do-tel*
hungry (to be)	**(avoir) faim**	*av-war fa^n*
knife	**le couteau**	*koo-toh*
main course	**le plat principal**	*pla pra^n -see-pal*
menu	**le menu/la carte**	*me^r -nu^{el}/kart*
napkin	**la serviette**	*sair-vyet*
oil	**l'huile** *f*	*weel*
pepper	**le poivre**	*pwavr*
plate	**l'assiette** *f*	*as-yet*
salt	**le sel**	*sel*
sauce	**la sauce**	*sohs*
saucer	**la soucoupe**	*soo-koop*
self-service restaurant	**le self**	*self*
service	**le service**	*sair-vees*
set menu	**le menu (à prix fixe)**	*me^r-nu^e (a pree feeks)*
snack bar	**le snack bar**	*snak-bar*
spoon	**la cuillère**	*kwee-yair*
straw	**la paille**	*pa-y*
sweetener	**le sucre de régime/ les sucrettes** *f*	*su^e kr de^r ray-zheem/ su^e -kret*

table	**la table**	*tabl*
tablecloth	**la nappe**	*nap*
thirsty (to be)	**(avoir) soif**	*a-vwar swaf*
tip	**le pourboire**	*poor-bwar*
toilets	**les toilettes** *f*	*twa-let*
toothpick	**le cure-dent**	*ku^e r-dah^n*
tomato ketchup	**le ketchup**	*kay-chop*
vegetarian	**végétarien**	*vay-zhay-ta-rya^n*
vinegar	**le vinaigre**	*vee-negr*
waiter	**le garçon**	*gar-so^n*
waitress	**la serveuse**	*sair-vœz*
water	**l'eau** *f*	*oh*
wine list	**la carte des vins**	*kart day va^n*

THE MENU

Hors D'œuvres / Starters

anchois / anchovy

artichaut / artichoke

asperges / asparagus

assiette anglaise / assorted cold cuts

assiette de charcuterie / assorted salamis and similar sausages

belons / belon oysters

boutargue / cured fish roe

brandade de morue / salt cod with potato, cream and garlic

claires / oysters

coquilles St Jacques / scallops

crudités / selection of dressed raw vegetables

escargots / snails

foie gras truffé / goose liver pâté with truffles

(cuisses de) grenouilles / frogs (legs)

huîtres / oysters

jambon / ham

jambon de Bayonne / cured ham

jambon persillé / ham with parsley and garlic in white wine jelly

maquereau au vin blanc / mackerel marinated in white wine

melon / melon

moules marinières / mussels in white wine sauce

œuf dur mayonnaise / egg mayonnaise

pâté (de campagne) / pâté

pâté de foie de volaille / chicken liver pâté

quiche lorraine / quiche

rillettes / potted pork, or goose and pork/duck and pork/rabbit and pork

saucisson / sausage (salami type)

saumon fumé / smoked salmon

tarte à l'oignon / onion tart

tête de veau vinaigrette / calf's head with vinaigrette sauce

terrine (de lapin/canard/poisson) / pâté/terrine (rabbit/duck/fish)

Soupes/Potages/Soups

bisque (de homard) / a rich soup made from shellfish (lobster)

consommé / a clear soup made with beef or chicken

crème/velouté d'asperges/de tomates / cream of asparagus/tomato

crème vichyssoise / a cold soup of potato, leeks and cream

garbure / hearty cabbage soup from SW France

petite marmite / a substantial clear soup with a predominant flavour of chicken

potage aux champignons / mushroom soup

potage Crécy / carrot soup

potage au cresson / watercress soup

potage julienne / clear soup with finely shredded vegetables

potage parmentier / potato and leek soup

potage au poulet / chicken soup

potage printanière / spring vegetable soup

potage Saint-Germain / pea soup

soupe à l'ail / garlic soup

soupe aux choux / cabbage soup

soupe de légumes / vegetable soup

soupe à l'oignon gratinée / onion soup poured over slices of bread covered with grated cheese

soupe à l'oseille / sorrel soup

soupe au pistou / thick vegetable soup with basil

soupe de poisson / fish soup

soupe à la tomate / tomato soup

soupe du jour / soup of the day

Poisson / Fish

alose / shad

anguille / eel

araignée de mer / spider crab

barbue / brill

blanchaille, petite friture / whitebait

bouillabaisse / Mediterranean fish stew

bourride / Provençal fish stew with aïoli

brochet / pike

cabillaud / cod

calmar / squid

carpe / carp

carrelet / plaice/flounder

colin / hake

congre / conger eel

cotriade / Breton fish stew

crabe / crab

crevette grise / small shrimp

crevette (rose) / prawn

crustacés / shellfish

darne / thick fillet of fish

daurade / gilthead bream

écrevisses (à la nage) / freshwater crayfish (in a light wine and vegetable sauce)

espadon / swordfish

flétan / halibut

fruits de mer / shellfish

grondin / gurnard

hareng / herring

homard / lobster

huîtres / oysters

langouste / rock lobster

limande / lemon sole

lotte / monkfish

loup de mer / sea bass

maquereau / mackerel

matelote / fish stew

merlan / whiting

merluche / hake

mérou / grouper

morue / salt cod

mouclade / mussels in a creamy sauce with anis and saffron

moules / mussels

mulet / grey mullet

oursin / sea urchin

palourdes / clams

panaché de poissons / a variety of fish, usually fried or grilled

plie / plaice

poulpe / octopus

praires / clams

quenelle (de brochet) / fish (pike) dumpling

raie / skate

rouget / red mullet

St Pierre / John Dory

sandre / pike/perch

sardines / sardines

saumon / salmon

seiche / cuttlefish

sole / sole

thon / tuna

tourteau / crab

truite / trout

turbot / turbot

Viande / Meat

bœuf: / *beef:*

bavette aux échalotes / grilled flank steak with shallots

bifteck / steak

bœuf bourguignon / beef cooked in red wine with mushrooms and onions

bœuf à la ficelle / beef poached in stock

bœuf à la mode / beef braised in red wine and served hot with vegetables or cold in its jelly

bœuf en daube / beef braised in red wine and seasoned with herbs

carbonnade de bœuf / a rich beef stew made with beer

châteaubriand / steak taken from the middle of a fillet of beef

côte/entrecôte / T-bone/rib steak

filet/contre-filet / fillet/loin steak

jarret de bœuf en daube / shin slow-cooked in wine

pot-au-feu / beef stewed with root vegetables

queue de bœuf / oxtail

rôti / roast

steak au poivre / pepper steak

steak / steak

   bleu / very rare

   saignant / rare

   à point / medium

   bien cuit / well done

steak frites / steak and chips

steak tartare / raw minced fillet with egg yolk, capers and parsley

tournedos / a thick steak cut from the eye of the fillet

agneau/mouton: / lamb/mutton:

brochette / kebab

carré d'agneau à la Bretonne / loin of lamb with haricot beans

côtelette / chop

épaule d'agneau à la boulangère / shoulder baked with potatoes

gigot / leg

navarin d'agneau / lamb and vegetable stew

noisette / boned round cut from the loin

pieds et paquets / lamb tripe and trotters (Provence)

veau: / veal:

blanquette / veal stew in white sauce

côtelette / cutlet

foie de veau / calf's liver

jarret / shin/knuckle

longe / loin

médaillon / slice cut from the loin

paupiettes de veau / stuffed, rolled escalopes

poitrine / breast

ris de veau / sweetbreads

porc: / pork:

andouilles/andouillettes / sausages made of chitterlings, usually grilled

bacon / bacon

baeckeoffe / pork, lamb and potatoes slow cooked in white wine (Alsace)

basse-côtes / spare ribs

boudin blanc / white pudding/sausage

boudin (noir) / black pudding or blood sausage, fried or grilled

cassoulet / casserole of pork, sausage and beans, with preserved goose (South West)

charcuterie / assorted preserved pork products

choucroute garnie / sauerkraut with pork, ham, sausage and boiled potatoes

cochon de lait / suckling pig

côte de porc Vallée d'Auge / chop with cider sauce

enchaud / tenderloin

jambon au madère / ham in madeira sauce

longe / loin

oreilles / ears

pieds / trotters

abats / offal:

boulettes / meatballs/rissoles

cervelle / brains

crépinettes / small flat sausages flavoured with herbs and brandy

foie / liver

gras-double / tripe

langue / tongue

ragoût / stew

rognons / kidneys

saucisses de Francfort/de Strasbourg / frankfurters

saucisses de Toulouse / big sausages with thickly cut forcemeat, grilled or fried

tripes à la mode de Caen / tripe cooked with onions and carrots

Volaille et Gibier / Poultry and Game

ballottine de volaille / boned bird, stuffed, poached and served cold

bécasse / woodcock

blanc / breast

caille / quail

canard/caneton / duck / duckling

canard à l'orange / duck with orange sauce

canard aux olives / duck with olives

canard aux navets / duck with turnips

chevreuil / venison

civet de lièvre / jugged hare

confit de canard / preserved duck

confit d'oie / preserved goose

coq au vin / chicken cooked in red wine with bacon, mushrooms and onions

cuisse / leg

dinde / turkey

faisan / pheasant

lapereau / young rabbit

lapin / rabbit

lapin à la moutarde / rabbit in mustard sauce

lapin chasseur / rabbit in white wine

lapin de garenne / wild rabbit

lièvre / hare

magret de canard / duck breast

marcassin / wild boar

oie / goose

perdreau/perdrix / partridge

pigeon / pigeon

pintade / guinea fowl

poule-au-pot / chicken stewed with root vegetables

poularde/poulet / chicken

poulet à l'estragon / chicken with tarragon sauce

poulet basquaise / chicken with onion, tomatoes and peppers

poussin / spring chicken

sanglier / wild boar

suprême / breast

Légumes et Salades /
Vegetables and Salads

ail / garlic

artichaut / artichoke

asperges / asparagus

aubergine / aubergine/eggplant

basilic / basil

betterave / beetroot

carotte / carrot

céleri/céleri-rave / celery/celeriac

céleri en rémoulade / celeriac in mustard and mayonnaise dressing

champignon (cèpe/morille/chanterelle) / mushroom

chicorée / chicory/endive

chou / cabbage

choucroute / sauerkraut

chou-fleur / cauliflower

choux de Bruxelles / Brussels sprouts

ciboulette / chives

concombre / cucumber

courgette / courgette/zucchini

échalote / shallot

endive / chicory

épinards / spinach

estragon / tarragon

fenouil / fennel

fèves / broad beans

flageolets / green kidney beans

fonds d'artichaut / artichoke hearts

frisée aux lardons / curly endive salad with chopped bacon

gratin dauphinois / very thinly sliced potatoes cooked in cream and milk

haricots verts / green beans

laitue / lettuce

lentilles / lentils

mâche / lamb's lettuce/corn salad

maïs / sweet corn

menthe / mint

navet / turnip

oignon / onion

oseille / sorrel

petits pois / peas

poireau / leek

pois-chiches / chickpeas

poivron / pepper

pommes de terre / potatoes

    allumettes / chips

    chips / crisps

    en purée / creamed

    en robe de chambre / cooked in the skin/jacket potatoes

    frites / chips/French fries

    paille / game chips

potiron / pumpkin

radis / radish

ratatouille / sautéd onion, aubergine, tomato, pepper and courgette

riz / rice

salade (verte) / salad (even without *verte* it usually means a green salad)

salade composée/mixte / mixed salad

salade de gésiers / salad with gizzards

salade de saison / seasonal salad

salade niçoise / salad with tuna, anchovies, egg and olives

tomate / tomato

topinambour / Jerusalem artichoke

truffe/truffé / truffle/with truffles

Oeufs / Eggs

à la coque / boiled

brouillés / scrambled

en gelée / in aspic

en meurette / in red wine sauce

mollets / soft boiled

omelette (nature/aux fines herbes/aux champignons) / omelette (plain/with herbs/with mushrooms)

pipérade / scrambled eggs with peppers, tomatoes and onion (Basque)

pochés / poached

soufflé / soufflé

sur le plat / fried

Fromage / Cheese

Beaufort / hard mountain cheese from Savoie

Bleu de Bresse / soft blue cheese

brebis / cheese made from sheeps' milk

Cantal / hard cheese from Auvergne

chèvre / any cheese made of goats' milk

Comté / hard cheese from the Jura

Emmenthal / hard-pressed Swiss cheese with large holes

Époisses / strong, fine-textured cheese from Burgundy

Gruyère / hard-pressed Swiss cheese, with small holes

Munster / small semi-hard cheese with a powerful aroma

Pont l'évêque / soft cheese which increases in pungency with age

Port Salut / medium-hard and of medium taste, France's all-purpose cheese

Roquefort / semi-hard blue cheese made of ewes' milk

Saint Paulin / mild semi-soft cheese, much like Port Salut

Vacherin / soft, aromatic cheese from Franche-Comté

croque-monsieur / toasted ham and cheese sandwich

fondue / hot dip of cheese and white wine, eaten with chunks of bread

raclette / grilled cheese, eaten with potatoes and pickles

Desserts / Desserts

beignets / fritters

blanc-manger / dessert of almonds, sugar and cream

choux à la crème / cream puffs

clafoutis aux cerises / batter pudding with cherries

coupe glacée / ice-cream sundae

crème caramel / baked custard with caramel

crêpes / pancakes

crêpes Suzette / thin pancakes flamed with brandy and orange liqueur

diplomate / cold custard-based dessert with sponge fingers and candied fruits

fromage blanc/fromage frais / soft cream cheese

gâteau / cake

gâteau Saint-Honoré / choux pastry gâteau with cream

glaces / ice cream

   à la vanille / vanilla

   au café / coffee

   au chocolat / chocolate

granités / water ices

kugelhopf / yeast cake with sultanas (Alsace)

œufs à la neige / floating islands

omelette au rhum / rum omelette

sabayon / whipped egg yolks, sugar and Marsala

salade de fruits / fruit salad

soufflé au Grand Marnier / soufflé flavoured with orange liqueur

soufflé Rothschild / soufflé with candied fruits

tarte (aux pommes) / (apple) tart

tarte frangipane / tart with almond cream

tarte Tatin / apple tart

Fruits et Noix / Fruit and Nuts

abricot / apricot

airelle / cranberry

amande / almond

ananas / pineapple

banane / banana

brugnon / nectarine

cacahuètes / peanuts

cajou / cashew

cassis / blackcurrant

cerise / cherry

citron / lemon

citron vert / lime

coing / quince

figue / fig

figue de barbarie / prickly pear

fraise (des bois) / (wild) strawberry

framboise / raspberry

grenade / pomegranate

groseille / redcurrant

groseille à maquereau / gooseberry

marron / chestnut

melon / melon

mûre / blackberry/mulberry

noisette / hazelnut

noix / walnut

orange / orange

pamplemousse / grapefruit

pastèque / watermelon

pêche / peach

pistache / pistachio

poire / pear

pomme / apple

prune / plum

pruneau / prune

raisin / grape

raisin sec / raisin

reine-claude / greengage

Some Cooking Methods

à l'ail / with garlic

à la broche / barbecued on a spit

à l'étuvée / steamed

au beurre/à l'huile / with butter/oil

au four / baked

au poivre (vert) / with (green) pepper

bouilli / boiled

braisé / braised

chaud/froid / hot/cold

cru / raw

en cocotte / casseroled

duxelles / with chopped mushrooms

en gelée / in aspic

fait maison / homemade

farci / stuffed

frit / fried

fumé / smoked

grillé / grilled

mariné / marinated

mijoté/en ragoût / stewed

persillé / with parsley

poché / poached

râpé / grated

rôti / roast

Sauces et Garnitures /
Sauces and Garnishes

aïoli / garlic mayonnaise

à l'américaine / cooked in white wine with brandy, tomatoes and onions

béarnaise / egg yolk and butter sauce flavoured with shallots and tarragon

béchamel / white sauce

bercy / butter sauce with white wine and shallots

beurre blanc / white butter sauce with white wine vinegar and shallots

beurre maître d'hôtel / parsley butter

beurre noir / browned butter sauce

bigarrade / with orange

bordelaise / mushrooms, shallots and red wine

bourguignonne / red wine and herbs

Café de Paris / butter with brandy and herbs

chasseur / (red) wine, mushrooms, shallots and herbs

financière / madeira, olives and mushrooms

fines herbes / with herbs

florentine / with spinach

hollandaise / egg yolk, butter and lemon juice sauce

lyonnaise / with onions

marchand de vin / with red wine and shallots

marinière / white wine, own broth and egg yolk

meunière / brown butter, parsley and lemon juice

mornay / cheese sauce

moutarde / mustard sauce

normande / cream with mushrooms and egg

parmentier / with potatoes

provençale / olive oil, tomatoes and garlic

ravigote / herbs, capers, gherkins in thick vinaigrette

rémoulade / mustard-flavoured mayonnaise

rouille / chilli and garlic sauce for bouillabaisse

soubise / onion sauce

tartare / gherkins, capers and herbs

thermidor / cream sauce

vinaigrette / oil and vinegar dressing

Boissons / Drinks

bière / beer

   blonde / lager

   brune / (brown) ale

   à la pression / draught

   en bouteille / bottled

café / espresso

   café au lait / coffee with milk

   café crème / white coffee

   café viennois / coffee with whipped cream

   décaféiné / decaffeinated

chocolat chaud / hot chocolate

cidre / cider

citron pressé / freshly squeezed lemon juice

cognac / cognac/brandy

crème de cassis / blackcurrant liqueur

demi / small glass of beer

digestif / liqueur

eau de vie / spirit distilled from fruit (dry)

eau minérale plate/gazeuse / still/sparkling mineral water

eau du robinet / tap water

fine / fine cognac

frappé / chilled, on ice

glaçon / ice cube

jus de fruit / fruit juice

   jus d'orange / orange juice

   jus de pamplemousse / grapefruit juice

   jus de pomme / apple juice

   jus de raisin / grape juice

   jus de tomate / tomato juice

kir / white wine with blackcurrant liqueur

kir royale / champagne with blackcurrant liqueur

lait / milk

limonade / lemonade

millésime / vintage

orangeade / orangeade

orange pressée / fresh orange juice

pastis / aniseed drink (alcoholic), served with water and ice

pétillant / lightly sparkling

porto / port

rhum / rum

thé au lait / tea with milk

thé de Chine / China tea

thé citron / tea with lemon

thé indien / Indian tea

camomille / camomile

menthe / mint

tilleul / limeflowers

tisane / herbal tea

verveine / verbena

vin / wine

   blanc / white

   rosé / rosé

   rouge / red

   doux / sweet

   sec / dry

   pétillant/mousseux / sparkling

xérès / sherry

EMERGENCIES[1]

Key Phrases

Fire brigade	**les pompiers**	in France dial 18
Police[2]	**la police ou la gendarmerie**	in France dial 17
Emergency medical service	**SOS médecin**	France dial 3624
Emergency ambulance service	**SAMU (Services d'Aide Médicale d'Urgence),**	in France dial 15
Help!	**Au secours!**	*Oh skoor*
Danger!	**Danger!**	*Dah^n-zhay*
Call the police	**Appelez la police**	*Ap-lay la po-lees*
Call a doctor/an ambulance	**Appelez un médecin/ une ambulance**	*Ap-lay e^n mayd-sa^n/u^e n ah^n-bu^e-lah^n s*
Where is the nearest A&E hospital?	**Où est le service des urgences le plus proche?**	*Oo ay le^r sair-vees day zu^e r-zhah^n s le^r plu^e prosh*
My son/daughter is lost	**Mon fils/ma fille s'est perdu(e)**	*Mo^n fees/ma fee-y say pair-du^e*

1. For car breakdowns see AT A GARAGE OR PETROL STATION (p. 39). For problems with a house rental see APARTMENTS and VILLAS (p. 79).

2. In towns and cities police duties are performed by **agents (de police)**, addressed as **Monsieur l'agent**. The police station is called **le commissariat de police**. In very small towns and in the country police duties are performed by **gendarmes** and the police station is called **la gendarmerie**. There is a special police branch whose main duty is to patrol the roads and enforce traffic regulations. This is known as **la police de la route** and the policemen are familiarly known as **motards**.

Where's the police station[1]	Où est le commissariat de police/la gendarmerie?	*Oo ay le^r ko-mee-sar-ya de^r po-lees/la zhah^n -dar-me^r -ree*
Where is the British consulate?	Où est le consulat britannique?	*Oo ay le^r ko^n -su^e -la bree-ta-neek*
I want to speak to someone from the embassy	Je veux parler à quelqu'un de l'ambassade	*Zhe^r ve^r par-lay a kel-ke^n de^r lah^n -ba-sad*
I want a lawyer who speaks English	Je voudrais un avocat qui parle anglais	*Zhe voo-dray e^n a-vo-ka kee parl ah^n -gle*
It's urgent	C'est urgent	*Say-tu^e r-zhah^n*
Can you help me?	Pouvez-vous m'aider?	*Poo-vay voo meh-day*

Accidents[1]

There has been an accident[2]	Il y a eu un accident	*Eel-ya-u^e e^n nak-see-dah^n*
Is anyone hurt?	*Y a-t-il des blessés?	*Ee-ya-teel day blay-say*
Do you need help?	*Vous avez besoin d'aide?	*Voo za-vay be^r -zwa^n ded*

1. Dial the police on 17 and the ambulance service on 15 anywhere in France. If you are involved in an accident in a town get the **agent de police** to make a report (**dresser un constat**). In the country if there has been injury to people, advise the **gendarmerie**. In other cases engage a **huissier** (sheriff's officer) from the nearest town to make a report. Try to get names and addresses of witnesses.
2. see also Doctor p. 158

emergency exit	la sortie de secours	sor-tee de' se' -koor
fire extinguisher	l'extincteur	eks-ta^n k-tœr
lifeguard	le maître-nageur	metr-na-zhoer
paramedics	les secouristes	Se'-Koo-Reeset
He's badly hurt	Il est grièvement blessé	Eel ay greeayv-mah^n ble-say
He has fainted	Il s'est évanoui	Eel say-tay-va-noo-ee
He's losing blood	Il perd du sang	Eel pair du^e sah^n
Her arm is broken	Son bras est cassé	So^n bra ay ka-say
Please get	Allez chercher	A-lay shair-shay
some bandages	des pansements	day pah^n s-mah^n
a blanket	une couverture	u^e n koo-vair-tu^e r
some water	un peu d'eau, s'il vous plaît	e^n pe' doh, seel-voo-ple
I've broken my glasses	J'ai cassé mes lunettes	Zhay ka-say may lu^e -net
I can't see	Je ne peux pas voir	Zhe' ne' pe' pa vwar
A child has fallen in the water	Un enfant est tombé à l'eau	E^n nah^n -fah^n ay to^n -bay a loh
She is drowning	Elle se noie	El se' nwa
She can't swim	Elle ne sait pas nager	El ne say pa na-zhay
There's a fire	Il y a un incendie	Eel-ya e^n na^n -sah^n -dee
I had an accident	J'ai eu un accident	Zhay u^e e^n ak-see-dah^n
The other driver hit my car	Le conducteur de l'autre véhicule a heurté ma voiture	Le' ko^n -du^e -ktœr de' lotr vay-ee-k u^e la œr-tay ma vwa-tu^e r

It was my fault/his fault	C'était de ma faute/ sa faute	Say-tay de' ma fot/ sa fot
I didn't understand the sign	Je n'ai pas compris le panneau (de signalisation)	Zhe' nay pa koⁿ -pree le' pa-noh (de' seen-ya-lee-za-syoⁿ)
May I see your	*Je voudrais voir votre	Zhe' voo-dre vwar votr
driving licence	permis de conduire	pair-mee de' koⁿ -dweer
insurance certificate	certificat/ attestation d'assurance	votr'sair-tee-fee-ka/ a-tes-ta-syoⁿ da-su^e -rahⁿ s
vehicle registration papers	carte grise	kart greez
What are the name and address of the owner?	Quels sont le nom et l'adresse du propriétaire?	Kel soⁿ le' noⁿ ay la-dres du^e pro-pree-ay-tair
Are you willing to act as a witness?	Voulez-vous bien servir de témoin?	Voo-lay-voo byaⁿ sair-veer de' tay-mwaⁿ
Could I have your name and address, please?	Pourrais-je avoir votre nom et adresse, s'il vous plaît?	Poo-rezh a-vwar votr noⁿ ay votr a-dres, seel-voo-ple
You must make a statement	*Vous devez faire une déclaration	Voo de' -vay fair u^e n day-kla-ra-syoⁿ
I want a copy of the police report	Je voudrais une copie du constat	Zhe' voo-dre u^e n ko-pee du^e koⁿ s-ta
You were speeding	* Vous avez commis un excès de vitesse	Voo-za-vay ko-mee eⁿ ekse de' vee-tes
How much is the fine?	L'amende est de combien?	La-mahⁿ d ay de' koⁿ -byaⁿ

Lost Property

Lost property office	**Le bureau des objets trouvés**	*Le' bu[e] -roh day zob-zhay troo-vay*
My luggage is missing	**Mes bagages ne sont pas arrivés**	*May ba-gazh ne so[n] pa za-ree-vay*
Has my luggage been found yet?	**Est-ce que mes bagages ont finalement été retrouvés?**	*Es-ke' may ba-gazh o[n] fee-nal-mah[n] ay-tay re-troo-vay?*
My luggage has been damaged/broken into	**Mes bagages ont été endommagés/ouverts**	*May ba-gazh o[n] ay-tay ah[n] -do-ma-zhay/oo-vair*
I have lost	**J'ai perdu**	*Zhay pair-du[e]*
my luggage	**mes bagages**	*may ba-gazh*
my passport	**mon passeport**	*mo[n] pas-por*
my credit card	**ma carte de crédit**	*ma kart de' cray-dee*
my (video) camera	**mon appareil photo (caméscope)**	*mo[n] a-pa-re-y fo-to (ka-mays-kop)*
my mobile phone	**mon portable**	*mo[n] por-tabl*
my keys	**mes clés**	*may klay*
I've locked myself out	**Je me suis enfermé dehors**	*Zhe' me' swee zah[n] -fair-may de' -or*
I found this in the street	**J'ai trouvé ceci dans la rue**	*Zhay troo-vay se' -see dah[n] la ru[e]*

Missing Persons

My son/daughter is lost	**Mon fils/ma fille s'est perdu(e)**	*Mo^n fees/ma fee-y say pair-du^e*
He is . . . years old, and wearing a blue shirt and shorts	**Il a . . . ans et il porte une chemise bleue et un short**	*Eel-a . . . ah^n ay eel port u^e n she^r -meez ble^r ay e^n short*
This is his/her photo	**Voici sa photo**	*Vwa-see sa fo-to*
Could you help me find him/her?	**Pourriez-vous m'aider à le/la retrouver?**	*Poor-yay-voo meh-day a le^r la re^r -troo-vay*
Have you seen a small girl with brown curly hair?	**Avez-vous vu une petite fille aux cheveux bruns et frisés?**	*A-vay-voo vu^e u^e n pe^r -teet fee-y oh she^r -ve^r bre^n ay free-zay*
I've lost my wife	**J'ai perdu ma femme**	*Zhay pair-du^e ma fam*
Could you please ask for Mrs . . . over the loudspeaker?	**Pourriez-vous lancer un appel pour Madame . . . par haut-parleur?**	*Poor-yay-voo lah^n -say e^n a-pel poor madam . . . par oh par-lœr*

Theft

I've been robbed/ mugged	**On m'a volé(e)/ agressé(e)**	*O^n ma vo-lay/a-gray-say*
Did you have any jewellery/valuables on you?	***Est-ce que vous portiez des bijoux/ des objets de valeur?**	*Es-ke^r voo por-tyay day bee-zhoo/day zob-zhay de va-lœr*

Were there any witnesses?	*Y avait-il des témoins?	Y a-vay-teel day tay-mwa^n
My bag/wallet has been stolen	On m'a volé mon sac/mon portefeuille	O^n ma vo-lay mo^n sak/mo^n port-fœ-y
Some things have been stolen from our car	On a volé des affaires dans notre voiture	O^n na vo-lay day za-fair dah^n notr vwa-tu^e r
It was stolen from our room	On l'a volé dans notre chambre	O^n la vo-lay dah^n notr shah^n br

ENTERTAINMENT

Key Phrases

Is there an entertainment guide?	**Y a-t-il un guide des spectacles?**	*Ee-ya-teel eⁿ gheed day spek-takl*
What is there for children?	**Est-ce qu'il y a des choses à faire pour les enfants?**	*Es-keel-ee-ya day shozh a fair poor lay zahⁿ -fahⁿ*
Do you have a programme for the festival?	**Vous avez le programme du festival?**	*Voo za-vay leʳ pro-gram duᵉ fay-stee-val*
The cheapest seats, please	**Les places les moins chères, s'il vous plaît**	*Lay plas lay mwaⁿ shair, seel-voo-ple*

What is there to see/ to do here?	**Qu'est-ce qu'on peut voir/faire ici?**	*Kes-koⁿ peʳ vwar/ fair ee-see*
Is the circus on?	**Est-ce qu'il y a un spectacle de cirque?**	*Es-keel-ee-ya eⁿ spek-takl deʳ seerk*
Is there a son et lumière show at the château?	**Y a-t-il un spectacle son et lumière au château?**	*Ee-ya-teel eⁿ spek-takl soⁿ ay luᵉ -myair oh sha-toh*
What time is the firework display?	**À quelle heure sont les feux d'artifice?**	*A ke-lœr soⁿ lay fœ dar-tee-fees*
How far is it to the amusement park?	**Le parc d'attractions, c'est loin?**	*Leʳ park da-trak-syoⁿ, say lwaⁿ*
Is there a casino?	**Y a-t-il un casino?**	*Ee-ya-teel eⁿ ka-zee-no*

Booking Tickets

I want two seats for tonight/for the matinée tomorrow	**Je voudrais deux places pour ce soir/ pour la matinée de demain**	*Zhe' voo-dre de' plas poor se' swar/poor la ma-tee-nay de' de' -ma^n*
I want to book seats for Thursday	**Je voudrais réserver des places pour jeudi**	*Zhe' voo-dre ray-zayr-vay day plas poor zhe' -dee*
Is the matinée sold out?	**Est-ce qu'il reste des places pour la matinée?**	*Es-keel rest day plas pour la ma-tee-nay*
Where do you want to sit?	***Quelles places désirez-vous?**	*Kel plas day-zee-ray voo*
I'd like seats	**Je voudrais des places**	*Zhe' voo-dre day plas*
in the stalls	**à l'orchestre**	*a lor-kestr*
in the circle	**au balcon**	*oh bal-ko^n*
in the gallery	**au dernier balcon**	*oh dair-nyay bal-ko^n*
I'd like a table at the front	**Je voudrais une table devant la scène**	*Zhe' voo-dre u^e n tabl de' -vah^n la sayn*
Are there any concessions?	**Y a-t-il des réductions?**	*Ee-ya-teel day ray-du^e k-syo^n*
The cheapest seats, please	**Les places les moins chères, s'il vous plaît**	*Lar plas lar mwa^n shaik, seel-voo-ple*
Where are these seats?	**Où sont ces places?**	*Oo so^n say plas*

We're sold out (for this performance)	***Tout est complet (pour cette représentation)**	*Too-tay ko^n -play (poor set re^r -pray-zah^n -ta-syo^n)*
Everything is sold out	***Tout est complet**	*Too-tay ko^n -play*
Standing room only (at the back of the stalls/in the upper balcony)	***Il ne reste que des places debout (en fond de parterre/au dernier balcon[1])**	*Eel ne^r rest ke^r day plas de^r -boo (ah^n fo^n de^r par-tair/ oh dair-nyay bal-ko^n)*
Pick the tickets up before the performance	***Retirez les billets avant le début du spectacle**	*Re^r -tee-ray lay bee-yay a-vah le^r day-bu^e du^e spek-takl*
This is your seat	***Voici votre place**	*Vwa-see votr plas*

Cinema, Theatre and Live Music

chamber music	**la musique de chambre**	*mu^e -zeek de^r shah^n br*
film	**le film**	*feelm*
modern dance	**la danse moderne**	*dah^n s mo-dairn*
musical	**la comédie musicale**	*ko-may-dee mu^e -zee-kal*
opera	**l'opéra**	*o-pay-ra*
play	**la pièce**	*pyes*
recital	**le récital**	*ray-see-tal*

1. In spoken French the standing area on the upper balcony is called **poulailler**.

Can you recommend a film/musical?	Pourriez-vous nous recommander un film/une comédie musicale?	Poor-yay-voo noo re' -ko-mah^n -day e^n feelm/ u^e n ko-may-dee mu^e -zee-kal
What's on at the theatre/cinema?[1]	Qu'est ce qu'on joue au théâtre/au cinéma?	Kes-ko^n zhoo oh tay-atr/ oh see-nay-ma
Can you recommend a good show?	Pouvez-vous me recommander un bon spectacle?	Poo-vay-voo me' re' -ko-mah^n -day e^n bo^n spek-takl
Is it the original version?	Est-ce la version originale?	Es la vayr-syo^n o-ree-zhee-nal
Are there subtitles?	Y a-t-il des sous-titres?	Ee-ya-teel day soo-teetr
Is it dubbed?	Est-ce doublé?	Es doo-blay
Is there a concert tonight?	Est-ce qu'il y a un concert ce soir?	Es-keel-ee-ya e^n ko^n -sair se swar
Is there a support band?	Qui est-ce qui joue en première partie?	Kee-es-kee zhoo ah^n pre' -myair par-tee
What time does the main band start?	À quelle heure joue le groupe principal?	A ke-lœr zhoo le' groop pra^n -see-pal
Who is	Qui est	Kee ay
acting?	l'acteur?	lak-tœr
conducting?	le chef d'orchestre?	le' shef dor-kestr

1. Theatres always close one day each week, but are open for the matinée performance (around 2 p.m.) on Sundays. Seats can be reserved at the theatre every day from 11 a.m. to 7 p.m.; they are normally only on sale about a week before any given performance. Cinemas in Paris and other large French cities are open from 10 a.m. to midnight. Many are **cinémas permanents** – i.e., performances are continuous, the others have set hours for performances.

directing?	le metteur en scène?	*le' me-tœr ah[n] sen*
singing?	le chanteur?	*le' shan -tœr*
When does the ballet start?	À quelle heure commence le ballet?	*A ke-lœr ko-ma[n] s le ba-lay*
What time does the performance end?	À quelle heure finit le spectacle?	*A ke-lœr fee-nee le' spek-takl*
Where is the cloakroom?	Où est le vestiaire?	*Oo ay le' ves-tyair*
A programme, please	Un programme, s'il vous plaît	*E[n] pro-gram, seel-voo-ple*

Clubs and Discos

Which is the best club?	Quel est la meilleure boîte de nuit?	*Kel ay le' me-yœr bwat de' nwee*
Is there a jazz club here?	Y a-t-il un club de jazz ici?	*Ee-ya-teel e[n] klœb de' dzhaz ee-see*
Where can we go dancing?	Où pourrions-nous aller danser?	*Oo poor-yo[n] -noo a-lay dah[n] -say*
Where is the best disco?	Où se trouve la meilleure discothèque?	*Oo se' troov la me-yœr dees-ko-tek*
Would you like to dance?	Voulez-vous danser?	*Voo-lay-voo dah[n] -say*

HEALTH

Dentist

Key Phrases

I need to see a dentist	**Je dois voir un dentiste**	*Zhe[r] dwa vwar e[n] dah[n] -teest*
Can you recommend one?	**Pouvez-vous m'en recommander un?**	*Poo-vay-voo mah[n] re[r]-ko-mah[n]-day e[n]*
I've lost a filling	**J'ai perdu un plombage**	*Zhay pair-du[e] e[n] plo[n] -bazh*
Can you do it now?	**Pouvez-vous le faire maintenant?**	*Poo-vay-voo le[r] fair ma[n] -te[r] -nah[n]*
Can you fix it (temporarily)?	**Pouvez-vous le réparer (provisoirement)?**	*Poo-vay-voo le[r] ray-pa-ray (pro-vee-zwar-mah[n])*

Can I make an appointment with the dentist as soon as possible?	**Puis-je prendre rendez-vous *chez* le dentiste le plus tôt possible?**	*Pwee-zh prah[n] dr rah[n] -day-voo shay le[r] dah[n] -teest le[r] plu[e] toh po-seebl*
I have toothache	**J'ai mal aux dents**	*Zhay mal oh dah[n]*
This tooth hurts	**Cette dent me fait mal**	*Set dah[n] me[r] fe mal*
I have a broken tooth/an abscess	**J'ai une dent cassée/ un abcès**	*Zhay u[e] n dah[n] ka-say/ e[n] nap-se*

I've lost a filling	**J'ai perdu un plombage**	*Zhay pair-due en plon -bazh*
Can you fill the tooth?	**Pouvez-vous plomber la dent?**	*Poo-vay-voo plon -bay la dahn*
Can you do it now?	**Pouvez-vous le faire maintenant?**	*Poo-vay-voo ler fair man -ter -nahn*
I do not want the tooth taken out	**Je ne veux pas que la dent soit arrachée**	*Zher ner ver pa ker la dahn swa-ta-ra-shay*
Please give me an injection first	**Insensibilisez-moi la dent d'abord, s'il vous plaît**	*An -sahn -see-bee-lee-zay mwa la dahn da-bor, seel-voo-ple*
My gums are swollen/keep bleeding	**Mes gencives sont enflées/saignent souvent**	*May zhahn -seev son -tahn -flay/sen-y soo-vahn*
I have broken/ chipped my dentures	**J'ai cassé/ébréché mon dentier**	*Zhay ka-say/ay-bray-shay mon dahn -tyay*
You're hurting me	**Vous me faites mal**	*Voo mer fet mal*
Please rinse your mouth	***Rincez-vous la bouche, s'il vous plaît***	*Ran -say-voo la boosh, seel-voo-ple*
I will X-ray your teeth	***Je vais faire une radio de vos dents***	*Zher ve fair ue n ra-dyo der voh dahn*
You have an abscess	***Vous avez un abcès***	*Voo-za-vay en nap-se*
The nerve is exposed	***Le nerf est à vif***	*Ler nair ay-ta veef*

This tooth can't be saved	*Cette dent est perdue	*Set dahⁿ ay pair-du^e*
How much do I owe you?	Combien vous dois-je?	*Koⁿ -byaⁿ voo dwazh*
When should I come again?	Quand dois-je revenir?	*Kahⁿ dwa-zh re' -ve' -neer*

Doctor

Key Phrases

I must see a doctor; can you recommend one?	Il faut que je consulte un médecin; pouvez-vous m'en recommander un?	*Eel fo ke' zhe' koⁿ -su^e lt eⁿ mayd-saⁿ; poo-vay-voo mahⁿ re' -ko-mahⁿ -day eⁿ*
Please call a doctor	Faites venir un médecin, s'il vous plaît	*Fet ve' -neer eⁿ mayd-saⁿ, seel-voo-ple*
I suffer from . . .; here is a list of my medication	J'ai. . . .; voici les médicaments que je prends	*Zhay . . .; vwa-see lay may-dee-ka-mahⁿ ke' zhe' prahⁿ*
I have a heart condition	Je suis cardiaque	*Zhe' swee kar-dyak*
I am diabetic	Je suis diabétique	*Zhe' swee dya-bay-teek*
I suffer from asthma	Je souffre d'asthme	*Zhe' soofr dazm*
I've had a high temperature since yesterday	J'ai de la fièvre depuis hier	*Zhay de' la fyevr de' -pwee yair*
My stomach¹ is upset	J'ai mal au ventre	*Zhay mal oh vahⁿ tr*

Is there a doctor's surgery nearby?	**Y a-t-il un cabinet de consultation médicale près d'ici?**	*Ee-ya-teel e^n ka-bee-nay de^r ko^n -su^e l-ta-syo^n may-dee-kal pre dee-see*
When can the doctor come?	**Quand est-ce que le médecin pourra venir?**	*Kah^n es-ke^r le^r mayd-sa^n poo-ra ve^r -neer*
Does the doctor speak English?	**Est-ce que le médecin parle anglais?**	*Es-ke^r le^r mayd-sa^n parl ah^n -gle*
I'd like to find a paediatrician	**Je cherche un pédiatre**	*Zhe^r shairsh e^n pay-dyatr*

Medication

I take daily medication for ...	**Je suis sous traitement pour ...**	*Zhe^r swee soo tret-mah^n poor*
I suffer from ...; here is a list of my medication	**J'ai....; voici les médicaments que je prends**	*Zhay ...; vwa-see lay may-dee-ka-mah^n ke^r zhe^r prah^n*
This is a copy of my UK prescription, could you please prescribe ... for me?	**Voici une copie de ma prescription anglaise, pourriez-vous me prescrire ..., s'il vous plaît?**	*Vwa-see u^e n ko-pee de^r ma pray-skreep-syo^n ah^n -glez, poor-yay-voo me^r pray-skreer ..., seel-voo-ple*

Symptoms and Conditions

I am ill	**Je suis malade**	*Zhe^r swee ma-lad*
I feel weak	**Je me sens faible**	*Zhe^r me^r sah^n faibl*
I have high/low blood pressure	**Je fais de l'hypertension/de l'hypotension**	*Zhe^r fe de^r lee-pair-tah^n -syo^n/de^r lee-po-tah^n -syo^n*

I have a heart condition	**Je suis cardiaque**	*Zhe' swee kar-dyak*
I am diabetic	**Je suis diabétique**	*Zhe' swee dya-bay-teek*
I suffer from asthma	**Je souffre d'asthme**	*Zhe' soofr dazm*
I have a fever	**J'ai de la fièvre**	*Zhay de' la fyevr*
I've had a high temperature since yesterday	**J'ai de la fièvre depuis hier**	*Zhay de' la fyevr de' -pwee yair*
I've a pain in my right arm	**J'ai une douleur au bras droit**	*Zhay u' n doo-lœr oh bra drwa*
It's a sharp pain/a persistent pain	**Je ressens une vive douleur/une douleur continue**	*Zhe' re' -sah' u' n veev doo-lœr/u' n doo-lœr ko' -tee-nu' .*
My wrist hurts	**Mon poignet me fait mal**	*Mo' pwan-yay me' fe mal*
I think I've sprained/broken my ankle	**Je crois que je me suis foulé/cassé la cheville**	*Zhe' krwa ke' zhe' me' swee foo-lay/ka-say la she' -vee-y*
I fell down and my back hurts	**Je suis tombé et je me suis fait mal au dos**	*Zhe' swee to' -bay ay zhe' me' swee fe mal oh doh*
My foot is swollen	**Mon pied est enflé**	*Mo' pyay ay tah' -flay*
I've burned/cut/hurt myself	**Je me suis brûlé/coupé/fait mal**	*Zhe' me' swee bru' -lay/koo-pay/fe rnal*
I think it is infected	**Je crois que c'est infecté**	*Zhe' krwa ke' say ta' -fek-tay*
I've developed a rash	**J'ai développé une éruption cutanée**	*Zhay day-vlo-pay u' n ay-ru' p-syo' ku' -ta-nay*

My appetite's gone	**Je n'ai plus d'appétit**	*Zhe' nay plu* *da-pay-tee*
I think I've got food poisoning	**Je crois souffrir d'une intoxication alimentaire**	*Zhe' krwa soo-freer du* *n a* *-tok-see-ka-syo* *a-lee-mah* *-tair*
I've got indigestion/ diarrhoea	**J'ai une indigestion/ de la diarrhée**	*Zhay u* *n a* *-dee-zhest-yo* */de' la dya-ray*
I keep vomiting	**Je vomis souvent**	*Zhe' vo-mee soo-vah*
I can't eat/sleep	**Je ne peux pas manger/dormir**	*Zhe' ne' pe' pa mah* *-zhay/dor-meer*
My nose keeps bleeding	**Je saigne constamment du nez**	*Zhe' sen-y ko* *-sta-mah* *-du* *-nay*
I have earache	**J'ai mal à l'oreille (*one ear*)/aux oreilles (*two ears*)**	*Zhay mal a lo-re-y/oh zo-re-y*
I have difficulty in breathing	**J'ai du mal à respirer**	*Zhay du* *mal a res-pee-ray*
I feel dizzy/sick/ shivery	**J'ai des vertiges/ nausées/frissons**	*Zhay day vair-teezh/ noh-zay/free-so*
I think I've caught flu	**Je crois que j'ai attrapé la grippe**	*Zhe' kraw ke' zhay a-tra-pay la greep*
I've got a cold	**Je suis enrhumé**	*Zhe' swee ah* *-ru* *-may*
I've had it since yesterday/for a few hours	**J'ai cela depuis hier/ depuis quelques heures**	*Zhay se' -la de' -pwee yair/de' -pwee kelk zœr*
abscess	**l'abcès *m***	*ap-se*
ache	**le mal/la douleur**	*mal/doo-lœr*

allergy	l'allergie *f*	a-lair-zhee
appendicitis	l'appendicite *f*	a-pa^n-dee-seet
asthma	l'asthme *m*	asm
back pain	le mal au dos/la lombalgie	mal oh doh/ lo^n-bal-zhee
blister	l'ampoule *f*	ah^n-pool
boil	le furoncle	fu^e-ro^n kl
bruise	le bleu/la contusion	ble^r/ko^n-tu^e-zyo^n
burn	la brûlure	bru^e-lu^e r
chill	le refroidissement	re-frwa-dees-mah^n
cold	le rhume	ru^e m
constipation	la constipation	ko^n-stee-pa-syo^n
cough	la toux	too
cramp	la crampe	krah^n p
diabetic	diabétique	dya-bay-teek
diarrhoea	la diarrhée	dya-ray
earache	le mal à l'oreille	mal a lo-re-y
epilepsy	l'épilepsie *f*	ay-pee-lay-psee
fever	la fièvre	fyevr
food poisoning	l'intoxication alimentaire *f*	a^n-tok-see-ka-syo^n a-lee-mah^n-tair
fracture	la fracture	frak-tu^e r
hay fever	le rhume des foins	ru^e m day fwa^n
headache	le mal de tête	mal de^r tet

heart attack	la crise cardiaque	*kreez kar-dyak*
high blood pressure	l'hypertension *f*	*ee-pair-tah^n -syo^n*
ill, sick	malade	*ma-lad*
illness	la maladie	*ma-la-dee*
indigestion	l'indigestion *f*	*a^n -dee-zhest-yo^n*
infection	l'infection *f*	*a^n -fek-syo^n*
influenza	la grippe	*greep*
insect bite	la piqûre d'insecte	*pee-ku^e r da^n -sekt*
insomnia	l'insomnie *f*	*a^n -som-nee*
itch	la démangeaison	*day-mah^n -zhay-zo^n*
nausea	la nausée	*no-zay*
nose bleed	la saignement de nez	*sen-ye^r -mah^n de^r nay*
pain	la douleur	*doo-lœr*
rheumatism	le rhumatisme	*ra^e -ma-teesm*
sore throat/throat infection	le mal de gorge/ l'angine *f*	*mal de^r gorzh/ah^n -zheen*
sprain	la foulure	*foo-lu^e r*
sting	la piqûre/(*pain*) la brûlure	*pee-ku^e r/bru^e -lu^e r*
stomach ache	le mal au ventre	*mal oh vah^n tr*
sunburn	le coup de soleil	*koo de so-le-y*
swelling	l'enflure *f*/(*lump*) la grosseur	*ah^n -flu^e r/gro-sœr*
tonsillitis	l'angine *f*	*ah^n -zheen*

toothache	le mal aux dents	*mal oh dah^n*
ulcer	l'ulcère *m*	*u^e l-sair*
wound	la blessure	*ble-su^e r*

Diagnosis and treatment

Where does it hurt?	*Où avez-vous mal?	*Oo a-vay-voo mal*
Have you a pain here?	*Avez-vous mal là?	*A-vay-voo mal la*
How long have you had the pain?	*Depuis quand avez-vous cette douleur?	*De^r -pwee kah^n a-vay-voo set doo-lœr*
Open your mouth	*Ouvrez la bouche	*Oo-vray la boosh*
Put out your tongue	*Montrez-moi votre langue	*Mo^n -tray-mwa votr lah^n g*
Breathe in	*Respirez/inspirez	*Res-pee-ray/a^n s-pee-ray*
Breathe out	*Soufflez/expirez	*Soo-flay/eks-pee-ray*
Does that hurt?	*Est-ce que cela vous fait mal?	*Es-ke^r se^r -la voo fe mal*
You're hurting me	Vous me faites mal	*Voo me^r fet mal*
A lot?/A little? *pain*	*Très mal?/Un peu?	*Tre mal/e^n pe^r*
Please lie down	*Allongez-vous, s'il vous plaît	*A-lo^n -zhay-voo, seel-voo-ple*
You must have a blood/urine test	*Vous devez faire des analyses de sang/d'urine	*Voo de^r -vay-fair day za-na-leez de^r sah^n /du^e -reen*
What medicines have you been taking?	*Quels médicaments/ remèdes prenez-vous?	*Kel may-dee-ka-mah^n /re^r -med pre^r -nay-voo*

I am pregnant	**Je suis enceinte**	*Zher swee zahn -san t*
I am allergic to . . .	**Je suis allergique à . . .**	*Zher swee za-lair-zheek a*
Are you being treated for these symptoms?	***Suivez-vous un traitement pour ces symptômes?**	*Swee-vay-voo en tret-mahn poor say san -tom*
Can you please prescribe a sleeping pill?	**Pouvez-vous me prescrire un somnifère?**	*Poo-vay-voo mer pray-skreer en som-nee-fair*
I'll give you	***Je vais vous donner**	*Zher ve voo do-nay*
an antibiotic	**un antibiotique**	*en ahn -tee-byo-teek*
some medicine	**des médicaments**	*day may-dee-ka-mahn*
a painkiller	**un analgésique/ un antalgique**	*en na-nal-zhay-zeek/en nahn -tal-zheek*
a sedative	**un sédatif/un calmant**	*en say-da-teef/ en kal-mahn*
Take this prescription to the chemist's	***Allez chez le pharmacien avec cette ordonnance**	*A-lay shay ler far-ma-syan a-vek set or-do-nahn s*
Take this three times a day	***Prenez ceci trois fois par jour**	*Prer -nay ser -see trwa fwa par zhoor*
I'll give you an injection	***Je vais vous faire une piqûre**	*Zher ve voo fair ue n pee-kue r*
Roll up your sleeve	***Retroussez votre manche**	*Rer -troo-say votr mahn sh*
I'll put you on a diet	***Je vais vous mettre au régime**	*Zher ve voo metr oh ray-zheem*

You must go to the hospital	***Il faut que vous alliez à l'hôpital**	*Eel fo ke' voo za-lyay a lo-pee-tal*
You must be X-rayed	***Il faut vous faire radiographier**	*Eel fo voo fair ra-dyo-gra-fyay*
You've pulled a muscle	***Vous vous êtes fait une élongation musculaire**	*Voo-voo-zayt fe u' n ay-lo'' -ga-syo'' mu' sku' -lair*
You have a fracture/ sprain	***Vous avez une fracture/une entorse**	*Voo-za-vay u' n fra-ktu' r/ u'n ah''-tors*
You need a few stitches	***Vous avez besoin de points de suture**	*Voo-za-vay be' -zwa'' de' pwa'' de' su' -tu' r*
You must stay in bed	***Vous devez rester au lit**	*Voo de' -vay res-tay oh lee*
Come and see me again in two days' time	***Revenez me voir dans deux jours**	*Re' -ve' -nay me' vwar dah'' de' zhoor*
Will you call again?	**Est-ce que vous repasserez me voir?**	*Es-ke' voo re' -pa-se' -ray me' vwar*
Is it serious/ contagious?	**Est-ce grave/ contagieux?**	*Es grav/ko'' -ta-zhye'*
It's nothing to worry about	***Ce n'est pas grave/ Ce n'est rien**	*Se' nay pa grav/ se' nay rya''*
I feel better now	**Je me sens mieux maintenant**	*Zhe' me' sah'' mye' ma'' -te' -nah''*
When can I travel again?	**Quand pourrai-je repartir?**	*Kah'' poo-rezh re' -par-teer*
You should not travel until . . .	***Vous ne devriez pas voyager avant . . .**	*Voo ne' de' -vryay pa vwa-ya-zhay a-vah''*

How much do I owe you?	**Combien vous dois-je?**	*Ko^n -bya^n voo dwa-zh*
I'd like a receipt for the health insurance	**J'ai besoin d'un reçu pour mon assurance médicale**	*Zhay be^r -zwa^n de^n re^r -su^e poor mo^n na-su^e -rah^n s may-dee-kal*
ambulance	**l'ambulance** *f*	*ah^n -bu^e -lah^n s*
anaesthetic	**l'anesthésique** *m*	*a-nay-stay-zeek*
bandage	**le pansement/la bande**	*pah^n -smah^n /bah^n d*
chiropodist	**le pédicure**	*pay-dee-ku^e r*
first aid station/A&E	**le poste de secours (services des) urgences**	*post de^r se^r -koor/(sair-vees dayz) u^e r-zhah^n s*
hospital	**l'hôpital** *m*	*o-pee-tal*
injection	**la piqûre**	*pee-ku^e r*
laxative	**le laxatif**	*lak-sa-teef*
nurse	**l'infirmière** *f*	*a^n -feer-myair*
operation	**l'opération** *f*	*o-pay-ra-syo^n*
optician	**l'opticien** *m*	*op-tee-sya^n*
osteopath	**l'ostéopathe** *m*	*os-tay-o-pat*
paediatrician	**le pédiatre**	*pay-dyatr*
(adhesive) plaster	**le sparadrap**	*spa-ra-dra*
prescription	**l'ordonnance** *f*	*or-do-nah^n s*
X-ray	**la radio(-graphie)**	*ra-dyo(-gra-fee)*

Optician

Key Phrases

I have broken my glasses; can you repair them?	J'ai cassé mes lunettes; pouvez-vous les réparer?	Zhay ka-say may lu^e-net; poo-vay-voo lay ray-pa-ray
Can you give me a new pair of glasses to the same prescription?	Pourriez-vous me donner une nouvelle paire de lunettes selon la même ordonnance?	Poor-yay-voo me' do-nay u^e n noo-vel pair de lu^e-net se'-loⁿ la mem or-do-nahⁿ s
Please test my eyes	Pourriez-vous tester ma vue, s'il vous plaît	Poor-yay-voo tes-tay ma vu^e, seel-voo-ple
I am short-sighted/long-sighted	Je suis myope/presbyte	Zhe' swee myop/pres-beet
I have broken the frame/the arm	J'ai cassé la monture/la branche	Zhay ka-say la moⁿ-tu^e r/la brahⁿ sh
When will they be ready?	Quand seront-elles prêtes?	Kahⁿ se'-roⁿ-tel pret
I have difficulty with reading/with long-distance vision	J'ai de la difficulté à lire/à voir de loin	Zhay de la dee-fee-ku^e l-tay a leer/a vwar de' lwaⁿ
I have lost one of my contact lenses	J'ai perdu un de mes verres de contact	Zhay pair-du eⁿ de may vair de koⁿ-takt
I should like to have contact lenses	Je voudrais des verres de contact	Zhe voo-dre day vair de koⁿ-takt

| My vision is blurred | **Ma vision est floue** | *Ma vee-zyo^n ay floo* |
| I can't see clearly | **Je ne peux pas voir clairement** | *Zhe^r ne^r pe^r pa vwar klayr-mah^n* |

Parts of the Body

ankle	**la cheville**	*she^r -vee-y*
arm	**le bras**	*bra*
artery	**l'artère** *f*	*ar-tair*
back	**le dos**	*doh*
bladder	**la vessie**	*vay-see*
blood	**le sang**	*sah^n*
body	**le corps**	*kor*
bone	**l'os** *m*	*os*
bowels	**les intestins** *m*	*a^n -tes-ta^n*
brain	**le cerveau**	*sair-voh*
breast	**le sein**	*sa^n*
cheek	**la joue**	*zhoo*
chest	**la poitrine**	*pwa-treen*
chin	**le menton**	*mah^n -to^n*
collar-bone	**la clavicule**	*kla-vee-ku^e l*
ear	**l'oreille** *f*	*o-re-y*

elbow	le coude	kood
eye	l'œil m (pl les yeux)	œ-y (ye')
eyelid	la paupière	po-pyair
face	la figure	fee-gu^e r
finger	le doigt	dwa
foot	le pied	pyay
forehead	le front	fro^n
gall bladder	la vésicule (biliaire)	vay-zee-ku^e l (bee-lyair)
gum	la gencive	zhah^n -seev
hand	la main	ma^n
head	la tête	tet
heart	le cœur	kœr
heel	le talon	ta-lo^n
hip	la hanche	ah^n sh
jaw	la mâchoire	ma-shwar
joint	l'articulation f	ar-tee-ku^e -la-syo^n
kidney	le rein	ra^n
knee	le genou	zhe' -noo
knee-cap	la rotule	ro-tu^e l
leg	la jambe	zhah^n b
lip	la lèvre	levr
liver	le foie	fwa
lung	le poumon	poo-mo^n

mouth	**la bouche**	*boosh*
muscle	**le muscle**	*mu^e-skl*
nail	**l'ongle** *m*	*oh^r -gl*
neck	**le cou**	*koo*
nerve	**le nerf**	*nair*
nose	**le nez**	*nay*
pelvis	**le pelvis**	*payl-vees*
pulse	**le pouls**	*poo*
rib	**la côte**	*koht*
shoulder	**l'épaule** *f*	*ay-pol*
skin	**la peau**	*poh*
spine	**la colonne vertébrale**	*ko-lon vair-tay-bral*
stomach	**l'estomac** *m*	*es-to-ma*
temple	**la tempe**	*tah^n p*
thigh	**la cuisse**	*kwees*
throat	**la gorge**	*gorzh*
thumb	**le pouce**	*poos*
toe	**l'orteil** *m*	*or-te-y*
tongue	**la langue**	*lah^n g*
tonsils	**les amygdales** *f*	*a-mee-dal*
tooth	**la dent**	*dah^n*
vein	**la veine**	*ven*
wrist	**le poignet**	*pwa-nyay*

MEETING PEOPLE

Key Phrases

Glad to meet you	**Enchanté(e) de vous connaître**	*Ah^n -shah^n -tay de^r voo ko-netr*
How are you?	**Comment allez-vous?**	*Ko-mah^n ta-lay-voo*
My name is . . .	**Je m'appelle . . .**	*Zhe^r ma-pel*
I'm on holiday/a business trip	**Je suis en vacances/ en voyage d'affaires**	*Zhe^r swee ah^n va-kah^n s/ ah^n vwa-yazh da-fair*
What's your telephone number?	**Quel est votre numéro de téléphone?**	*Kel ay votr nu^e -may-ro de^r tay-lay-fon*
Thanks for the invitation	**Merci de l'invitation**	*Mair-see de^r la^n -vee-ta-syo^n*
Yes, I'd like to come	**Oui, j'aimerais bien venir**	*Wee, zhem-re bya^n ve^r -neer*
I'm sorry, I can't come	**Je regrette, je ne peux pas venir**	*Zhe^r re^r -gret zhe^r ne^r pe^r pa ve^r -neer*

Introductions[1]

May I introduce . . . ?	**Permettez que je présente . . .**	*Pair-may-tay ke^r zhe^r pray-zah^n t*
Have you met . . . ?	**Connaissez-vous . . . ?**	*Ko-ne-say-voo*

1. See ESSENTIALS (pp. 1–7).

How are things?	**Comment ça va?**	*Ko-mahⁿ sa va*
Fine, thanks; and you?	**Très bien, merci; et vous?**	*Tre byaⁿ, mair-see; ay voo*
What is your name?	**Comment vous appelez-vous?**	*Ko-manⁿ voo zap-lay-voo*
Am I disturbing you?	**Je vous dérange?**	*Zheʳ voo day-rahⁿ zh*
Sorry to have troubled you	**Excusez-moi de vous avoir dérangé(e)**	*Eks-kuᵉ -zay-mwa deʳ voo za-vwar day-rahⁿ -zhay*

Getting Acquainted

Are you on holiday?	**Êtes-vous en vacances?**	*Et voo zen va-kahⁿ s*
I'm on holiday/a business trip	**Je suis en vacances/en voyage d'affaires**	*Zheʳ swee ahⁿ va-kahⁿ s/ ahⁿ vwa-yazh da-fair*
Do you travel a lot?	**Vous voyagez beaucoup?**	*Voo vwa-ya-zhay boh-koo*
We've been here a week	**Nous sommes ici depuis une semaine**	*Noo som zee-see deʳ -pwee uᵉ n seʳ -men*
Do you live/are you staying here?	**Vous habitez/ séjournez ici?**	*Voo-za-bee-tay/ say-zhoor-nay ee-see*
Is this your first time here?	**C'est la première fois que vous venez ici?**	*Say la preʳ -myair fwa keʳ voo veʳ -nay ee-see*
Do you like it here?	**Vous vous plaisez ici?**	*Voo-voo play-zay ee-see*
Where do you come from?	**D'où venez-vous?**	*Doo veʳ -nay-voo*

I come from . . .	**Je viens de . . .**	*Zhe' vyaⁿ de'*
Have you been to Australia/America?	**Êtes-vous déjà allé(e) en Australie/ en Amérique?**	*Et-voo day-zha a-lay ahⁿ no-stra-lee/ahⁿ na-may-reek*
Are you on your own?	**Vous êtes seul(e)?**	*Voo zet sœl*
I am travelling alone	**Je voyage seul(e)**	*Zhe' vwa-yazh sœl*
It's been nice talking to you	**J'ai eu beaucoup de plaisir à vous parler**	*Zhay u^e boh-koo de' play-zeer a voo parlay*
Can I see you again?	**Est-ce qu'on peut se revoir?**	*Es-koⁿ pe' se' re' -vwar*

Personal Information

I am with	**Je suis avec**	*Zhe' swee a-vek*
a colleague	**un(e) collègue**	*eⁿ (u^en) ko-layg*
my family	**ma famille**	*ma fa-mee-y*
a friend	**un(e) ami(e)**	*eⁿ (u^en) na-mee*
my husband	**mon mari**	*moⁿ ma-ree*
my parents	**mes parents**	*may pa-rahⁿ*
my wife	**ma femme**	*ma fam*
I have a boyfriend/ girlfriend	**J'ai un petit ami/ une petite amie**	*Zhay eⁿ pe' -tee ta-mee/ u^e n pe' -tee ta-mee*
I live with my partner	**J'habite avec mon partenaire m/ ma partenaire f**	*Zha-beet a-vek moⁿ par-tnair ma par-tnair*
I am separated/ divorced	**Je suis séparé(e)/ divorcé(e)**	*Zhe' swee say-pa-ray/ dee-vor-say*

I am a widow (er)	**Je suis veuve/veuf**	*Zhe' swee vœv/vœf*
Are you married/ single?	**Êtes-vous marié(e)/ célibataire?**	*Et-voo mar-yay/ say-lee-ba-tair*
Do you have children/ grandchildren?	**Avez-vous des enfants/des petits-enfants?**	*A-vay-voo day zahⁿ-fahⁿ/day pe' -tee zahⁿ -fahⁿ*
What do you do?	**Qu'est-ce que vous faites dans la vie?**	*Kes-ke' voo fet dahⁿ la vee*
I work for . . .	**Je travaille chez . . .**	*Zhe' tra-va-y shay*
I am a student/ nurse/accountant	**Je suis étudiant(e)/ infirmier(ère)/ comptable**	*Zhe' swee zay-tu^e -dyahⁿ (te')/zaⁿ -feer-my-ay(air)/ koⁿ -tabl*
I work freelance	**Je travaille à mon compte**	*Zhe' tra-va-y a moⁿ koⁿ t*
I'm a consultant	**Je suis consultant(e)**	*Zhe' swee koⁿ -su^e l-taⁿ (t)*
We're retired	**Nous sommes à la retraite**	*Noo som a la re' -trait*
What are you studying?	**Qu'est-ce que vous étudiez?**	*Kes-ke' voo zay-tu^e -dyay*
What do you do in your spare time?	**Que faites-vous pendant votre temps libre?**	*Ke' fet-voo pahⁿ -dahⁿ votr tahⁿ leebr*
I like sailing/ swimming/walking	**J'aime faire de la voile/ natation/marche**	*Zhem fair de' la vwal/ na-ta-syoⁿ/marsh*
I don't like cycling/ tennis	**Je n'aime pas faire du vélo/tennis**	*Zhe' nem pa fair du^e vay-lo/te-nees*
I'm interested in art/ music	**Je m'intéresse à l'art/la musique**	*Zhe' maⁿ -te-rays a lar/ la mu^e -zeek*

Going Out

Would you like to have coffee/a drink?	**Vous prenez un café/ une boisson?**	*Voo pre' -nay e^n ka-fay/ u^e n bwa-so^n*
I'd like a . . . , please	**Je prendrai un . . . , s'il vous plaît**	*Zhe' prah^n -dray e^n . . . , seel-voo-ple*
Cheers!	**Santé!**	*Sah^n -tay*
Would you like to have lunch tomorrow?	**Voudriez-vous déjeuner avec moi demain?**	*Voo-dree-yay-voo day- zhe' -nay a-vek mwa de' -ma^n*
Can you come to dinner/for a drink?	**Pouvez-vous venir dîner/prendre un verre?**	*Poo-vay-voo ve' -neer dee-nay/prah^n dr e^n vair*
We're giving/there is a party; would you like to come?	**Nous organisons/il y a une fête; voulez- vous venir?**	*Noo zor-ga-nee-zoh^n /eel- ya u^e n fayt; voo-lay-voo ve' -neer*
May I bring a (girl) friend?	**Puis-je amener un ami (une amie)?**	*Pwee-zh a-me' -nay e^n na-mee/u^e n a-mee*
Shall we go	**On va**	*O^n va*
to the cinema?	**au cinéma?**	*oh see-nay-ma*
to the theatre?	**au théâtre?**	*oh tay-atr*
for a walk?	**se promener?**	*se' pro-me' -nay*
Would you like to go dancing/for a drive?	**Voulez-vous aller danser/faire une promenade en voiture?**	*Voo-lay-voo a-lay dah^n -say/fair u^e n pro-me' -nad ah^n vwa-tu^e r*
Do you know a good disco/restaurant?	**Connaissez-vous une bonne discothèque/ un bon restaurant?**	*Ko-nay-say-voo u^e n bon dees-ko-tek/e^n bo^n res- to-rah^n*

Let's go to a gay bar	Allons dans un bar gay	A-lo*n* dah*n* ze*n* bar gay

Arrangements

Where shall we meet?	Où nous retrouverons-nous?	Oo noo re' -troov-ro*n* -noo
What time shall I/we come?	À quelle heure dois-je/devons-nous venir?	A kel-œr dwa-zh/de' -vo*n* -noo ve' -neer
I could pick you up at your hotel	Je pourrais passer vous prendre à votre hôtel	Zhe' poo-re pa-say voo prah*n* dr a votr o-tel
Can you meet me at …?	Pouvez-vous me rejoindre à …?	Poo-vay-voo me' re' -zhwa*n* dr a
May I see you home?	Puis-je vous raccompagner chez vous?	Pwee-zh voo ra-ko*n* -pan-yay shay voo
Can we give you a lift home/to your hotel?	Pouvons-nous vous reconduire chez vous/à votre hôtel?	Poo-vo*n* -noo voo re' -ko*n* -dweer shay voo/a votr o-tel
Where do you live?	Où habitez-vous?	Oo a-bee-tay-voo
What's your telephone number?	Quel est votre numéro de téléphone?	Kel ay votr nu*e* -may-ro de' tay-lay-fon
I hope to see you again soon	J'espère vous revoir bientôt	Zhes-pair vous re-vwar bya*n* -to
See you soon/later/ tomorrow	À bientôt/à plus tard/à demain	A bya*n* -to/a plu*e* tar/ a de' -ma*n*
Are you free at the weekend?	Êtes-vous libre ce week-end?	Et voo leebr se' wee-kend

Accepting and declining

Thanks for the invitation	**Merci de l'invitation**	*Mair-see de' la^n -vee-ta-syo^n*
Yes, I'd like to come	**Oui, j'aimerais bien venir**	*Wee, zhem-re bya^n ve' -neer*
Did you enjoy it?	**Est-ce que vous avez aimé?**	*Es-ke' voo-za-vay ay-may*
It was lovely	**C'était très sympathique**	*Say-tay tre sa^n -pa-teek*
I've enjoyed myself very much	**Je me suis bien amusé(e)**	*Zhe' me' swee bya^n na-mu-zay*
It was interesting/ funny/fantastic	**C'était intéressant/ amusant/fantastique**	*Say-tay a^n -tay-re-sah^n/ amu^e -zah^n/fah^n -ta-steek*
Thanks for	**Merci pour**	*Mair-see poor*
the drink	**le pot**	*le' po*
the evening	**la soirée**	*la swa-ray*
the ride	**la promenade**	*la pro-me' -nad*
I'm sorry, I can't come	**Je regrette, je ne peux pas venir**	*Zhe' re' -gret zhe' ne' pe' pa ve' -neer*
Maybe another time	**Une autre fois peut-être**	*U^e n otr fwa pe' -tetr*
No thanks, I'd rather not	**Non merci, j'aimerais mieux pas**	*No^n mair-see, zhem-re mye' pa*
Go away	**Allez-vous en/Partez**	*A-lay-voo-zah^n/par-tay*
Leave me alone	**Laissez-moi tranquille**	*Le-say-mwa trah^n -keel*

MONEY[1]

Key Phrases

Where is the nearest ATM?	**Où est le distributeur de billets le plus proche?**	*Oo ay le^r dee-stree-bu^e -tœr de^r bee-yay le^r plu^e prosh*
Do you take credits card?	**Accepterez-vous les cartes de crédit?**	*Ak-sep-te^r -ray-voo/ lay kart de^r kray-dee*
Is there a bank/an exchange bureau near here?	**Y a-t-il une banque/un bureau de change près d'ici?**	*Ee-ya-teel u^e n bahⁿ k/eⁿ bu^e -roh de^r shahⁿ zh pre dee-see*
Can you give me some small change?	**Pourriez-vous me donner de la monnaie?**	*Poor-yay-voo me^r do-nay de^r la mo-nay*
I want to open a bank account	**Je voudrais ouvrir un compte**	*Zhe^r voo-dre oo-vreer eⁿ koⁿ t*

1. In France most banks are open from 9 a.m. to 4.30 p.m. All banks are closed on Sundays. Some are closed on Saturdays, some on Mondays. In Switzerland they are open from 8 or 8.30 a.m. to 5 p.m., closed Saturday and Sunday. In Belgium most banks are open from 9 a.m. to 4 p.m., closed Saturday and Sunday. Some banks may close from noon to 2 p.m.

Credit and Debit Cards

I'll pay with a credit card	**Je payerai avec une carte de crédit**	*zhe pe-yer-ay-avek u^e n kart de' kray-dee*
I'd like to get some cash with my	**Pourrais-je retirer de l'argent avec ma**	*Poo-rezh re-tee-ray de' lar-zhahⁿ a-vek ma*
credit card	**carte de crédit**	*kart de' kray-dee*
debit card	**carte de paiement**	*kart de' pay-mahⁿ*
Please enter your pin number	***Veuillez saisir votre code**	*Vœ-yay say-zeer votr kod*
The ATM has swallowed my card	**Le distributeur de billets a avalé ma carte**	*Le' dee-stree-bu^e-tœr de' bee-yay a a-va-lay ma kart*

Exchange

Do you cash traveller's cheques?	**Acceptez-vous les chèques de voyage?**	*Ak-sep-tay-voo lay shek de' vwa-yazh*
Where can I cash traveller's cheques?	**Où puis-je encaisser des chèques de voyage?**	*Oo pwee-zh ahⁿ-kay-say day shek de' vwa-yazh*
I want to change some English/ American money	**Je voudrais changer des livres sterling/ des dollars**	*Zhe' voo-dre shahⁿ-zhay day leevr stair-laⁿ/ day do-lar*
Your passport, please	***Votre passeport, s'il vous plaît**	*Votr pa-spor, seel-voo-ple*
Where do I sign?	**Où dois-je signer?**	*Oo dwa-zh seen-yay*

Sign here, please	*Signez ici, s'il vous plaît	*Seen-yay ee-see seel-voo-ple*
Go to the cashier	*Allez à la caisse	*A-lay a la kes*
What is the rate of exchange?	Quel est le taux de change?	*Kel-ay le' toh de' shah" zh*
How much is your commission?	Quelle commission est-ce que vous prenez?	*Kel ko-mee-syo" es-ke' voo pre' -nay*
Can you give me some small change?	Pourriez-vous me donner de la monnaie?	*Poor-yay-voo me' do-nay de' la mo-nay*
I'd like small notes, please	Je voudrais de petites coupures, s'il vous plaît	*Zhe' voo-dre de' pe' -teet koo-pu^e r, seel-voo-ple*

General Banking

I arranged for money to be transferred from the UK; has it arrived yet?	J'ai fait transférer de l'argent/du Royaume Uni; est-il arrivé?	*Zhay fe trah" s-fay-ray de' lar-zhah" du^e rwa -yom u^enee; ay-teel a-ree-vay*
I want to open a bank account	Je voudrais ouvrir un compte	*Zhe' voo-dre oo-vreer e" koh" t*
Please credit this to my account	Veuillez verser ceci sur mon compte	*Voe-yay vair-say se' -see sur mo" ko" t*
I'd like to withdraw some cash with my debit card	Je voudrais retirer de l'argent avec ma carte de paiement	*Zhe' voo-dre re' -tee-ray de' lar-zhah" a-vek ma kart de' pay-mah"*
I want to make a transfer	Je veux effectuer un virement	*Zhe' ve' ay-fay-ktu^e -ay e" vee-re' -mah"*

balance	**le solde**	*sold*
bank card	**la carte bancaire**	*kart bahⁿ -kair*
cheque book	**le carnet de chèques/le chéquier**	*kar-nay de' shek/shay-kyay*
current account	**le compte courant**	*koⁿ t koo-rahⁿ*
deposit account	**le compte de dépôt**	*koⁿ t de' day-poh*
foreign currency	**la devise étrangère**	*de-veez ay-trahⁿ -zhair*
statement	**le relevé de compte**	*re' -le' -vay de' koⁿ t*

SHOPS[1] AND SERVICES

Where to Go

antique shop	**le magasin d'antiquités**	*rna-ga-zaⁿ dahⁿ -tee kee-tay*
audio equipment shop	**le magasin d'équipements audio**	*ma-ga-zaⁿ day-kee-pe^r -mahⁿ o-dyo*
bakery	**la boulangerie**	*boo-lahⁿ -zhe^r -ree*
bank	**la banque**	*bahⁿ k*
barber (see p. 205)	**le coiffeur**	*kwa-fœr*
beauty and spa treatments (see p. 193)	**l'esthéticienne** *f*	*ay-stay-tee-syayn*
bicycle repair shop (see p. 50)	**le magasin de réparation de vélo**	*ma-ga-zaⁿ de^r ray-pa-ra-syoⁿ de^r vay-lo*
bookshop (see p. 194)	**la librairie**	*lee-brai-ree*
builder	**le maçon/**(*contractor*) **l'entrepreneur** *m*	*ma-soⁿ/ahⁿ -tre^r -pre^r -nœr*
butcher (see p. 126)	**la boucherie/la charcuterie**	*boo-she^r -ree/shar-ku^e -te^r -ree*
cake shop	**la pâtisserie**	*pa-tee-se^r -ree*
camping equipment (see p. 82 and 207)	**le matériel de camping**	*ma-tay-ryel de^r kahⁿ -ping*

1. Most smaller shops are open by 8.30 a.m.; they close for lunch and stay open until seven or eight in the evening.

carpenter	le menuisier	me' -nwee-zyay
chemist's (see pp. 159 and 197)	la pharmacie	far-ma-see
consulate (see p. 243)	le consulat	koⁿ -su^e -la
craft shop	la boutique d'artisanat	boo-teek dar-tee-za-na
decorator/painter	le peintre décorateur	paⁿ tr day-ko-ra-tœr
delicatessen	l'épicerie fine f	ay-pee-sree feen
dentist (see p. 156)	le dentiste	dahⁿ -teest
department store	le grand magasin	grahⁿ ma-ga-zaⁿ
DIY shop (see p. 209)	le magasin de bricolage	ma-ga-zaⁿ de' bree-ko-lazh
doctor (see p. 158)	le médecin	may-de' -saⁿ
dry cleaner (see p. 209)	la teinturerie	taⁿ -tu^e -re' -ree
electrical appliances	les appareils électriques	a-pa-re-y ay-lek-treek
electrician	l'électricien m	ay-lek-tree-syaⁿ
embassy (see p. 145)	l'ambassade f	ahⁿ -ba-sad
fishmonger (see p. 122)	la poissonnerie	pwa-so-ne' -ree
florist	le fleuriste	flœ-reest
furniture shop (see p.83)	le magasin de meubles	ma-ga-zaⁿ de' mœbl
garden centre	la jardinerie	zhar-dee-ne' -ree

gift shop	**la boutique de cadeaux**	*boo-teek de^r ka-doh*
greengrocer (see pp. 131 and 137)	**le marchand de légumes**	*mar-shah^n de lay-gu^e m*
grocery	**l'épicerie**	*uy-pee-se^r-ree*
hairdresser (see p. 205)	**le coiffeur**	*kwa-fœr*
handyman	**l'homme à tout faire** *m*	*om a too fair*
hardware store (see p. 207)	**la quincaillerie**	*ka^n-ka-ye^r-ree*
health food shop	**le magasin de produits bio**	*ma-ga-za^n de^r pro-dwee byo*
home entertainment shop	**le magasin de multimédia**	*ma-ga-za^n de^r mu^e l-tee-may-dya*
hypermarket	**l'hypermarché** *m*	*ee-pair-mar-shay*
interior design shop	**le magasin de décoration d'intérieur**	*ma-ga-za^n de^r day-ko-ra-syo^n da^n-tay-ryœr*
jeweller	**le bijoutier**	*bee-zhoo-tyay*
kitchen shop	**le magasin de meubles de cuisine**	*ma-ga-za^n de^r mœbl de^r kwee-zeen*
launderette	**la laverie (automatique)**	*la-ve^r-ree (oh-toh-ma-teek)*
laundry (see p. 209)	**la blanchisserie**	*blah^n-shee-se^r-ree*
lighting shop	**le magasin de luminaires**	*ma-ga-za^n de^r lu^e-mee-nair*
market	**le marché**	*mar-shay*

mobile/cell phone shop (see p. 95)	le magasin de téléphonie mobile	*ma-ga-zaⁿ deʳ tay-lay-fo-nee mo-beel*
newsagent (see p. 194)	le marchand de journaux	*mar-shahⁿ de zhoor-noh*
notary	le notaire	*no-tair*
optician (see p. 168)	l'opticien *m*	*op-tee-syaⁿ*
outdoor equipment shop (see p. 207)	le magasin d'équipements de plein air	*ma-ga-zaⁿ day-kee-peʳ mahⁿ deʳ plaⁿ nair*
pastry shop (see p. 136)	la pâtisserie	*pa-tees-ree*
photographer	le photographe	*fo-to-graf*
photographic equipment (see p. 211)	le marchand d'appareils photo	*mar-shahⁿ da-pa-rey fo-to*
plasterer	le plâtrier	*pla-tree-ay*
plumber	le plombier	*ploⁿ -byay*
police	la police	*po-lees*
post office (see p. 93)	la poste/le bureau de poste	*post/buᵉ -ro deʳ post*
shoe repairs	le cordonnier	*kor-do-nyay*
shoeshop	le magasin de chaussures	*ma-ga-zaⁿ deʳ sho-suᵉ r*
shopping centre	le centre commercial	*sahⁿ tr ko-mair-syal*
souvenir shop	la boutique de souvenirs	*boo-teek deʳ soo-veʳ -neer*
sports shop	le magasin de sports	*ma-ga-zaⁿ deʳ spor*
stationer (see p. 194)	la papeterie	*pa-pe-tree*

supermarket	**le supermarché**	*su^e -pair-mar-shay*
sweet shop	**la confiserie**	*ko^n -feez-ree*
tobacconist	**le bureau de tabac**	*bu^e -roh de ta-ba*
tourist information office	**l'office du tourisme** *f*	*o-fees du^e too-reezm*
toy shop	**le magasin de jouets**	*ma-ga-za^n de^r zhoo-ay*
travel agency	**l'agence de voyages** *f*	*a-zhah^n s de^r wa-yazh*
travel goods shop	**la boutique d'articles de voyage**	*boo-teek dar-teekl de^r vwa-yazh*
wine merchant	**le marchand de vin**	*mar-shah^n de^r va^n*

Key Phrases

Which is the best …?	**Quel(le) est le meilleur/ la meilleure …?**	*Kel-ay le^r me-yœr/ la me-yœr*
Where is the nearest …?	**Où est le/la … le/ la plus proche?**	*Oo-ay le^r/la … le^r/ la plu^e prosh*
Can you recommend a …?	**Pouvez-vous me recommander un/une …?**	*Poo-vay-voo me^r re^r -ko-mah^n -day e^n/u^e n*
Where is the market?	**Où est le marché?**	*Oo-ay le^r mar-shay*
Is there a market every day?	**Est-ce qu'il y a un marché tous les jours?**	*Es-keel-ya e^n mar-shay too lay zhoor*
Where can I buy …?	**Où puis-je acheter …?**	*Oo pweezh ash-tay*
When are the shops open?	**Quand est-ce que les magasins sont ouverts?**	*Kah^n es-ke^r lay ma-ga-za^n so^n too-vair*

In the Shop

check-out/cash desk	**caisse**	*kes*
manager	**le directeur/la directrice, le gérant/ la gérante**	*dee-rek-tœr/dee-rek-trees zhay-rahⁿ/zhay-rant*
sale (*clearance*)	**soldes**	*sold*
self-service	**libre-service/ self-service**	*leebr-sair-vees/ self-sair-vees*
shop assistant	**le vendeur/la vendeuse**	*vahⁿ -dœr/vahⁿ -dœz*
Where can I get a trolley?	**Où puis-je prendre un chariot?**	*Oo pwee-zh prahⁿ dr eⁿ sha-ryo?*
Can I help you?	***Vous désirez?**	*Voo day-zee-ray*
I want to buy . . .	**Je voudrais acheter . . .**	*Zheʳ voo-dre ash-tay*
Do you sell . . .?	**Est-ce que vous avez . . .?**	*Es-keʳ voo-za-vay*
I'm just looking round	**Je jette un coup d'œil/je regarde**	*Zheʳ zhet eⁿ koo dœ-y/ zheʳ reʳ -gard*
I don't want to buy anything now	**Je ne veux rien acheter maintenant**	*Zheʳ neʳ veʳ ryaⁿ ash-tay maⁿ -teʳ -nahⁿ*
Could you show me . . .?	**Pouvez-vous me montrer . . .?**	*Poo-vay-voo meʳ moⁿ -tray*
I don't like this	**Je n'aime pas ça**	*Zheʳ nem pa sa*
I'll have this	**Je prendrai ça**	*Zheʳ prahⁿ -dre sa*

Will you gift wrap it, please?	**Pouvez-vous faire un paquet-cadeau, s'il vous plaît?**	*Poo-vay-voo fair eⁿ pa-kay ka-doh, seel-voo-ple*
We do not have that	***Nous n'avons pas ça**	*Noo na-voⁿ pa sa*
You'll find them at that counter	***Vous trouverez cela à ce rayon**	*Voo troo-veʳ -ray seʳ -la a seʳ ray-yoⁿ*
We've sold out but we'll have more tomorrow	***Nous n'en avons plus, mais nous en aurons d'autres demain**	*Noo nahⁿ na-voⁿ plueᵉ may noo zahⁿ no-roⁿ dotr deʳ -maⁿ*
Anything else?	***Vous faut-il autre chose?**	*Voo fo-teel otr shoz*
That will be all	**Ce sera tout**	*Seʳ seʳ -ra too*
Will you take it with you?	***C'est pour emporter?**	*Say poor ahⁿ -por-tay*
I will take it with me	**Je l'emporte**	*Zheʳ lahⁿ -port*
Please send them to this address/ hotel . . .	**Envoyez-les à cette adress/ à cet hôtel . . .**	*Ahⁿ -vwa-yay-lay a set a-dres/a set o-tel*

Choosing

I like the one in the window	**J'aime celui/celle qui est en vitrine**	*Zhem seʳ -lwee/sel kee ay tahⁿ vee-treen*
Can I see that one?	**Puis-je voir celui-là/ celle-là?**	*Pwee-zh vwar seʳ -lwee-la/sel-la*
Is it handmade?	**Est-ce fait à la main?**	*Es fay a la maⁿ*
What is it made of?	**En quoi est-ce?**	*Ahⁿ kwa es*

I like the colour but not the style	**J'aime la couleur mais pas le style**	*Zhem la koo-lœr may pa le' steel*
I want a darker/lighter shade	**Je veux une teinte plus foncée/plus claire**	*Zhe' ve' u^e n taⁿ t plu^e foⁿ -say/plu^e klair*
Do you have one in another colour/size?	**En avez-vous un(e) dans une autre couleur/taille?**	*Ahⁿ a-vay-voo eⁿ (u^e n) dahⁿ zu^e n otr koo-lœr/ta-y*
It's for a three-year-old	**C'est pour un enfant de trois ans**	*Say poor eⁿ ahⁿ -fahⁿ de' trwa zahⁿ*
Have you anything better/cheaper?	**Avez-vous quelque chose de mieux/de meilleur marché?**	*A-vay-voo kel-ke' -shoz de' mye'/de' me-yœr mar-shay*
How much is this?	**Combien coûte ceci?**	*Koⁿ -byaⁿ koot se' -see*
That is too much for me	**C'est trop cher pour moi**	*Say troh shair poor mwa*

Colours

beige	**beige**	*bezh*
black	**noir**	*nwar*
blue	**bleu**	*ble'*
brown	**brun/marron**	*breⁿ/ma-roⁿ*
gold	**doré**	*do-ray*
green	**vert**	*vair*
grey	**gris**	*gree*
mauve	**mauve**	*mohv*

orange	**orange**	*orah^n zh*
pink	**rose**	*roz*
purple	**violet**	*vee-o-lay*
red	**rouge**	*roozh*
silver	**argent**	*ar-zhah^n*
white	**blanc**	*blah^n*
yellow	**jaune**	*zhohn*

Materials

canvas	**la toile**	*twal*
cotton	**le coton**	*ko-to^n*
glass	**le verre**	*vair*
lace	**la dentelle**	*dah^n -tel*
leather	**le cuir**	*kweer*
linen	**le lin**	*la^n*
muslin	**la mousseline**	*moo-se^r -leen*
plastic	**le plastique**	*plas-teek*
silk	**la soie**	*swa*
suede	**le daim**	*da^n*
synthetic	**synthétique**	*sa^n -tay-teek*
velvet	**le velours**	*ve^r -loor*
wood	**le bois**	*bwa*
wool	**la laine**	*len*

Paying

How much is this?	**Combien coûte ceci?**	*Ko^n-bya^n koot se^r-see*
That's ... euros, please	***Cela fait ... euros**	*Se^r-la fe ... e^r-roh*
They are ... euros each	***Ils/elles coûtent ... euros la pièce**	*Eel/el koot ... e^r-roh la pyes*
It's too expensive	**C'est trop cher**	*Say tro shair*
Is that your best price?	**C'est votre meilleur prix?**	*Say votr me-yœr pree*
Can you give me a discount?	**Pouvez-vous me faire une réduction?**	*Poo-vay-voo me^r fair u^{e}n ray-du^{e}k-syo^n*
How much does that come to?	**Combien est-ce que cela fait?**	*Ko^n-bya^n es-ke^r se^r-la fe*
How would you like to pay?	***Comment voulez-vous payer?**	*Ko-mah^n voo-lay-voo pe-yay*
Cash only, please	***En espèces uniquement, s'il vous plaît**	*Ah^n nays-pays u^e -nee-ke^r-mah^n, seel-voo-ple*
Do you take credit cards/traveller's cheques?	**Acceptez-vous les cartes de crédit/les chèques de voyage?**	*Ak-sep-tay-voo lay kart de^r kray-dee/lay shek de^r vwa-yazh*
Do I have to pay VAT?	**Dois-je payer la TVA?**	*Dwa-zh pe-yay la tay-vay-a*
Please pay at the cash desk	***Payez à la caisse, s'il vous plaît**	*Pay-yay a la kes seel-voo-ple*
May I have a receipt, please?	**Pourriez-vous me donner un reçu?**	*Poor-yay-voo me^r do-nay e^n re^r-su^e*
You've given me the wrong change	**Vous vous êtes trompé en me rendant la monnaie**	*Voo-voo-zet tro^n-pay ah^n me^r rah^n-dah^n la mo-nay*

Complaints

I want to see the manager	**Je veux voir le patron/le gérant**	*Zhe' ve' vwar le' patroⁿ/le' zhay-rahⁿ*
I bought this yesterday	**J'ai acheté ceci hier**	*Zhay ash-tay se'-see yair*
It doesn't work	**Cela ne marche pas**	*Se'-la ne' marsh pa*
It doesn't fit	**Ça ne va pas**	*Sa ne' va pa*
This is	**C'est**	*Say*
bad	**mauvais**	*mo-ve*
broken	**cassé**	*ka-say*
cracked	**fêlé**	*fay-lay*
dirty	**sale**	*sal*
stained	**taché**	*ta-shay*
torn	**déchiré**	*day-shee-ray*
I want to return this	**Je voudrais rendre ceci**	*Zhe' voo-dre rahⁿ dr se'-see*
Will you change it?	**Pouvez-vous me le changer?**	*Poo-vay-voo me' le' shahⁿ-zhay*
Will you refund my money?	**Pouvez-vous me rembourser?**	*Poo-vay-voo me' rahⁿ-boor-say*
Here is the receipt	**Voici le reçu**	*Vwa-see le' re'-su^e*

Beauty and Spa Treatments

I'd like a manicure/ pedicure	**Je voudrais une manucure/pédicure**	*Zhe' voo-dre u^en ma-nu^e-ku^er/pay-dee-ku^er*
I'd like a facial massage	**Je voudrais un massage du visage**	*Zhe' voo-dre eⁿ ma-sazh du^e vee-zazh*

Do you do waxing?	**Vous faites l'épilation à la cire?**	*Voo fet lay-pee-la-syoⁿ a la seer*
I'd like my eyebrows shaped	**Je voudrais qu'on m'épile les sourcils**	*Zhe^r voo-dre koⁿ may-peel lay soor-seel*
Do you do aromatherapy?	**Vous faites de l'aromathérapie?**	*Voo fet de^r la-ro-ma-tay-ra-pee*
Is there a sauna/ steam room?	**Y a-t-il un sauna/un bain de vapeur?**	*Ee-ya-teel eⁿ so-na/eⁿ baⁿ de va-pœr*
What spa packages are available?	**Quelles sont vos formules spa?**	*Kel soⁿ vo for-mu^el spa*
How much does it cost?	**Combien ça coûte?**	*Koⁿ-byaⁿ sa koot*

Books, Newspapers and Stationery

Do you sell English/American newspapers/ magazines?	**Avez-vous des journaux/des périodiques anglais/ américains?**	*A-vay-voo day zhoor-noh/ day payr-yo-deek ahⁿ -gle/a-may-ree-kaⁿ*
Can you get ... for me?	**Pourriez-vous faire venir ... pour moi?**	*Poor-yay-voo fair ve^r -neer ... poor mwa*
Where can I get the ...?	**Où pourrais-je trouver le ...?**	*Oo poo-rezh troo-vay le^r*
I want a map of the city/road map	**Je voudrais un plan de la ville/une carte**	*Zhe^r voo-dre eⁿ plahⁿ de^r la veel/u^e n kart*
I'd like a guide to the city in English	**Je voudrais un guide de la ville en anglais**	*Zhe^r voo-dre eⁿ gheed de la veel ahⁿ nahⁿ -gle*

I want an entertainment guide[1]	**Je voudrais un guide des spectacles**	*Zhe' voo-dre e^n gheed day spek-takl*
Do you have any books in English?	**Avez-vous des livres en anglais?**	*A-vay-voo day leevr ahn ahn-gle*
Have you any books by . . .?	**Avez-vous des livres de . . .?**	*A-vay-voo day leevr de'*
I want some postcards	**Je voudrais des cartes postales**	*Zhe' voo-dre day kart pos-tal*
Do you sell souvenirs/toys?	**Est-ce que vous vendez des souvenirs/des jouets?**	*Es-ke' voo vah^n -day day soo-ve' -neer/ day zhoo-ay*
ballpoint pen	**le stylo-bille**	*stee-loh bee-y*
calculator	**la calculatrice/la calculette**	*kal-ku^e -la-trees/ kal-ku^e -let*
card	**la carte**	*kart*
dictionary	**le dictionnaire**	*deek-syo-nair*
drawing paper	**le papier à dessin**	*pa-pyay a day-sa^n*
drawing pin	**la punaise**	*pu^e -naiz*
elastic band	**l'élastique** *m*	*ay-las-teek*
envelope	**l'enveloppe** *f*	*ah^n -vlop*
felt-tip pen	**le feutre**	*fœtr*
glue	**la colle**	*kol*
guide book	**le guide**	*gheed*
ink	**l'encre** *f*	*ah^n kr*

1. In Paris, equivalents to *Time Out* are called *Pariscope* and *L'officiel des spectacles*.

notebook	**le carnet**	*kar-nay*
paperclip	**le trombone**	*tro^n -bon*
pen	**le stylo**	*stee-loh*
pen cartridge	**la cartouche d'encre**	*kar-toosh dah^n kr*
(coloured) pencil	**le crayon (de couleur)**	*kre-yo^n (de^r koo-lœr)*
pencil sharpener	**le taille-crayon**	*ta-y kre-yo^n*
postcard	**la carte postale**	*kart pos-tal*
rubber, eraser	**la gomme**	*gom*
sellotape	**le scotch**	*skotsh*
string	**la ficelle**	*fee-sel*
sketch pad	**le bloc à dessin**	*blok a day-sa^n*
wrapping paper	**le papier cadeau**	*pap-yay ka-doh*
writing paper	**le papier à lettre**	*pap-yay a letr*

CDs and DVDs

Can you recommend any CDs of local music?	**Pouvez-vous me recommander des CD avec de la musique locale?**	*Poo-vay-voo me re^r -ko-mah^n -day day say-day a-vek de la mu^e -zeek lo-kal*
Are there any new CDs by . . .?	**Avez-vous de nouveaux CD de . . .?**	*A-vay-voo de^r noo-voh say-day de^r*
Have you any CDs by . . .?	**Avez-vous des CD de . . .?**	*A-vay-voo day say-day de^r*
I'm looking for DVDs of . . .	**Je cherche des DVD de . . .**	*Zhe^r shairsh day day-vay-day de^r*

Chemist[1]

Can you prepare this prescription for me?	**Pouvez-vous me préparer cette ordonnance?**	*Poo-vay-voo me^r pray-pa-ray set or-do-nahⁿ s*
Have you a small first-aid kit?	**Avez-vous une petite trousse de secours?**	*A-vay-voo u^e n pe^r -teet troos de^r se^r -koor*
I want some aspirin	**Je voudrais de l'aspirine**	*Zhe^r voo-dre de^r las-pee-reen*
paracetamol	**du paracétamol**	*du^e pa-ra-say-ta-mol*
a packet of adhesive plasters	**une boîte de pansements adhésifs**	*u^e n bwat de^r pahⁿ -se-mahⁿ a-day-zeef*
sunscreen for children	**une crème solaire pour enfants**	*u^e n krem so-lair poor ahⁿ -fahⁿ*
Could you give me something for	**Pourriez-vous me donner quelque chose pour**	*Poor-yay voo me^r do-nay kel-ke^r -shoz poor*
constipation?	**la constipation?**	*la koⁿ s-tee-pa-syoⁿ*
diarrhoea?	**la diarrhée?**	*la dya-ray*
indigestion?	**l'indigestion?**	*laⁿ -dee-zhest-yoⁿ*
insect stings?	**les piqûres d'insecte?**	*lay pee-ku^e r daⁿ -saykt*
an upset stomach?	**les maux d'estomac?**	*lay moh des-to-ma*

1. See also DOCTOR (p. 158).

Do you sell contraceptives?	Est-ce que vous avez des préservatifs?	*Es-ke' voo za-vay day pray-zair-va-teef*
I'd like	Je voudrais	*Zhe' voo-dre*
an antiseptic cream/ointment	une crème/ pommade antiseptique	*u^e n krem/po-mad ah^n -tee-sep-teek*
a disinfectant	un désinfectant	*e^n day-za^n -fek-tah^n*
a mouthwash	une eau dentifrice/(*for gargling*) un gargarisme	*u^e n oh dah^n -tee-frees/ e^n gar-ga-reezm*
some nose drops	des gouttes nasales	*day goot na-zal*
something for sunburn	quelque chose pour les coups de soleil	*kel-ke' -shoz poor lay koo de' so-le-y*
some throat pastilles	des pastilles pour la gorge	*day pas-tee-y poor la gorzh*
Do you have	Est-ce que vous avez	*Es-ke' voo za-vay*
cotton wool?	du coton hydrophile?	*du^e ko-to^n ee-dro-feel*
sanitary towels?	des serviettes hygiéniques?	*day sair-vyet ee-zhee- ay-neek*
tampons?	des tampons?	*day tah^n -po^n*
I need something for a hangover/travel sickness	Je voudrais quelque chose pour les excès de boisson/le mal des transports	*Zhe' voo-dre kel-ke' -shoz poor lay zekse de' bwa- so^n/le' mal day trah^n -spor*

Clothes, Shoes and Accessories

I want a hat/sunhat	**Je voudrais un chapeau/un chapeau de soleil**	*Zhe' voo-dre e^n sha-poh/ e^n sha -poh de' so-le-y*
Where are the beach clothes?	**Où sont les vêtements pour la plage?**	*Oo so^n lay vet-mah^n poor la plazh*
The fashion department is on the second floor	***Le rayon des modes est au deuxième étage**	*Le' rai-yo^n day mod ay- toh de'-zyem ay-tazh*
I want a short/long-sleeved shirt	**Je voudrais une chemise à manches courtes/longues**	*Zhe' voo-dre u^en she'- meez a mah^nsh koort/ lo^ng*
Where can I find	**Où pourrais-je trouver**	*Oo poo-rezh troo-vay*
socks?	**des chaussettes?**	*day shoh-set*
tights?	**un collant?**	*e^n ko-lah^n*
I am looking for	**Je cherche**	*Zhe' shairsh*
a blouse	**un chemisier**	*e^n she'-mee-zyay*
a bra	**un soutien-gorge**	*e^n soo-tya^n gorzh*
a dress	**une robe**	*u^en rob*
a sweater	**un chandail**	*e^n shah^n -da-y*
I need	**Je voudrais**	*Zhe' voo-dre*
a coat	**un manteau**	*e^n mah^n-toh*
a jacket	**une veste**	*u^en vest*
a raincoat	**un imperméable**	*e^n a^n -pair-may-abl*
a pair of trousers	**un pantalon**	*pah^n-ta-lo^n*

Do you have other colours?	**Avez-vous d'autres couleurs?**	*A-vay-voo dotr koo-lœr*
I want it to match this	**Je veux quelque chose qui aille avec ceci**	*Zhe' ve' kel-ke'-shoz kee a-y a-vek se'-see*
What size is this?[1]	**C'est quelle taille/ quelle pointure?**	*Say kel ta-y/kel pwan-tu^e r*
I take size . . .	**Je prends du . . .**	*Zhe' prahn du^e*
I don't know the French size	**Je ne connais pas la taille française**	*Zhe' ne' ko-ne pa la ta-y frahn -sez*
Can you measure me?	**Pouvez-vous prendre mes mesures?**	*Poo-vay-voo prahndr may me'-zu^{e}r*
May I try it on?	**Puis-je l'essayer?**	*Pwee-zh lay-say-yay*
Is there a mirror?	**Y a-t-il une glace/ un miroir?**	*Ee-ya-teel u^{e}n glas/ en mee-rwar*
This doesn't fit	**Ceci ne me va pas**	*Se'-see ne' me' va pa*
It's too	**C'est trop**	*Say troh*
short	**court**	*koor*
long	**long**	*lon*
tight	**serré**	*say-ray*
loose	**ample**	*ahn-pl*
Have you a larger/ smaller one?	**Avez-vous plus grand/plus petit?**	*A-vay-voo plu^e grahn/ plu^e pe'-tee*
I need something warmer/thinner	**Je veux quelque chose de plus chaud/ de plus léger**	*Zhe' ve' kel-ke'-shoz de' plu^e shoh/de' plu^e lay-zhay*

1. Size = **taille** except for shoes, gloves and hats, when **pointure** should be used. See table (p. 201) for continental sizes.

Is it colour-fast?	Est-ce garanti bon teint?	*Es ga-rah^n-tee bo^n ta^n*
Is it machine-washable?	Est-ce qu'on peut laver cela à la machine?	*Es-ko^n pe^r la-vay se^r-la a la ma-sheen*
Will it shrink?	Est-ce que cela va rétrécir?	*Es-ke^r se^r-la va ray-tray-seer*
I need a pair of walking shoes	J'ai besoin d'une paire de chaussures pour la marche	*Zay be^r-zwa^n du^e-n pair de^r sho-su^{e}r poor la mar-sh*
I want a pair of boots	Je voudrais une paire de	*Zhe^r voo-dre u^{e}n pair de^r*
beach sandals	nu-pieds	*nu-pyay*
black shoes	chaussures noires	*sho-su^{e}r nwar*
boots	bottes	*bot*
trainers	baskets	*bas-ket*

Clothing sizes

WOMEN'S CLOTHING

coats, dresses, skirts, tops, trousers

UK/Australia	8	10	12	14	16	18
USA/Canada	6	8	10	12	14	16
Europe	38	40	42	44	46	48

shoes

UK	4	5	6	7	8	9	10
USA/Canada	$5^1/2$	$6^1/2$	$7^1/2$	$8^1/2$	$9^1/2$	$10^1/2$	$11^1/2$
Europe	37	38	39/40	41	42	43	44

MEN'S CLOTHING

suits and coats

UK/USA/Canada	36	38	40	42	44	46
Europe	46	48	50	52	54	56

shirts

UK/USA/Canada	14	14½	15	15½	16	16½	17
Europe	36	37	38	39	40	41	42

shoes

UK	9½	10	10½	11	11½
USA/Canada	10	10½	11	11½	12
Europe	43	44	44	45	45

Food[1]

Give me a kilo/half a kilo (a pound) of . . . , please	**Donnez-moi un kilo/ un demi-kilo (une livre) de . . . , s'il vous plaît**	*Do-nay mwa e^n kee-lo/e^n de^r -mee kee-lo (u^e n lee-vr) de^r . . . , seel-voo-ple*
100 grammes of sweets, please	**Cent grammes de bonbons, s'il vous plaît**	*Sah^n gram de^r bo^n -bo^n, seel-voo-ple*
A bottle of	**Une bouteille de**	*U^e n boo-te-y de*
beer, please	**bière, s'il vous plaît**	*byair, seel-voo-ple*
wine	**vin**	*va^n*

1. See also the various MENU sections (pp. 121–43) and WEIGHTS AND MEASURES (p. 257).

A litre of semi-skimmed/full-fat milk, please	**Un litre de lait demi-écrémé/ lait entier, s'il vous plaît**	*E^n leetr de^r le de^r -mee ay-kray-may/ le e^n -tyay, seel-voo-ple*
a carton of plain yogurt	**un pot de yaourt nature**	*e^n po de^r ya-oort na-tu^e r*
a dozen eggs	**une douzaine d'œufs**	*u^e n doo-zen de^r*
a bottle of mineral water	**une bouteille d'eau minérale**	*u^e n boo-te-y doh mee-nay-ral*
I want	**Je voudrais**	*Zhe^r voo-dre*
a jar of . . .	**un pot de . . .**	*e^n poh de^r*
a can of . . .	**une boîte de . . .**	*u^e n bwat de^r*
a packet of . . .	**un paquet de . . .**	*e^n pa-kay de^r*
. . . slices of ham, please	**. . . tranches de jambon, s'il vous plaît**	*trah^n sh de^r zhah^n -bo^n, seel-voo-ple*
300g . . . cheese, please	**trois cents grammes de fromage, s'il vous plaît**	*trwa sah^n gram de^r fro-mazh, seel-voo-ple*
Do you sell frozen foods?	**Vendez-vous des aliments surgelés?**	*Vah^n -day-voo day za-lee-mah^n su^e r -zhe^r -lay*
Is it fresh or frozen?	**Est-ce frais ou congelé?**	*Es fre oo ko^n -zhe^r -lay*
These pears are too hard/soft	**Ces poires sont trop dures/molles**	*Say pwar so^n troh du^e r/ mol*
Are they ripe?	**Sont-ils mûrs?**	*So^n -teel mu^e r*

This is bad	C'est mauvais	*Say mo-ve*
This is stale	Ce n'est pas frais	*Se' nay pas fre*
A loaf of bread, please[1]	Un pain, s'il vous plaît	*E^n pa^n, seel-voo-ple*
How much is a kilo/a bottle?	Combien est-ce le kilo/la bouteille?	*Ko^n -bya^n es le' kee-lo/ la boo-te-y*
a kilo of sausages	un kilo de saucisses	*e^n kee-lo de' soh-sees*
four pork chops	quatre côtes de porc	*katr kot de' por*
Could you mince the meat?	Pourriez-vous hacher la viande?	*Poor-yay-voo a-shay la vyah^n d*
Could you bone the fish?	Pourriez-vous ôter les arêtes du poisson?	*Poor-yay-voo oh-tay les za-ret du^e pwa-so^n*
Could you clean the fish?	Pourriez-vous vider le poisson?	*Poor-yay-voo vee-day le' pwa-so^n*
Leave/take off the head	Laissez/enlevez la tête	*Lay-say/ah^n -le' -vay la tet*
Please fillet the fish	Pourriez-vous découper le poisson en filets?	*Poor-yay-voo day-koo-pay le' pwa-so^n ah^n fee-lay*
Is there any shellfish?	Avez-vous des fruits de mer?	*A-vay-voo day frwee de mair*
Shall I help myself?	Puis-je me servir?	*Pwee-zh me' sair-veer*

1. French loaves: **une flûte** – a small thin stick; **une baguette** – a longer, slightly thicker stick (the most common French bread); **un bâtard** – shorter and thicker than a **baguette**; **un pain de mie** – sandwich loaf. **Un pain intégral** is a wholemeal loaf.

Hairdresser and Barber

May I make an appointment for this morning/tomorrow afternoon?	Pourrais-je prendre un rendez-vous pour ce matin/demain après-midi?	Poo-rezh prah^n dr e^n rah^n -day-voo poor se^r ma-ta^n/de^r -ma^n a-pre mee-dee
What time?	À quelle heure?	A kel-œr
I want my hair cut	Je voudrais me faire couper les cheveux	Zhe^r voo-dre me^r fair koo-pay lay she^r -ve^r
Just a trim, please	Simplement rafraîchir, s'il vous plaît	Sa^n -ple^r -mah^n ra-fre-sheer, seel-voo-ple
Not too short at the sides	Pas trop courts sur le côté	Pa troh koor su^e r le^r ko-tay
I'll have it shorter at the back, please	Je les voudrais un peu plus courts derrière, s'il vous plaît	Zhe^r lay voo-dre e^n pe^r plu^e koor der-yair, seel-voo-ple
Shorter on top	Plus courts sur le haut	Plu^e koor su^e r le^r oh
No shorter	Pas plus courts	Pa plu^e koor
That's fine	C'est très bien comme ça	Say tre bya^n kom sa
I'd like a shave, please	Je voudrais me faire raser, s'il vous plaît	Zhe^r voo-dre me^r fair ra-zay, seel-voo-ple
Please trim my beard/my moustache	Veuillez me tailler légèrement la barbe/la moustache	Vœ-yay me^r ta-yay lay-zhair-mah^n la barb/la moos-tash

My hair is oily/dry	Mes cheveux sont gras/secs	*May she' -ve' soⁿ gra/sek*
I want a shampoo	Je voudrais un shampooing	*Zhe' voo-dre eⁿ shahⁿ -pwaⁿ*
Please use conditioner	Utilisez une crème 'après shampooing', s'il vous plaît	*U^e -tee-lee-zay u^e n krem a-pre shahⁿ -pwaⁿ, seel-voo-ple*
I want my hair washed, styled and blow-dried	Je voudrais un shampooing, une coupe et un brushing	*Zhe' voo-dre eⁿ shahⁿ -pwaⁿ, u^e n koop ay eⁿ bra-shing*
Please do not use any hairspray	N'utilisez pas de laque, s'il vous plaît	*Nu^e -tee-lee-zay pa de' lak seel-voo-ple*
I want a colour rinse	Je voudrais un rinçage	*Zhe' voo-dre eⁿ raⁿ -sazh*
I'd like to see a colour chart	Puis-je voir la gamme des coloris?	*Pwee-zh vwar la gam day ko-lo-ree*
I'd like a darker/lighter shade	Je voudrais une teinte plus foncée/plus claire	*Zhe' voo-dre u^e n taⁿ t plu^e foⁿ -say/plu^e klair*
I want a tint/highlights	Je voudrais un colorant/un balayage	*Zhe' voo-dre eⁿ ko-lo-rahⁿ/eⁿ ba-lay-yazh*
The water is too cold	L'eau est trop froide	*Loh ay troh frwad*
The dryer is too hot	Le séchoir est trop chaud	*Le' say-shwar ay troh shoh*
I want a manicure	Je voudrais une manucure	*Zhe' voo-dre u^e n ma-nu^e -ku^e r*
Thank you, I like it very much	Merci, c'est très bien	*Mair-see say tre byaⁿ*

Hardware and Outdoors[1]

Where is the camping equipment?	**Où se trouve le matériel de camping?**	*Oo se^r troov le^r ma-ter-yel de^r kahⁿ -ping*
Do you have a battery for this?	**Avez-vous une pile pour cet appareil?**	*A-vay-voo u^e n peel poor set a-pa-re-y*
Where can I get butane gas?	**Où pourrais-je trouver du gaz butane?**	*Oo poo-rezh troo-vay du^e gaz bu^e -tan*
I need	**J'ai besoin**	*Zhay be^r -zwaⁿ*
a bottle-opener	**d'un décapsuleur**	*deⁿ day-kap-su^e -lœr*
a corkscrew	**d'un tire-bouchon**	*deⁿ teer-boo-shoⁿ*
a tin-opener	**d'un ouvre-boîte**	*deⁿ oovr-bwat*
I'd like some candles/ matches	**Je voudrais des bougies/des allumettes**	*Zhe^r voo-dre day boo-zhee/day-za-lu^e -met*
I want	**Je veux**	*Zhe^r ve^r*
a flashlight	**une lampe de poche**	*u^e n lahⁿ p de^r posh*
a pen-knife	**un canif**	*eⁿ ka-neef*
a pair of scissors	**une paire de ciseaux**	*u^e n pair de^r see-zoh*
Do you sell string/ rope?	**Vendez-vous de la ficelle/de la corde?**	*Vahⁿ -day-voo de^r la fee-sel/de^r la kord*

1. See also CAMPING (p. 71) and APARTMENTS AND VILLAS (p. 79).

Where can I find	**Où puis-je trouver**	*Oo pwee-zh troo-vay*
scouring powder?	**de la poudre à récurer?**	*de^r la poodr a re-ku^e-ray*
soap pads?	**des tampons à récurer?**	*day tah^n-po^n a re-ku^e-ray*
washing-up liquid?	**du liquide pour la vaisselle?**	*du^e lee-keed poor la vay-sel*
Do you have tea towels?	**Avez-vous des torchons?**	*A-vay-voo day tor-sho^n*
I need	**J'ai besoin**	*Zhay be^r-zwa^n*
a brush	**d'une brosse**	*du^e n bros*
a bucket	**d'un seau**	*de^n soh*
a frying pan	**d'une poêle à frire**	*du^e n pwal a freer*
a groundsheet	**d'un tapis de sol**	*de^n ta-pee de^r sol*
I want to buy a barbecue	**Je voudrais acheter un barbecue**	*Zhe^r voo-dre ash-tay e^n bar-be^r-ku^e*
Do you sell charcoal?	**Vous vendez du charbon de bois?**	*Voo vah^n-day du^e shar-bo^n de^r bwa*
adaptor	**la prise multiple, l'adaptateur**	*preez mu^e l-teepl, la-dap-ta-tœr*
basket	**le panier**	*pan-yay*
duster	**le chiffon (à poussière)**	*shee-fo^n (a poo-syair)*
electrical flex	**le fil électrique**	*feel ay-lek-treek*
extension lead	**la rallonge**	*ra-lo^n zh*
fuse	**le fusible**	*fu^e-zeebl*

fuse wire	**le fil à fusible**	*feel a fu^e -zeebl*
insulating tape	**le chatterton**	*sha-tair-ton*
lightbulb	**l'ampoule électrique** *f*	*ahⁿ -pool ay-lek-treek*
plug (*bath*)	**la bonde**	*boⁿ d*
plug (*electric*)	**la prise électrique**	*preez ay-lek-treek*

Laundry and Dry Cleaning

Where is the nearest launderette/ dry cleaner?	**Où se trouve la laverie/la teinturerie la plus proche?**	*Oo se^r troov la la-ve^r -ree/la taⁿ -tu^e -re^r -ree la plu^e prosh*
I want to have these things washed/ cleaned	**Je voudrais faire laver/faire nettoyer ces affaires**	*Zhe^r voo-dre fair la-vay/fair ne-twa-yay say za-fair*
Can you get this stain out?	**Pouvez-vous faire disparaître cette tache?**	*Poo-vay-voo fair dees-pa-raitr set tash*
It is	**C'est**	*Say*
coffee	**du café**	*du^e ka-fay*
grease	**de la graisse**	*de^r la gres*
wine	**du vin**	*du^e vaⁿ*
It only needs to be pressed	**Ceci n'a besoin que d'être repassé**	*Se^r -see na be^r -zwaⁿ ke^r detr re^r -pa-say*
This is torn; can you mend it?	**Ceci est déchiré; pouvez-vous le réparer?**	*Se^r -see ay day-shee-ray; poo-vay-voo le^r ray-pa-ray*

There's a button missing	Il manque un bouton	*Eel mah^n k e^n boo-to^n*
Will you sew on another one, please?	Pouvez-vous le remplacer, s'il vous plaît?	*Poo-vay-voo le' rah^n -pla-say, seel-voo-ple*
When will they be ready?	Quand est-ce que ce sera prêt?	*Kah^n es-ke' se' se' -ra pre*
I need them by this evening/tomorrow	J'en ai besoin pour ce soir/pour demain	*Zhah^n nay be' -zwa^n poor se' swar/poor de' -ma^n*
Call back around five o'clock	*Revenez vers cinq heures	*Re' -ve' -nay vair sa^n k œr*
We can't do it before Tuesday	*Nous ne pouvons pas le faire avant mardi	*Noo ne' poo-vo^n pa le' fair a-vah^n mar-dee*
It will take three days	*Cela prendra trois jours	*Se' -la prah^n -dra trwa zhoor*
This isn't mine	Ceci n'est pas à moi	*Se' -see nay pa za mwa*
I've lost my ticket	J'ai perdu mon ticket	*Zhay pair-du^e mo^n tee-kay*

Household laundry

bath towel	la serviette de bain	*sair-vyet de' ba^n*
blanket	la couverture	*koo-vair-tu^e r*
napkin	la serviette de table	*sair-vyet de' tabl*
pillow case	la taie d'oreiller	*te do-re-yay*
sheet	le drap	*dra*
tablecloth	la nappe	*nap*
tea towel	le torchon	*tor-sho^n*

Markets

Which day is market day?	**Quel jour a lieu le marché?**	*Kel zhoor a lye[r] le[r] mar-shay*
Where is the market held?	**Où a lieu le marché?**	*Oo a lye[r] le[r] mar-shay*
Is it a permanent/ covered market?	**Est-ce un marché permanent/couvert?**	*Es e[n] mar-shay per-ma-nah[n]/koo-ver*
What time does it start/finish?	**À quelle heure commence-t-il/ termine-t-il?**	*A ke-lœr ko-mah[n] s-teel/ ter-meen-teel*
Is there a market today in a nearby town?	**Y a-t-il un marché aujourd'hui dans une ville près d'ici?**	*Ee-ya-teel e[n] mar-shay oh-zhoor-dwee dah[n] u[e] n veel pre dee-see*

Photography

I'd like . . .	**Je voudrais**	*Zhe[r] voo-dre*
a digital camera	**un appareil photo numérique**	*e[n] a-pa-re-y fo-to nu[e] -may-reek*
a disposable camera	**un appareil photo jetable**	*e[n] a-pa-re-y fo-to zhe[r] -tabl*
a camcorder	**une caméra**	*ka-me-ra*
Do you have a memory card for this camera?	**Vous avez une carte mémoire pour cet appareil photo?**	*Voo-za-vay u[e] n kart may-mwar poor set apa-re-y fo-to*
Can you print photos from this card/ disk/USB?	**Pouvez-vous imprimer des photos à partir de cette carte/ce disque/ cette clé USB?**	*Poo-vay-voo a[n] -pree-may day fo-to a par-teer de[r] set kart/se[r] deesk/ set klay u[e] -es-bay*

I'd like ... prints/ enlargements of this image	**Je voudrais ... épreuves/ agrandissements de cette image**	*Zhe′ voo-dre ... ay-prœv/ a-grah′ -dees-mah′ de′ set ee-mazh*
I'd like the express service	**Je voudrais ce service dans les plus courts délais**	*Zhe′ voo-dre se′ sair-vees dah′ lay plu′ koor day-lay*
When will it be ready?	**Quand est-ce que ce sera prêt?**	*Kah′ es-ke′ se′ se′ -ra pre*
Will it be done tomorrow?	**Est-ce que ce sera fait demain?**	*Es-ke′ se′ se′ -ra fe de′ -ma′*
My camera's not working; can you look at it?	**Mon appareil ne marche pas; pouvez-vous l'examiner?**	*Mo′ napa-re-y ne′ mar-sh pa; poo-vay-voo lek-za-mee-nay*
You will have to leave the camera with us for a few days	***Vous devrez nous laisser votre appareil pendant quelques jours**	*Voo de′ -vray noo lay-say votr a-pa-re-y pah′ -dah′ kel-ke′ zhoor*
battery	**la pile**	*peel*
camera case	**le boîtier pour caméra**	*bwa-tyay poor ka-me-ra*
filter	**le filtre**	*feeltr*
glossy	**brillant**	*bree-y-ah′*
lens	**l'objectif**	*ob-zhek-teef*
lens cap	**le capuchon d'objectif**	*ka-pu′ -sho′ dob-zhek-teef*
light meter	**la cellule**	*se-lu′ l*
matt	**matte**	*mat*

Repairs

This is broken; can it be mended?	**Ceci est cassé; est-ce qu'on peut le réparer?**	*Se' -see ay ka-say; es-ko^n pe' le' ray-pa-ray*
Can you do it while I wait?	**Pouvez-vous le faire tout de suite?**	*Poo-vay-voo le' fair too de' sweet*
When should I come back for it?	**Quand dois-je revenir le/ la chercher?**	*Kah^n dwa-zh re' -ve' -neer le'/la shair-shay*
I want these shoes soled	**Je voudrais faire ressemeler ces chaussures**	*Zhe' voo-dre fair re' -se' m-lay say sho-su^e r*
I want leather soles	**Je voudrais des semelles en cuir**	*Zhe' voo-dre day se' -mel ah^n kweer*
I want these shoes heeled with rubber	**Je voudrais faire mettre des talons en caoutchouc à cette paire de chaussures**	*Zhe' voo-dre fair metr day ta-lo^n ah^n ka-oo-tshoo a set pair de' sho-su^e r*
Do you sell shoelaces?	**Vendez-vous des lacets?**	*Vah^n -day-voo day la-say*
My watch is broken	**Ma montre est cassée**	*Ma mo^n tr ay ka-say*
I have broken the glass/the strap	**J'ai cassé le verre/ le bracelet**	*Zhay ka-say le' vair/ le' bras-lay*
Can you mend this bag for me, please?	**Pouvez-vous raccommoder ce sac pour moi, s'il vous plaît?**	*Poo-vay-voo ra-ko-mo-day se' sak poor mwa, seel-voo-ple*

Could you put in a new zip?	**Pourriez-vous remplacer la fermeture éclair?**	*Poor-yay-voo rah^{n} -pla-say la fair-me^{r} -tu^{e} r ay-klair*
The stone/charm/ screw has come loose	**La pierre/l'amulette/ la vis est desserrée**	*La pyrair/la-mu^{e} -let/ la vees ay day-say-ray*
The fastener/clip/ chain is broken	**Le fermoir/la pince/ la chaîne est cassé(e)**	*Le^{r} fair-mwar/la pa^{n} s/ la shen ay ka-say*
It can't be repaired	***C'est irréparable**	*Say-tee-ray-pa-rabl*
You need a new one	***Vous avez besoin d'en acheter un nouveau (une nouvelle)**	*Voo-za-vay be^{r} -zwa^{n} dah^{n} -nash-tay e^{n} noo-voh (u^{e}n noo-vel)*
How much would a new one cost?	**Un neuf/une neuve me coûterait combien?**	*E^{n} nœf/u^{e} n nœv me^{r} koo-te^{r} -re ko^{n} -bya^{n}*

Toiletries

Some razor blades, please	**Des lames de rasoir, s'il vous plaît**	*Day lam de^{r} ra-zwar, seel-voo-ple*
How much is this after-shave lotion?	**Combien coûte cette lotion après-rasage?**	*Ko^{n} -bya^{n} koot set loh-syo^{n} a-pre ra-zazh*
A tube of toothpaste, please	**Un tube de dentifrice, s'il vous plaît**	*E^{n} tu^{e} b de^{r} dah^{n} -tee-frees, seel-voo-ple*
A box of paper handkerchiefs, please	**Une boîte de mouchoirs en papier, s'il vous plaît**	*U^{e} n bwat de^{r} moo-shwar ah^{n} pap-yay, seel-voo-ple*

I want some cologne/ perfume	Je voudrais de l'eau-de-cologne/du parfum	Zhe' voo-dre de' loh de' ko-lon-y/du^e par-feⁿ
May I try it?	Puis-je l'essayer?	Pwee-zh le-say-yay
Do you have any sun cream?	Avez-vous de la crème solaire?	A-vay-voo de' la krem so-lair
I'd like	Je voudrais	Zhe' voo-dre
a bar of soap	un savon	eⁿ sa-voⁿ
a bottle/tube of shampoo for dry/ greasy hair	un flacon/un tube de shampooing pour cheveux secs/gras	eⁿ fla-koⁿ/eⁿ tu^e b de' shahⁿ -pwaⁿ poor she' -ve' sek/gra
a cleansing cream/ lotion	une crème/ une lotion démaquillante	u^e n krem/u^e n loh-syoⁿ day-ma-kee-yahⁿ t
a hair conditioner	une crème après-shampooing	u^e n krem a-pre shahⁿ -pwaⁿ
a hand cream	une crème pour les mains	u^e n krem poor lay maⁿ
a lipsalve	un stick/une pommade pour les lèvres	eⁿ steek/u^e n po-mad poor lay levr
a moisturizer	une crème hydratante	u^e n krem ee-dra-tahⁿ t
a razor	un rasoir	eⁿ ra-zwar
a roll of toilet paper	un rouleau de papier hygiénique	eⁿ roo-loh de' pap-yay ee-zhee-ay-neek

SIGHTSEEING[1]

Key Phrases

Where is the tourist office?	Où se trouve le syndicat d'initiative/l'office du tourisme?	*Oo se' troov le' san -dee-ka dee-nee-sya-teev/ lo-fees du' too-reezm*
Is there a map/plan of the places to visit?	Y a-t-il une carte/un plan des endroits à visiter?	*Ee-ya-teel u' n kart/e'' plahn day zahn -drwa a vee-zee-tay*
Is there a good sightseeing tour?	Y a-t-il une visite touristique intéressante?	*Ee-ya-teel u' n vee-zeet too-rees-teek an -tay-re-sahn t*
Is there a walking tour of the town?	Y a-t-il une visite guidée de la ville?	*Ee-ya-teel u' n vee-zeet ghee-day de' la veel*
How much does the tour cost?	Combien coûte la visite?	*Kon -byan koot la vee-zeet*
Is there access for wheelchairs?	Est-ce accessible aux fauteuils roulants?	*Es ak-say-seebl oh fo- tœ-y roo-lahn*
Is there an audio guide in English?	Y a-t-il un guide audio en anglais?	*Ee-ya-teel en gheed o-dyo ahn nahn -gle*

1. See also GETTING AROUND (p. 15) and DIRECTIONS (p. 57).

What should we see here?	**Que faut-il voir ici?**	*Ke^r fo-teel vwar ee-see*
I want a guide book	**Je voudrais un guide touristique**	*Zhe^r voo-dre e^n gheed too-rees-teek*
Can you suggest an interesting half-day excursion?	**Pouvez-vous me recommander une excursion d'une demi-journée?**	*Poo-vay-voo me^r re^r-ko-mah^n-day u^e n alk-sku^e r-syo^n du^e n de^r-mee zhoor-nay*
Can we take a boat cruise/a balloon flight?	**Peut-on prendre un bateau de croisière/un vol en mongolfière?**	*Pe^r-to^n prah^n dr e^n ba-toh de^r krwa-zyair/e^n vol ah^n mo^n-gol-fyair*
We want to go hiking	**On voudrait faire de la randonnée**	*O^n voo-dray fair de^r la rah^n-do-nay*
Do we need a guide?	**Est-ce qu'on a besoin d'un guide?**	*Es-ko^n na be^r-zwa^n de^n gheed*
It's	**C'est**	*Say*
beautiful	**beau**	*boh*
funny	**amusant**	*amu^e-zah^n*
impressive	**impressionnant**	*a^n-pray-syo-nah^n*
romantic	**romantique**	*ro-mah^n-teek*
stunning	**sensationnel**	*sah^n-sa-syo-nayl*
unusual	**extraordinaire**	*ex-tra-or-dee-nair*

Exploring

Where is the old part of the city?	Où se trouve la vieille ville?	*Oo se' troov la vye-y veel*
I'd like to walk round the old town	J'aimerais faire une promenade dans la vieille ville	*Zhem-re fair u^e n promnad dahⁿ la vye-y veel*
Is there a good street plan showing the buildings?	Est-ce qu'il y a un plan détaillé indiquant les monuments?	*Es-keel-yo eⁿ plan day-ta-yay aⁿ -dee-kahⁿ lay mo-nu^e -mahⁿ*
We want to visit	Nous voudrions visiter	*Noo voo-dree-yoⁿ vee-zee-tay*
the cathedral	la cathédrale	*la ka-tay-dral*
the cloister	le cloître	*le' klwatr*
the fortress	la forteresse	*la for-te' -res*
the library	la bibliothèque	*la bee-blee-o-tek*
the monastery	le monastère	*le' mo-nas-tair*
the palace	le palais	*le' pa-le*
the ruins	les ruines	*lay rween*
May we walk around the walls?	Est-ce qu'on peut se promener le long des murs/des remparts?	*Es-koⁿ pe' se' prom-nay le' loⁿ day mu^e r/day rahⁿ -par*
May we go up the tower?	Est-ce qu'on peut monter à la tour?	*Es-koⁿ pe' moⁿ -tay a la toor*
What is that building?	Qu'est-ce que ce bâtiment?	*Kes ke' se' ba-tee-mahⁿ*

Where is the church/ the cemetery?	**Où se trouve l'église/le cimetière?**	*Oo se^r troov lay-gleez/le^r seem-tyair*
Where is the antiques market/flea market?	**Où se trouve le marché aux antiquités/le marché aux puces?**	*Oo se^r troov le^r mar-shay oh zahⁿ -tee-kee-tay/le^r mar-shay oh pu^e s*

Gardens, Parks and Zoos

Where is the botanic garden/zoo?	**Où est le jardin botanique/le zoo?**	*Oo ay le^r zhar-daⁿ bo-ta-neek/le^r zohoh*
How do I get to the park?	**Comment puis-je me rendre au parc?**	*Ko-mahⁿ pwee-zh me^r rahⁿ dr oh park*
Can we walk there?	**Est-ce qu'on peut y aller à pied?**	*Es-koⁿ pe^r ee a-lay a pyay*
Can we drive through the park?	**Est-ce qu'on peut circuler en voiture dans le parc?**	*Es-koⁿ pe^r seer-ku^e -lay ahⁿ vwa-tu^e r dahⁿ le^r park*
Are the gardens open to the public?	**Les jardins sont-ils ouverts au public?**	*Lay zhar-daⁿ soⁿ -teel oo-vair oh pu^e -bleek*
What time do the gardens close?	**À quelle heure les jardins ferment-ils?**	*A ke-lœr lay zhar-daⁿ fairm-teel*
Is there a plan of the gardens?	**Est-ce qu'il y a un plan des jardins?**	*Es-keel-ya eⁿ plahⁿ day zhar-daⁿ*
Who designed the gardens?	**Qui a dessiné les jardins?**	*Kee a day-see-nay lay zhar-daⁿ*
Where is the tropical plant house/the lake?	**Où se trouve le pavillon des plantes tropicales/le lac?**	*Oo se^r troov le^r pa-vee-yoⁿ day plahⁿ t tro-pee-kal/ le^r lak*

Historic Sites

We want to visit . . .; can we get there by car?	**Nous voudrions visiter . . .; est-il possible d'y aller en voiture?**	*Noo voo-dree-yon vee-zee-tay . . .; ay-teel poseebl dee a-lay ahn vwa-tue r*
Is it far to walk?	**Est-ce que c'est loin à pied?**	*Es-ker say lwan a pyay*
Is it an easy walk?	**Peut-on y aller à pied facilement?**	*Per -ton ee a-lay a pyay fa-see-ler -mahn*
Is it far to	**Est-ce que e'est loin,**	*Es-ker say lwan,*
the aqueduct?	**l'aqueduc?**	*lak-due k*
the castle?	**le château?**	*ler sha-toh*
the fort?	**le fort?**	*ler for*
the fortifications?	**les fortifications?**	*lay for-tee-fee-ka-syon*
the fountain?	**la fontaine?**	*la fon-ten*
the gate?	**la porte?**	*la port*
the walls?	**les murs/les remparts**	*la mue r/lay rahn -par*
When was it built?	**À quelle époque cela a-t-il été construit?**	*A kel ay-pok ser -la a-teel ay-tay kon -strwee*
Who built it?	**Qui l'a construit?**	*Kee la kon -strwee*

Museums and Galleries

When does the museum open/close?	À quelle heure ouvre/ferme le musée?	A ke-lœr oovr/fairm le[r] -mu[e] -zay
Is it open every day?	Est-il ouvert tous les jours?	Ay-teel oo-vair too lay zhoor
The gallery is closed on Mondays	*La galerie est fermée le lundi	La gal-ree ay fair-may le[r] le[n] -dee
Is there wheelchair access?	Y a-t-il un accès pour les fauteuils roulants?	Ee-ya-teel e[n] ak-say poor lay fo-tœ-y roo-lah[n]
How much does it cost?	Combien coûte l'entrée?	Ko[n] -bya[n] koot lah[n] -tray
Are there reductions	Y a-t-il des réductions	Ee-ya-teel day ray-du[e] k-syo[n]
for children?	**pour les enfants?**	poor lay zah[n] -fah[n]
for students?	**pour les étudiants?**	poor lay zay-tu[e] -dyah[n]
for seniors?	**pour les personnes âgées?**	poor lay pair-son za-zhay
Are admission fees lower on any special day?	Est-ce que le tarif d'entrée est réduit certains jours de la semaine?	Es-ke[r] le[r] ta-reef dah[n] -tray ay ray-dwee sair-ta[n] zhoor de[r] la se[r] -men
Admission free	*Entrée libre/ gratuite	Ah[n] -tray leebr/gra-tweet
Have you got a ticket?	*Avez-vous un billet/ ticket?	A-vay-voo e[n] bee-yay/ tee-kay*
Where do I buy a ticket?	Où puis-je acheter un billet?	Oo pwee-zh ash-tay e[n] bee-yay

Is there a family ticket?	Y a-t-il un tarif de famille?	*Ee-ya-teel e^n ta-reef de^r fa-mee-y*
Are there guided tours of the museum?	Y a-t-il des visites guidées du musée?	*Ee-ya-teel day vee-zeet ghee-day du^e mu^e -zay*
Does the guide speak English?	Est-ce que le guide parle anglais?	*Es-ke^r le^r gheed parl ah^n -gle*
Is there an audio guide in English?	Y a-t-il un guide audio en anglais?	*Ee-ya-teel e^n gheed o-dyo ah^n nah^n -gle*
We don't need a guide	Nous n'avons pas besoin de guide	*Noo na-vo^n pa be^r -zwa^n de^r gheed*
I would prefer to go round alone; is that all right?	Je préférerais faire la visite seul(e); est-ce possible?	*Zhe^r pray-fay-re^r -re fair la vee-zeet sœl; es po-seebl*
Where is the ... collection/exhibition?	Où se trouve la collection/ l'exposition ...?	*Oo se^r troov la ko-lek-syo^n/leks-po-zee-syo^n*
Please leave your bag in the cloakroom	*Veuillez déposer votre sac au vestiaire	*Vœ-yay day-po-zay votr sak oh vest-yair*
It's over there	*C'est là-bas	*Say la-ba*
Can I take photographs?	Est-ce que je peux prendre des photos?	*Es-ke^r zhe^r pe^r prah^n dr day fo-to*
Can I use a tripod?	Puis-je utiliser un tripode?	*Pwee-zh u^e -tee-lee-zay e^n tree-pod*
Photographs are not allowed	*Défense de prendre des photos/Les appareils de photo sont interdits	*Day-fah^n s de^r prah^n dr day fo-to/lay za-pa-re-y de^r fo-to so^n ta^n tair-dee*
I want to buy a catalogue	Je voudrais acheter un catalogue	*Zhe^r voo-dre ash-tay e^n katalog*

Places of Worship

Where is the	Où est	Oo ay
catholic church?	l'église catholique?	lay-gleez ka-to-leek
protestant church?	l'église protestante?	lay-gleez pro-tays-tah^{n}t
cathedral?	la cathédrale?	la ka-tay-dral
mosque?	la mosquée?	la mos-kay
shrine?	le sanctuaire?	le^r sah^n k-tu^e -air
synagogue?	la synagogue?	la see-na-gog
When is the mass/service?	À quelle heure est la messe/l'office?	A ke-lœr ay la mays/lo-fees
I'd like to look round the church	Je voudrais visiter l'église	Zhe^r voo-dre vee-zee-tay lay-gleez
When was the church built?	Quand l'église a-t-elle été construite?	Kah^n lay-gleez a-tel ay-tay ko^n -strweet

Tours

We want to take a coach tour round the sights	Nous voulons faire une visite touristique en autocar	Noo voo-lo^n fair u^e n vee-zeet too-rees-teek ah^n noh-toh-kar
Is there a sightseeing tour?	Y a-t-il un circuit touristique?	Ee-ya-teel e^n seer-kwee too-rees-teek
Is there a walking tour of the town?	Y a-t-il une visite guidée de la ville?	Ee-ya-teel u^e n vee-zeet ghee-day de^r la veel

Is there an excursion to . . . tomorrow?	Est-ce qu'il y a une excursion à . . . demain?	*Es-keel-ya u^e n ek-sku^e r-syo^n a . . . de^r -ma^n*
How long does the tour take?	Combien de temps dure la visite?	*Ko^n -bya^n de^r tah^n du^e r la vee-zeet*
When does it leave/ return?	À quelle heure ça commence/ça se termine?	*A ke-lœr sa ko-mah^n s/sa se^r tayr-meen*
Does the bus/coach stop at our hotel?	Est-ce que l'autobus/ le car s'arrête à notre hôtel?	*Es-ke^r loh-toh-bu^e s/le^r kar sa-ret a notr o-tel*
How much does the tour cost?	Combien coûte la visite?	*Ko^n -bya^n koot la vee-zeet*
Are all admission fees included?	Cela comprend-t-il tous les droits d'entrée?	*Se^r -la ko^n -prah^n -teel too lay drwa dah^n -tray*
Does it include lunch?	Est-ce que le déjeuner est compris?	*Es-ke^r le^r day-zhe^r -nay ay ko^n -pree*
Could we stop here to take photographs?	Peut-on s'arrêter ici pour prendre des photos?	*Pe^r -to^n sa-ray- tay eesee poor prah^n dr day fo-to*
buy souvenirs?	acheter des souvenirs?	*ash-tay day soo-ve^r -neer*
get a bottle of water?	acheter une bouteille d'eau?	*ash-tay u^e n boo-te-y doh*
use the toilets?	utiliser les toilettes?	*u^e -tee-lee-zay lay twa-let*
How long do we stay here?	Combien de temps allons-nous rester ici?	*Ko^n -bya^n de^r tah^n a-lo^n noo res-tay ee-see*

SPORTS AND LEISURE[1]

Where is the nearest tennis court/golf course?	Où est le court de tennis/le terrain de golf le plus proche?	Oo ay le' koor de' te-nees/le' te-ra'' de golf le' plu'' prosh
Is there a gym/a running track?	Y a-t-il une salle de gym/une piste d'athlétisme?	Ee-ya-teel u'' n sal de' zheem/u'' n peest da-tlay-teezm
What is the charge	Quel est le tarif	Kel ay le' ta-reef
game?	de la partie?	de' la par-tee
hour?	de l'heure?	de' lœr
day?	de la journée?	de' la zhoor-nay
Is it a club?	Est-ce un club?	Es e'' klœb
Do I need temporary membership?	Dois-je faire une demande d'adhésion temporaire?	Dwazh fair u'' n de'-mah'' d da-day-zyo'' tah'' -po-rair
Where can we go fishing?	Où peut-on aller pêcher?	Oo pe' -to'' a-lay pe-shay
Can I hire	Puis-je louer	Pwee-zh loo-ay
a racket?	une raquette?	u'' n ra-ket
clubs?	des clubs?	day klœb
fishing tackle?	du matériel de pêche?	du'' ma-tay-ryel de pesh

1. See also BY BIKE (p. 50).

Do I need a permit?	Est-ce que j'ai besoin d'un permis?	*Es-ke' zhay be' -zwaⁿ deⁿ pair-mee*
Where do I get a permit?	Où puis-je obtenir un permis?	*Oo pwee-zh ob-te' -neer eⁿ pair-mee*
Is there a skating rink?	Y a-t-il une patinoire?	*Ee-ya-teel uᵉ n pa-tee-nwar*
Can I hire skates?	Puis-je louer des patins à glace?	*Pwee-zh loo-ay day pa-taⁿ a glas*
I'd like to ride	J'aimerais faire du cheval	*Zhem-re fair duᵉ she' -val*
Is there a riding stable nearby?	Y a-t-il un centre d'équitation près d'ici?	*Ee-ya-teel eⁿ sahⁿ tr day-kee-ta-syoⁿ pre dee-see*
Do you give lessons?	Donnez-vous des leçons?	*Do-nay-voo day le' -soⁿ*
I am an inexperienced rider/a good rider	Je suis débutant(e)/je monte bien à cheval	*Zhe' swee day-buᵉ -tahⁿ(t)/zhe' moⁿ t byaⁿ a she' -val*

Winter Sports

Can I hire skis/ski boots?	Puis-je louer des skis/des chaussures de ski?	*Pwee-zh loo-ay day skee/day sho-suᵉ r de' skee*
Can I take lessons here?	Puis-je prendre des leçons ici?	*Pwee-zh prahⁿ dr day le' -soⁿ ee-see*
I've never skied before	Je n'ai jamais fait de ski	*Zhe' nay zha-me fe de' skee*

Are there ski runs for beginners/average skiers?	**Y a-t-il des pistes pour débutants/les skieurs moyens?**	*Ee-ya-teel day peest poor day-bu^e-tah^n/lay skee-œr mwa-ya^n*
I'd like to go cross-country skiing	**Je voudrais faire du ski de fond**	*Zhe^r voo-dre fair du^e skee de^r fo^n*
Where are the ski lifts?	**Où sont les remonte-pentes?**	*Oo so^n lay re-mo^n t pah^n t*
Can we go snowboarding?	**Peut-on faire du snowboard?**	*Pe^r -to^n fair du^e snoh-bord*
Can I buy a lift pass?	**Puis-je acheter un forfait pour les remontées mécaniques?**	*Pwee-zh ash-tay e^n for-fay poor lay re^r -mo^n tay may-ka-neek*

At the Beach

Which is the best beach?	**Quelle est la meilleure plage?**	*Kel ay la me-yœr plazh*
Is there a quiet beach near here?	**Y a-t-il une plage tranquille près d'ici?**	*Ee-ya-teel u^e n plazh trah^n -keel pre dee-see*
Is it far to walk?	**Est-ce loin à pied?**	*Es-lwan a pyay*
Is there a bus to the beach?	**Y a-t-il un autobus qui va à la plage?**	*Ee-ya-teel e^n oh-toh-bu^e s kee va a la plazh*
Is the beach sand or shingle?	**Est-ce une plage de sable ou de galets?**	*Es-u^e n plazh de^r sabl oo de^r ga-lay*
Is it safe for swimming?	**Est-ce qu'on peut se baigner sans danger?**	*Es-ko^n pe^r se^r ben-yay sah^n dah^n -zhay*
Is there a lifeguard?	**Y a-t-il un maître-nageur?**	*Ee-ya-teel e^n metr-na-zhœr*

Is it safe for small children?	La plage est-elle sûre pour les jeunes enfants?	*La plazh ay-tel su^e r poor lay zhœn zah^n -fah^n*
Bathing prohibited	*Baignade interdite	*Ben-yad a^n -tair-deet*
It's dangerous	*C'est dangereux	*Say dah^n -zhe^r -re^r*
What time is high/ low tide?	À quelle heure est la marée haute/basse?	*A ke-lœr ay la ma-ray ot/bas*
Is the tide rising/ falling?	Est-ce que la marée monte/descend?	*Es-ke^r la ma-ray mo^n t/ de-sah^n*
Does the sea get very rough?	La mer peut-elle être très mauvaise ici?	*La mair pe^r -tel etr tre mo-vez ee-see*
I want to hire a cabin for	Je voudrais louer une cabine pour	*Zhe^r voo-dre loo-ay u^e n ka-been poor*
the day	la journée	*la zhoor-nay*
the morning	la matinée	*la ma-tee-nay*
two hours	deux heures	*de^r zœr*
I want to hire a deckchair/sunshade	Je voudrais louer une chaise longue/ un parasol	*Zhe^r voo-dre loo-ay u^e n shez lo^n g/e^n pa-ra-sol*
Where can I buy	Où pourrais-je acheter	*Oo poo-rezh ash-tay*
a bucket and spade?	un seau et une pelle?	*e^n soh ay u^e n pel*
flippers?	des palmes?	*day palm*
a snorkel?	un tuba?	*e^n tu^e -ba*
ball	le ballon	*ba-lo^n*
beach bag	le sac de plage	*sak de^r plazh*

boat	**le bateau**	*ba-toh*
crab	**le crabe**	*krab*
first aid	**le poste de secours**	*post de^r se^r -koor*
jellyfish	**la méduse**	*may-du^e z*
lifebuoy	**la bouée de sauvetage**	*boo-ay de^r sov-tazh*
lifevest	**le gilet de sauvetage**	*zhee-lay de^r sov-tazh*
lighthouse	**le phare**	*far*
outboard motor	**le moteur hors-bord**	*mo-tœr or-bor*
rock	**le rocher**	*ro-shay*
sandbank	**le banc de sable**	*bahⁿ de^r sabl*
sandcastle	**le château de sable**	*sha-toh de^r sabl*
shell	**le coquillage**	*ko-kee-y-azh*
sunglasses	**les lunettes de soleil** f	*lu^r -net de^r so le y*
sunshade	**le parasol**	*pa-ra-sol*
wave	**la vague**	*vag*

Swimming

Is there an open air/ indoor swimming pool?	**Y a-t-il une piscine en plein air/ couverte?**	*Ee-ya-teel u^e n pee-seen ahⁿ plaⁿ nair/koo-vairt*
Is it heated?	**Est-elle chauffée?**	*Ay-tel shoh-fay*
Is the water cold?	**Est-ce que l'eau est froide?**	*Es-ke^r loh ay frwad*

It's warm	**Elle est chaude/bonne**	*El ay shod/bon*
Is it salt or fresh water?	**Est-ce de l'eau salée ou de l'eau douce?**	*Es de' loh sa-lay oo de' loh doos*
Can one swim in the lake/river?[1]	**Peut-on se baigner dans le lac/le fleuve/la rivière?**	*Pe' -toⁿ se' ben-yay dahⁿ le' lak/le' flœv/la reev-yair*
There's a strong current here	***Le courant est violent ici**	*Le' koo-rahⁿ ay vyo-lahⁿ ee-see*
Are you a strong swimmer?	***Êtes vous bon nageur (bonne nagause)?**	*Et-voo boⁿ na-zhœr (bon na-zhoez)*
Is it deep?	**Est-ce que c'est profond?**	*Es-ke' say pro-foⁿ*
You will be out of your depth	***Vous n'aurez pas pied**	*Voo no-ray pa pyay*
Are there showers?	**Y a-t-il des douches?**	*Ee-ya-teel day doosh*
No lifeguard on duty	***Baignade non surveillée**	*Ben-yad noⁿ sur-vay-y-lay*
armbands	**le bracelet de natation**	*bra-se' -lay de' na-ta-syoⁿ*
goggles	**les lunettes de plongée**	*lu^e -net de' ploⁿ -zhay*
rubber ring	**la bouée**	*boo-ay*
swimsuit	**le maillot de bain**	*ma-yo de' baⁿ*
towel	**la serviette**	*sair-vyet*
trunks	**le maillot de bain pour hommes**	*ma-yo de' baⁿ poor om*

1. There are two words for 'river' in French. **Fleuve** is used for rivers that flow into the sea and **rivière** for rivers that flow into **fleuves**.

Watersports

I'd like to try water-skiing	**Je voudrais faire du ski nautique**	*Zhe' voo-dre fair du^e skee no-teek*
I've never water-skied before	**Je n'ai jamais fait de ski nautique**	*Zhe' nay zha-me fe de' skee no-teek*
Can I hire a wetsuit?	**Est-ce que je peux louer une combinaison (isothermique)?**	*Es-ke' zhe' pe' loo-ay u^e n koⁿ -bee-nay-zoⁿ (ee-zo-tair-meek)*
Should I wear a life-jacket?	**Est-ce que je dois porter un gilet de sauvetage?**	*Es-ke' zhe' dwa por-tay e' zhee- lay de' sov-tazh*
Can I hire	**Est-ce que je peux louer**	*Es-ke' zhe' pe' loo-ay*
diving equipment?	**un équipement de plongée?**	*eⁿ ay-keep-mahⁿ de' ploⁿ -zhay*
a jet ski?	**un jet ski?**	*eⁿ zhet skee*
a motor boat?	**un canot à moteur?**	*eⁿ ka-no a mo-tœr*
a rowing boat?	**une barque/un bateau à rames?**	*u^e n bark/eⁿ ba-toh a ram*
sailing boat?	**un bateau à voile?**	*eⁿ ba-toh a vwal*
a surf board?	**une planche (de surf)?**	*u^e n plahⁿ sh (de' sœrf)*
waterskis?	**des skis nautiques?**	*day skee no-teek*
a windsurfer?	**une planche à voile?**	*u^e n plahⁿ sh a vwal*

Do you have a course on windsurfing for beginners?	Ya-t-il un cours de/ planche à voile pour débutants?	*Ee-ya-teel e^n koor de^r plah^{n}sh a vwal poor day-bu^e -tah^n*
Is there a map/chart of the river?	Y a-t-il une carte du fleuve/de la rivière?	*Ee-ya-teel u^e n kart du^e flœv/de^r la reev-yair*
Are there many locks to pass?	Y a-t-il beaucoup d'écluses à franchir?	*Ee-ya-teel boh-koo day-klu^e z a frah^n -sheer*
Can we get fuel here?	Peut-on acheter du carburant ici?	*Pe^r -to^n ash-tay du^e kar-bu^e -rah^n ee-see*
Where's the harbour?	Où est le port?	*Oo ay le^r por*
Can we go out in a fishing boat?	Peut-on aller faire une promenade en bateau de pêche?	*Pe^r -to^n a-lay fair u^e n prom-nad ah^n ba-toh de^r pesh*
What does it cost by the hour?	Combien coûte l'heure de location?	*Ko^n -bya^n koot lœr de^r lo-ka-syo^n*

Walking[1]

I'd like a map of the area showing walking trails	Je voudrais une carte des chemins de randonnées de la région	*Zhe^r voo-dre u^e n kart day she-ma^n de^r rah^n -do-nay de^r la ray-zhyo^n*
Can we walk?	Peut-on y aller à pied?	*Pe^r -to^n ee a-lay a pyay*
How far is the next village?	À quelle distance se trouve le prochain village?	*A kel dees-tah^n s se^r troov le^r pro-sha^n vee-lazh*

1. See also DIRECTIONS (p. 57).

How long is the walk to …?	Combien met-on à pied jusqu'à …?	*Ko^n -bya^n met-o^n a pyay zhu^e s-ka*
It's an hour's walk to …	*Il faut une heure jusqu'à …	*Eel fo u^e n œr zhu^e s-ka*
Which way is	C'est par où	*Say par oo*
the nature reserve?	la réserve naturelle?	*la ray-zairv na-tu^e -rel*
the lake?	le lac?	*le' lak*
the waterfall?	la cascade?	*la kas-kad*
Is there a scenic walk to …	Y a-t-il une randonnée panoramique pour …?	*Ee-ya-teel u^e n rah^n -do-nay pa-no-ra-meek poor*
Is it steep/far/ difficult?	Est-ce en pente raide/loin/difficile?	*Es ah^n pah^n t rayd/ lwa^n/dee-fee-seel*
Is there a footpath to …?	Y a-t-il un sentier qui mène à …?	*Ee-ya-teel e^n sah^n -tyay kee men a*
Is it possible to go across country?	Est-il possible d'y aller à travers champs?	*Ay-teel po-seebl dee a-lay a tra-vair shah^n*
Is there a shortcut?	Y a-t-il un raccourci?	*Ee-ya-teel e^n ra-koor-see*
Is this a public footpath?	Est-ce que ce sentier est public?	*Es-ke' se' sah^n -tyay e pu^e -bleek*
Is there a bridge across the stream?	Y a-t-il un pont qui traverse le cours d'eau?	*Ee-ya-teel e^n po^n kee tra-vairs le' koor doh*
Can you give me a lift to …?	Pourriez-vous m'emmener à …?	*Poor-yay-voo mah^n m-nay a*

Spectator Sports and Indoor Games

We want to go to a football match/the tennis tournament	**Nous voulons aller voir un match de football/le tournoi de tennis**	*Noo voo-lon a-lay vwar en matsh der foot-bol/ler toor-nwa der te-nees*
Can you get us tickets?	**Pouvez-vous nous procurer des billets?**	*Poo-vay-voo noo pro-kue-ray day bee-yay*
Are there seats in the grandstand?	**Y a-t-il des places aux tribunes?**	*Ee-ya-teel day plas oh tree-bue n*
How much are the cheapest seats?	**Combien coûtent les places les moins chères?**	*Kon-byan koot lay plas lay mwan shair*
Are they in the sun or the shade?	**Est-ce que ce sont des places au soleil ou à l'ombre?**	*Es-ker ser son day plas oh so-le-y oo a lon br*
Who is playing?	**Qui est-ce qui joue?**	*Kee es-kee zhoo*
When does it start?	**À quelle heure est-ce que cela commence?**	*A ke-lœr es-ker ser-la ko-mahn s*
Who is winning?	**Qui gagne?**	*Kee gan-y*
What is the score?	**Quel est le score** (*rugby and soccer*)/ **où en est la partie** (*tennis*)?	*Kel ay ler skor/oo ahn nay la par-tee*
Where is the race course?	**Où est le champ de courses/ l'hippodrome?**	*Oo ay ler shahn der koors/ lee-po-drom*

Which is the favourite?	**Quel est le favori?**	*Kel-ay le' fa-vo-ree*
Who is the jockey?	**Qui est le jockey?**	*Kee ay le' zho-kay*
Where can I place a bet?[1]	**Où puis-je placer un pari?**	*Oo pwee-zh pla-say e'' pa-ree*
Do you play cards?	**Jouez-vous aux cartes?**	*Zhoo-ay-voo oh kart*
Would you like a game of chess?	**Cela vous dit de faire une partie d'échecs?**	*Se' -la voo dee de' fair u'' n par-tee day-shek*
I'd like to play a game of checkers (draughts)	**J'aimerais faire une partie de dames**	*Zhem-re fair u'' n par-tee de' dam*

1. The equivalent of the tote in France is the **PMU (Pari mutuel urbain)**. Bets can be placed at the offices at the race course or at any café or newsagent with the sign PMU.

TRAVELLING WITH CHILDREN

Key Phrases

Are children allowed?	**Les enfants sont-ils admis?**	*Lay zah[n] -fah[n] so[n] -teel ad-mee*
Is there a lower price for children?	**Y a-t-il une réduction pour les enfants?**	*Ee-ya-teel u[e] n ray-du[e] k-syo[n] poor lay zah[n] -fah[n]*
Are there any organized activities for children?	**Y a-t-il des activités organisées pour les enfants?**	*Ee-ya-teel day zak-tee-vee-tay or-ga-nee-zay poor lay zah[n] -fah[n]*
Can you put a child's bed/cot in our room?	**Pouvez-vous installer un petit lit dans notre chambre?**	*Poo-vay-voo a[n] s-ta-lay e[n] pe[r] -tee lee dah[n] notr sha[n] br*
Where may I feed/ change my baby?	**Où pourrais-je faire manger/changer mon bébé?**	*Oo poo-rezh fair mah[n] -zhay/shah[n] -zhay mo[n] bay-bay*
My son/daughter is missing	**J'ai perdu mon fils/ ma fille**	*Zhay pair-du[e] mo[n] fees/ ma fee-y*

Out and About[1]

Is there	Y a-t-il	Ee-ya-teel
an amusement park	un parc d'attractions	e^n park da-trak-syo^n
a park	un parc	e^n park
a zoo	un zoo	e^n zo-oh
a toy shop?	un magasin de jouets?	e^n ma-ga-za^n de^r zhoo-ay
a playground?	un terrain de jeux?	e^n te-ra^n de^r zhe^r
a games room?	une salle de jeux?	u^e n sal de^r zhe^r
a paddling pool?	une pataugeoire?	u^e n pa-to-zhwar
a children's swimming pool?	une piscine pour enfants?	u^e n pee-seen poor ah^n-fah^n
Where is the aquarium?	Où se trouve l'aquarium?	Oo se^r troov la-kwa-ryom
Is the beach safe for children?	Est-ce que la plage est sans danger pour les enfants?	Es ke^r la plazh ay sah^n dah^n-zhay poor lay zah^n-fah^n
Can we hire a canoe/ paddle boat?	Pouvons-nous louer un canoë/pédalo?	Poo-vo^n noo loo-ay e^n ka-no-ay/pay-da-lo
Are there snorkelling/ skiing/riding lessons for children?	Y a-t-il des cours de plongée libre/ de ski/d'équitation pour les enfants?	Ee-ya-teel day koor de^r plo^n-zhay leebr/de^r skee/ day-kee-ta-syo^n poor lay zah^n-fah^n
I'd like	Je voudrais	Zhe^r voo-dre

1. See also AT THE BEACH (p. 227).

a doll	une poupée	*u^e n poo-pay*
some playing cards	un jeu de cartes	*e^n zhe^r de^r kart*
rollerblades	des patins en ligne	*day pa-ta^n e^n leegn*
He has lost his toy	Il a perdu son jouet	*Eel a pair-du^e so^n zhoo-ay*
I'm sorry if they have bothered you	Excusez-moi s'ils vous ont ennuyé(e)	*Ek-sku^e -zay-mwa seel voo zo^n tah^n -nwee-yay*

Everyday Needs

Can you put a child's bed/cot in our room?	Pouvez-vous installer un petit lit dans notre chambre?	*Poo-vay-voo a^n s-ta-lay e^n pe^r -tee lee dah^n notr sha^n br*
Can you give us adjoining rooms?	Pouvez-vous nous donner des chambres l'une à côté de l'autre?	*Poo-vay-voo noo do-nay day shah^n br lu^e n a ko-tay de^r lotr*
Does the hotel have a babysitting service?	Est-ce que l'hôtel a un service de garde d'enfants?	*Es-ke^r lo-tel a e^n sair-vees de^r gard dah^n -fah^n*
Can you find me a babysitter?	Pourriez-vous me trouver un baby sitter?	*Poor-yay-voo me^r troo-vay e^n ba-bee see-tair*
We shall be out for a couple of hours	Nous sortons pour deux heures environs	*Noo sor-to^n poor de^r zœr ah^n -vee-ro^n*
We shall be back at . . .	Nous serons de retour à . . .	*Noo se^r -ro^n de^r re^r -toor a*

You can reach me at ...	**Vous pouvez me joindre au ...**	*Voo poo-vay me zhwaⁿ -dre' o*
This is my mobile (cell) number	**Voici mon numéro de portable**	*Vwa-see moⁿ nu^e -may-ro de' por-tabl*
Is there a children's menu?	**Y a-t-il un menu pour les enfants?**	*Ee-ya-teel eⁿ me^e -nu^e poor lay zahⁿ -fahⁿ*
Do you have half portions for children?	**Servez-vous des demi-portions pour les enfants?**	*Sair-vay-voo day de' -mee por-syoⁿ poor lay zahⁿ -fahⁿ*
Have you got a high chair?	**Avez-vous une chaise haute?**	*A-vay-voo u^e n shez oht*
Where can I feed/ change my baby?	**Où pourrais-je faire manger/ changer mon bébé?**	*Oo poo-rezh fair mahⁿ -zhay/shahⁿ -zhay moⁿ bay-bay*
Can you heat this bottle for me?	**Pourriez-vous me réchauffer ce biberon?**	*Poor-yay-voo me' ray-sho-fay se' bee-broⁿ*
I want	**Je voudrais**	*Zhe' voo-dre*
some baby food	**des produits alimentaires pour bébé**	*day pro-dwee a-lee-mahⁿ -tair poor bay-bay*
baby wipes	**des lingettes pour bébé**	*day laⁿ -zhet poor bay-bay*
a bib	**un bavoir**	*eⁿ ba-vwar*
a feeding bottle	**un biberon**	*eⁿ bee-broⁿ*
(disposable) nappies	**des couches (à jeter)**	*day koosh (a zhe' -tay)*

Health and Emergencies[1]

My daughter suffers from travel sickness	**Ma fille est malade en voyage**	*Ma fee-y ay ma-lad ah^n vwa-yazh*
She has hurt herself	**Elle s'est fait mal**	*El say fay mal*
My son is ill	**Mon fils est malade**	*Mo^n fees ay ma-lad*
He is allergic to . . .	**Il est allergique à/ au . . .**	*Eel ay ta-layr-zheek a/o*
My son/daughter is missing	**J'ai perdu mon fils/ ma fille**	*Zhay pair-du^e mo^n fees/ ma fee-y*
He/she is . . . years old	**Il/elle a . . . ans**	*Eel/el a . . . ah^n*
He/she is wearing . . .	**Il/elle porte . . .**	*Eel/el port*

1. See also DOCTOR (p. 156).

WORK[1]

I'm here on business	**Je suis ici pour affaires**	*Zhe' swee zee-see poor a-fair*
Where is the conference centre?	**Où se trouve le centre de conférence?**	*Oo se' troov le sah^n tr de' ko^n -fay-rah^n s*
I'm here for the trade fair	**Je suis ici pour le salon**	*Zhe' swee zee-see poor le' sa-lo^n*
I've come to a conference/a seminar	**Je suis venu(e) pour une conférence/un séminaire**	*Zhe' swee ve' -nu^e poor u^e n ko^n -fay-rah^n s e^n say-mee-nair*
This is my colleague	**Voici mon/ma collègue**	*Vwa-see mo^n/ma ko-laygh*
I have an appointment with . . .	**J'ai un rendez-vous avec . . .**	*Zhay e^n rah^n -day-voo a-vek*
Here is my card	**Voici ma carte de visite**	*Vwa-see ma kart de' vee-zeet*
Can you provide us with an interpreter?	**Pouvez-vous nous fournir un interprète?**	*Poo-vay-voo noo foor-neer e^n a^n -tair-pret*

1. See also TELEPHONE, MOBILES AND SMS (p. 95).

TIME AND DATES

Time[1]

What time is it?	Quelle heure est-il?	Ke-lœr ay-teel
It's	Il est	Eel-ay
one o'clock	une heure	u^r n œr
two o'clock	deux heures	de^r zœr
five past eight	huit heures cinq	weet œr sa^n k
quarter past five	cinq heures et quart	sa^n k œr ay kar
twenty-five past eight	huit heures vingt-cinq	weet œr va^n -sa^n k
half past four	quatre heures et demie	katr-œr ay de^r -mee
twenty-five to seven	sept heures moins vingt-cinq	set-œr mwa^n va^n -sa^n k
quarter to ten	dix heures moins le quart	dee-zœr mwa^n le^r kar
7 a.m./7 p.m.	sept heures/ dix-neuf heures, sept heures du matin/du soir	set-œr/dee-zne^r -vœr; set-oer du^e ma-ta^n/du^e swar
second	la seconde	se^r -go^n d
minute	la minute	mee-nu^e t

1. France uses the 24-hour clock in formal contexts.

hour	l'heure	œr
It's early/late	Il est tôt/tard	Eel ay toh/tar
My watch	Ma montre	Ma mo^n tr
is slow	retarde	re^r -tard
is fast	avance	a-vah^n s
has stopped	s'est arrêtée	say-ta-re-tay
Sorry I am late	(Je suis) désolé d'être en retard	(Zhe^r swee) day-zo-lay detr ah^n re^r -tar

Days

Monday	lundi	le^n -dee
Tuesday	mardi	mar-dee
Wednesday	mercredi	mair-kre^r -dee
Thursday	jeudi	zhe^r -dee
Friday	vendredi	vah^n -dre^r -dee
Saturday	samedi	sam-dee
Sunday	dimanche	dee-mah^n sh

Months

January	janvier	zhah^n -vyay
February	février	fayv-ryay
March	mars	mars

April	**avril**	*a-vreel*
May	**mai**	*me*
June	**juin**	*zhwaⁿ*
July	**juillet**	*zhwee-ye*
August	**août**	*oot*
September	**septembre**	*sep-tahⁿ br*
October	**octobre**	*ok-tobr*
November	**novembre**	*no-vahⁿ br*
December	**décembre**	*day-sahⁿ br*

Seasons

Spring	**le printemps**	*praⁿ tahⁿ*
Summer	**l'été** *m*	*ay-tay*
Autumn	**l'automne** *m* or *f*	*oh-ton*
Winter	**l'hiver** *m*	*ee-vair*

Periods of Time

morning	**le matin/la matinée**	*ma-taⁿ/ma-tee-nay*
this morning	**ce matin**	*se' ma-taⁿ*
in the morning	**dans la matinée**	*dahⁿ la ma-tee-nay*
midday, noon	**midi**	*mee-dee*
afternoon	**l'après-midi** *m* or *f*	*a-pre-mee-dee*

yesterday afternoon	**hier après midi**	*yair a-pre-mee-dee*
evening	**le soir/la soirée**	*swar/swa-ray*
tomorrow evening	**demain soir**	*de^r -ma^n swar*
midnight	**minuit**	*meen-wee*
night	**la nuit**	*nwee*
at night	**de nuit**	*de^r nwee*
by day	**de jour**	*de^r zhoor*
today	**aujourd'hui**	*oh-zhoor-dwee*
yesterday	**hier**	*yair*
day before yesterday	**avant-hier**	*avah^n -tyair*
four days ago	**il y a quatre jours**	*eel-ya katr zhoor*
tomorrow	**demain**	*de^r -ma^n*
day after tomorrow	**après-demain**	*a-pre de^r -ma^n*
in ten days' time	**dans dix jours**	*dah^n dee zhoor*
on Tuesday	**mardi**	*mar-dee*
on Sundays	**les dimanches**	*lay dee-mah^n sh*
week	**la semaine**	*la se^r -men*
weekend	**le week-end**	*le^r wee-kend*
on weekdays	**en semaine**	*e^n se^r -men*
every week	**chaque semaine**	*shak se^r -men*
once a week	**une fois par semaine**	*u^e n fwa par se^r -men*
a fortnight	**une quinzaine**	*u^e n ka^n -zen*
month	**le mois**	*le^r mwa*
in January	**en janvier**	*e^n zhah^n -vyay*

since March	**depuis mars**	*de^r -pwee mars*
this year	**cette année**	*set a-nay*
last year	**l'année dernière**	*la-nay dair-nyair*
next year	**l'année prochaine**	*la-nay pro-shen*
in spring	**au printemps**	*oh pra^n -tah^n*
in summer/autumn/ winter	**en été/automne/ hiver**	*ah^n ay-tay/oh-ton/ee-vair*
during the summer	**pendant l'été**	*pah^n -dah^n lay-tay*
sunrise	**le lever du soleil**	*le^r -vay du^e so-le-y*
at sunrise	**au lever du soleil**	*oh le^r -vay du^e so-le-y*
dawn	**l'aube/l'aurore** *f*	*ohb/o-ror*
at dawn	**au point du jour**	*oh pwa^n du^e zhoor*
sunset	**le coucher du soleil**	*koo-shay du^e so-le-y*
dusk	**le crépuscule**	*kray-pu^e s-ku^e l*

Dates[1]

What's the date?	**Quelle est la date?**	*Kel ay la dat*
It's 9 December	**Nous sommes le neuf décembre**	*Noo som le^r nœf day-sah^n br*
We're leaving on 5 January	**Nous partons le cinq janvier**	*Noo par-to^n le^r sa^n k zhah^n -vyay*
We got here on 27 July	**Nous sommes arrivés le vingt-sept juillet**	*Noo som-za-ree-vay le^r va^n -tset zhwee-ye*

1. In French, cardinal numbers are used for dates except for the first, for which **premier** is used.

Public Holidays

1 January	**Le jour de l'An**	*New Year's Day*
	Le vendredi saint	*Good Friday (Switzerland only)*
	Le lundi de Pâques	*Easter Monday*
1 May	**La fête du Travail**	*Labour Day*
8 May	**Le 8 mai 1945**	*Victory in Europe Day (France only)*
	L'Ascension	*Ascension Day (sixth Thursday after Easter)*
	Le lundi de Pentecôte	*Whit Monday*
14 July	**La fête nationale**	*Bastille Day (France only)*
21 July	**La fête nationale**	*National holiday (Belgium only)*
1 August	**La fête nationale**	*National holiday (Switzerland only)*
15 August	**L'Assomption**	*The Assumption of the Virgin*
1 November	**La Toussaint**	*All Saints*
11 November	**Anniversaire de l'Armistice**	*Armistice Day*
25 December	**Le jour de Noël**	*Christmas Day*
26 December	**Saint-Étienne**	*Boxing Day (Switzerland only with the exception of few cantons)*

Switzerland has no Armistice Day; Labour Day is celebrated only in few cantons; All Saints day is celebrated only in cantons with mainly catholic citizens.

WEATHER

What is the weather forecast?	**Que prévoit la météo?**	*Ke^r pray-vwa la may-tay-oh*
What is the temperature?	**Combien de degrés fait-il aujourd'hui?**	*Ko^n -bya^n de^r de^r -gray fe-teel oh-zhoor-dwee*
Is it usually as hot as this?	**Est-ce qu'il fait aussi chaud que ça d'habitude?**	*Es-keel fe oh-see shoh ksa da-bee-tu^e d*
It's going to be hot/cold today	**Il va faire chaud/froid aujourd'hui**	*Eel va fair shoh/frwa oh-zhoor-dwee*
It's windy	**Il y a du vent**	*Eel-ya du^e vah^n*
It's misty/foggy	**Il y a de la brume/du brouillard**	*Eel-ya de^r la bru^e m/du^e broo-y-ar*
The mist will clear later	**La brume se dissipera plus tard**	*La bru^e m se^r dee-see-pe^r -ra plu^e tar*
Will it be fine tomorrow?	**Est-ce qu'il va faire beau demain?**	*Es-keel va fair boh de^r -ma^n*
What lovely/awful weather	**Quel beau/sale temps**	*Kel boh/sal tah^n*
Do you think it will rain/snow?	**Vous croyez qu'il va pleuvoir/neiger?**	*Voo krwa-yay keel va plœ-vwar/ne-zhay*
clear	**limpide**	*la^n -peed*
cloudy	**nuageux**	*nu^e -a-zhe^r*

frost	**la gelée**	*zheʳ -lay*
hail	**la grêle**	*grayl*
humid	**lourd**	*loor*
ice	**la glace**	*glas*
storm	**la tempête/l'orage**	*tahⁿ -pet/o-razh*

OPPOSITES

before/after	**avant/après**	*a-vah*[n] */a-pre*
early/late	**tôt/tard**	*toh/tar*
early (*ahead of schedule*)	**en avance**	*ah*[n] *na-vah*[n] *s*
late (*behind schedule*)	**en retard**	*ah*[n] *re*[r] *tar*
first/last	**premier/dernier**	*pre*[r] *m-yay/dair-nyay*
now/later/then	**maintenant/ plus tard/alors**	*ma*[n] *te*[r] *nah*[n] */plu*[e] *tar/ a-lor*
far/near	**loin/près**	*lwa*[n] */pre*
here/there	**ici/là**	*ee-see/la*
in/out	**dans/hors de**	*dah*[n] */or-de*[r]
inside/outside	**à l'intérieur, dedans/à l'extérieur, dehors**	*a la*[n] *-tay-ryœr, de*[r] *-dah*[n] */a lek-stay-ryœr, de*[r] *-or*
under/over	**au-dessous/ au-dessus**	*oh-de*[r] *-soo/oh-de*[r] *-su*[e]
big, large/small	**grand/petit**	*grah*[n] */pe*[r] *-tee*
deep/shallow	**profond/ peu profond**	*pro-fo*[n] */pe*[r] *pro-fo*[n]
empty/full	**vide/plein**	*veed/pla*[n]
fat/lean	**gras/maigre**	*gra/megr*
heavy/light	**lourd/léger**	*loor/lay-zhay*

high/low	**haut/bas**	*oh/ba*
long, tall/short	**grand/petit**	*grah^n/pe^r -tee*
narrow/wide	**étroit/large**	*ay-trwa/larzh*
thick/thin	**épais/mince**	*ay-pe/ma^n s*
least/most	**le moins/le plus**	*le^r mwa^n/le^r plu^e*
many/few	**beaucoup/peu**	*boh-koo/pe^r*
more/less	**plus/moins**	*plu^e/mwa^n*
much/little	**beaucoup/peu**	*boh-koo/pe^r*
beautiful/ugly	**beau/laid**	*boh/le*
better/worse	**meilleur/pire**	*me-yœr/peer*
cheap/expensive	**bon marché/cher**	*bo^n mar-shay/shair*
clean/dirty	**propre/sale**	*propr/sal*
cold/hot, warm	**froid/chaud**	*frwa/shoh*
easy/difficult	**facile/difficile**	*fa-seel/dee-fee-seel*
fresh/stale	**frais/pas frais**	*fre/pa fre*
good/bad	**bon/mauvais**	*bo^n/moh-ve*
new, young/old	**nouveau, jeune/ vieux**	*noo-voh, zhœn/vye^r*
nice/nasty	(*person*) **gentil/ méchant**, (*food, smell*) **bon/mauvais**	*zhah^n -tee/may-shah^n, bo^n/mo-ve*
right/wrong	**juste/faux**	*zhu^e st/foh*
right/left	**droite/gauche**	*drwa-t/gosh*
open/closed, shut	**ouvert/fermé**	*oo-vair/fair-may*

vacant/occupied	**libre/occupé**	*leebr/o-ku^e -pay*
quick/slow	**rapide/lent**	*ra-peed/lahⁿ*
quiet/noisy	**calme/bruyant**	*kalm/brwee-yahⁿ*
sharp/blunt	**pointu,** (*of blade*) **aiguisé/émoussé**	*pwaⁿ tu^e, e-gee-zay/ ay-moo-say*

NUMBERS

Cardinal

0	zéro	*zay-roh*
1	un	*e^n*
2	deux	*de^r*
3	trois	*trwa*
4	quatre	*katr*
5	cinq	*sa^n k*
6	six	*sees*
7	sept	*set*
8	huit	*weet*
9	neuf	*nœf*
10	dix	*dees*
11	onze	*o^n z*
12	douze	*dooz*
13	treize	*trez*
14	quatorze	*katorz*
15	quinze	*ka^n z*
16	seize	*sez*
17	dix-sept	*dees-set*

18	dix-huit	*deez-weet*
19	dix-neuf	*deez-nœf*
20	vingt	*va^n*
21	vingt et un	*va^n t-ay-e^n*
22	vingt-deux	*va^n t-de^r*
30	trente	*trah^n t*
31	trente et un	*trah^n t-ay-e^n*
32	trente-deux	*trah^n t-de^r*
40	quarante	*ka-rah^n t*
41	quarante et un	*ka-rah^n t-ay-e^n*
42	quarante-deux	*ka-rah^n t-de^r*
50	cinquante	*sa^n -kah^n t*
51	cinquante et un	*sa^n -kah^n t-ay-e^n*
52	cinquante-deux	*sa^n -kah^n t-de^r*
60	soixante	*swa-sah^n t*
61	soixante et un	*swa-sah^n t-ay-e^n*
62	soixante-deux	*swa-sah^n t-de^r*
70	soixante-dix	*swa-sah^n t-dees*
71	soixante et onze	*swa-sah^n t-ay-o^n z*
72	soixante-douze	*swa-sah^n t-dooz*
80	quatre-vingts	*katr-va^n*
81	quatre-vingt-un	*katr-va^n-e^n*
82	quatre-vingt-deux	*katr-va^n -de^r*

90	quatre-vingt-dix	*katr-va^n-dees*
91	quatre-vingt-onze	*katr-va^n-o^{n}z*
92	quatre-vingt-douze	*katr-va^n-dooz*
100	cent	*sah^n*
101	cent un	*sah^n e^n*
200	deux cents	*de' sah^n*
1000	mille	*meel*
2000	deux mille	*de' meel*
1,000,000	un million	*e^{n}mee-lyo^n*

Ordinal

1st	premier/première	*pre'-myay/pre'-myair*
2nd	deuxième/second	*de'-zyem/sego^n*
3rd	troisième	*trwa-zyem*
4th	quatrième	*ka-tryern*
5th	cinquième	*sa"-kyem*
6th	sixième	*see-zyem*
7th	septième	*se-tyem*
8th	huitième	*wee-tyem*
9th	neuvième	*ne'-vyem*
10th	dixième	*dee-zyem*
11th	onzième	*o^n-zyem*
12th	douzième	*doo-zyem*

13th	**treizième**	*tre-zyem*
14th	**quatorzième**	*ka-tor-zyem*
15th	**quinzième**	*ka^n-zyem*
16th	**seizième**	*sez-yem*
17th	**dix-septième**	*dees-se-tyem*
18th	**dix-huitième**	*dees-wee-tyem*
19th	**dix-neuvième**	*dees-ne^r-vyem*
20th	**vingtième**	*va^n-tyem*
21st	**vingt et unième**	*va^n-tay-u^e-nee-em*
30th	**trentième**	*trah^n-tyem*
40th	**quarantième**	*ka-ran-tyem*
50th	**cinquantième**	*sa^n-kah^n-tyem*
60th	**soixantième**	*swa-sah^n-tyem*
70th	**soixante-dixième**	*swa-sah^n t-dee-zyem*
80th	**quatre-vingtième**	*katr-va^n-tyem*
90th	**quatre-vingt-dixième**	*katr-va^n-dee-zyem*
100th	**centième**	*sah^n-tyem*
half	**demi**	*de^r-mee*
quarter	**quart**	*kar*
three quarters	**trois quarts**	*trwa kar*
a third	**un tiers**	*tyair*
two thirds	**deux tiers**	*de^r tyair*

In Belgium and Switzerland **septante, octante, nonante** are used for 70, 80, 90, with the intervening numbers corresponding to the pattern above.

WEIGHTS AND MEASURES

Distance

kilometres – miles

km	miles or km	miles	km	miles or km	miles
1.6	1	0.6	14.5	9	5.6
3.2	2	1.2	16.1	10	6.2
4.8	3	1.9	32.2	20	12.4
6.4	4	2.5	40.2	25	15.3
8	5	3.1	80.5	50	31.1
9.7	6	3.7	160.9	100	62.1
11.3	7	4.4	804.7	500	310.7
12.9	8	5			

A rough way to convert from miles to km: divide by 5 and multiply by 8; from km to miles: divide by 8 and multiply by 5.

Length and Height

centimetres – inches

cm	inch or cm	inch		cm	inch or cm	inch
2.5	1	0.4		17.8	7	2.8
5.1	2	0.8		20.3	8	3.2
7.6	3	1.2		22.9	9	3.5
10.2	4	1.6		25.4	10	3.9
12.7	5	2		50.8	20	7.9
15.2	6	2.4		127	50	19.7

A rough way to convert from inches to cm: divide by 2 and multiply by 5; from cm to inches: divide by 5 and multiply by 2.

metres – feet

m	ft or m	ft		m	ft or m	ft
0.3	1	3.3		2.4	8	26.2
0.6	2	6.6		2.7	9	29.5
0.9	3	9.8		3	10	32.8
1.2	4	13.1		6.1	20	65.6
1.5	5	16.4		15.2	50	164
1.8	6	19.7		30.5	100	328.1
2.1	7	23				

A rough way to convert from ft to m: divide by 10 and multiply by 3; from m to ft: divide by 3 and multiply by 10.

metres – yards

m	yds or m	yds	m	yds or m	yds
0.9	1	1.1	7.3	8	8.7
1.8	2	2.2	8.2	9	9.8
2.7	3	3.3	9.1	10	10.9
3.7	4	4.4	18.3	20	21.9
4.6	5	5.5	45.7	50	54.7
5.5	6	6.6	91.4	100	109.4
6.4	7	7.7	457.2	500	546.8

A rough way to convert from yds to m: subtract 10 per cent from the number of yds; from m to yds: add 10 per cent to the number of metres.

Liquid Measures

litres – gallons

litres	galls or litres	galls	litres	galls or litres	galls
4.6	1	0.2	36.4	8	1.8
9.1	2	0.4	40.9	9	2
13.6	3	0.7	45.5	10	2.2
18.2	4	0.9	90.9	20	4.4
22.7	5	1.1	136.4	30	6.6
27.3	6	1.3	181.8	40	8.8
31.8	7	1.5	227.3	50	41

1 pint – 0.6 litre   litre – 1.8 pints

A rough way to convert from galls to litres: divide by 2 and multiply by 9; from litres to galls: divide by 9 and multiply by 2.

Temperature

centigrade – Fahrenheit

centigrade °C	Fahrenheit °F	centigrade °C	Fahrenheit °F
0	32	20	68
5	41	30	86
10	50	40	104

To convert °F to °C: deduct 32, divide by 9, multiply by 5; to convert °C to °F: divide by 5, multiply by 9 and add 32.

Weight

kilogrammes – pounds

kg	lb or kg	lb	kg	lb or kg	lb
0.5	1	2.2	3.2	7	15.4
0.9	2	4.4	3.6	8	17.6
1.4	3	6.6	4.1	9	19.8
1.8	4	8.8	4.5	10	22
2.3	5	11	9.1	20	44.1
2.7	6	13.2	22.7	50	110.2

To convert lb to kg: divide by 11 and multiply by 5; to convert kg to lb: divide by 5 and multiply by 11.

grammes – ounces

grammes	oz
100	3.5
250	8.8
500	17.6
1000 (1 kg)	35

oz	grammes
2	56.7
4	113.4
8	226.8
16 (1 lb)	453.6

BASIC GRAMMAR

Gender of nouns

In French nouns are either masculine or feminine.

m	*f*
le livre (the book)	**la table** (the table)
le train (the train)	**la route** (the road)

Plural of nouns

To form the plural most nouns add **-s.** Those ending in **-eau,** **-eu** and some ending in **-ou** take **-x;** most ending in **-al** change to **-aux.**

sing	*pl*
le coiffeur (the hairdresser)	**les coiffeurs** (the hairdressers)
le bateau (the boat)	**les bateaux** (the boats)
l'animal (the animal)	**les animaux** (the animals)

The definite article (the)

	m	*f*
sing	**le père** (the father)	**la mère** (the mother)
pl	**les pères** (the fathers)	**les mères** (the mothers)

Before a singular noun beginning with a vowel or a silent 'h'
le (*m*), **la** (*f*) become **l'**

l'hôtel (the hotel)	**l'auto** (the car)
l'homme (the man)	**l'adresse** (the address)

The indefinite article (a, an)

	m	*f*
sing	**un hôtel** (a hotel)	**une auto** (a car)

The partitive article (some, any)

	m	*f*
sing	**du** (=de + le) **beurre** (some butter)	**de la confiture** (some jam)
pl	**des** (=de + les) **biscuits** (some biscuits)	**des pommes** (some apples)

Adjectives

Adjectives agree with the nouns they describe in gender
and number. To form the feminine most adjectives
add **-e** to the masculine (unless the masculine form already
ends with an 'e' – e.g. **immense**). To form the plural most
adjectives add **-s**.

	m	f
sing	**un camion vert** (a green lorry)	**une auto verte** (a green car)
pl	**des camions verts** (green lorries)	**des autos vertes** (green cars)

Adjectives are usually placed after the noun, but there are
some exceptions.

Possessive adjectives

These adjectives agree in gender and number with the object
possessed.

	m	f	pl
my	mon passeport	ma valise	mes enfants
your *familiar*	ton	ta	tes
his, her, its	son passeport	sa valise	ses enfants
our	notre passeport	notre valise	nos enfants
your *formal*	votre passeport	votre valise	vos enfants
their	leur passeport	leur valise	leurs enfants

Demonstrative adjectives (this, these, that, those)

	m	f
sing	ce monsieur (this/that gentleman)	cette dame (this/that lady)
pl	ces hommes (these/those men)	ces femmes (these/those women)

Before a masculine singular noun beginning with a vowel or a silent **'h'**, **cet** is used instead of **ce**.

e.g.	cet homme (this/that man)	cet arbre (this/that tree)

Relative pronouns (who, whom, which, that)

subject	qui	La rue qui mène à la gare (The street that leads to the station)
object	que	L'hôtelier que je connais (The hotel keeper whom I know)

Personal pronouns

subject		*direct object*		*indirect object of a verb*		*preceded by a preposition*
I	je	me	me	to me	me	moi
you *familiar*	tu	you	te	to you	te	toi

subject		*direct object*		*indirect object of a verb*		*preceded by a preposition*
he, it	il	him, it	le	to him, it	lui	lui
she, it	elle	her, it	la	to her, it	lui	elle
we	nous	us	nous	to us	nous	nous
you *formal*	vous	you	vous	to you	vous	vous
they	ils *m*	them	les *m, f*	to them	leur	eux *m*
they	elles *f*			to them	leur	elles *f*

Object pronouns are usually placed between the subject and the verb.

e.g.	**Je le vois** (I see him)	**Je l'aide** (I help him, her, it)
	Il me parle (He speaks to me)	**Nous les mangeons** (We eat them)

Verbs

Verb forms are too difficult to discuss in detail here, but we give present, future and perfect tenses of the regular verb patterns, and some of the more common irregular verbs. The perfect tense is made up of the present tense of **avoir**, or sometimes **être**, with the past participle of the verb. The verbs that usually form the past tense with **être** are: **aller**, **venir**, **arriver**, **partir**, **entrer**, **sortir**, **naître**, **mourir**, **devenir**, **rester**, **descendre**, **monter**.

The second person singular **tu** is only used when speaking to children, close friends or relatives, and animals. In all other cases use **vous**.

Être – *to be*

present		future		past	
je suis	*I am*	je serai	*I shall be, etc.*	j'ai été	*I was/have been, etc.*
tu es	*you are*	tu seras		tu as été	
il/elle est	*he/she is*	il sera		il a été	
nous sommes	*we are*	nous serons		nous avons été	
vous êtes	*you are*	vous serez		vous avez été	
ils/elles sont	*they are*	ils seront		ils ont été	

Avoir – *to have*

present		future		past	
j'ai	*I have*	j'aurai	*I shall have, etc.*	j'ai eu	*I had/have had, etc.*
tu as	*you have*	tu auras		tu as eu	
il/elle a	*he/she has*	il aura		il a eu	
nous avons	*we have*	nous aurons		nous avons eu	
vous avez	*you have*	vous aurez		vous avez eu	
ils/elles ont	*they have*	ils auront		ils ont eu	

Regular Verbs

Aimer – *to like*; verbs ending in **-er**

present	*future*	*past*
j'aime	j'aimerai	j'ai aimé, etc.
tu aimes	tu aimeras	
il aime	il aimera	
nous aimons	nous aimerons	
vous aimez	vous aimerez	
ils aiment	ils aimeront	

Finir – *to finish*; verbs ending in **-ir**

present	*future*	*past*
je finis	je finirai	j'ai fini, etc.
tu finis	tu finiras	
il finit	il finira	
nous finissons	nous finirons	
vous finissez	vous finirez	
ils finissent	ils finiront	

Vendre – *to sell*; verbs ending in **-re**

present	future	past
je vends	je vendrai	j'ai vendu, etc.
tu vends	tu vendras	
il vend	il vendra	
nous vendons	nous vendrons	
vous vendez	vous vendrez	
ils vendent	ils vendront	

Irregular Verbs

Aller – *to go*

present	future	past
je vais	j'irai	je suis allé(e)
tu vas	tu iras	tu es allé(e)
il va	il ira	il est allé
nous allons	nous irons	nous sommes allé(e)s
vous allez	vous irez	vous êtes allé(e)s
ils vont	ils iront	ils sont allés

Boire – *to drink*

present	future	past
je bois	je boirai	j'ai bu, etc.
tu bois	tu boiras	
il boit	il boira	
nous buvons	nous boirons	
vous buvez	vous boirez	
ils boivent	ils boiront	

Connaître – *to know (someone)*

present	future	past
je connais	je connaîtrai	j'ai connu, etc.
tu connais	tu connaîtras	
il connaît	il connaîtra	
nous connaissons	nous connaîtrons	
vous connaissez	vous connaîtrez	
ils connaissent	ils connaîtront	

Devoir – *to have to, must*

present	future	past
je dois	je devrai	j'ai dû, etc.
tu dois	tu devras	
il doit	il devra	
nous devons	nous devrons	
vous devez	vous devrez	
ils doivent	ils devront	

Dire – *to say*

present	future	past
je dis	je dirai	j'ai dit, etc.
tu dis	tu diras	
il dit	il dira	
nous disons	nous dirons	
vous dites	vous direz	
ils disent	ils diront	

Faire – *to make, do*

present	future	past
je fais	je ferai	j'ai fait, etc.
tu fais	tu feras	
il fait	il fera	
nous faisons	nous ferons	
vous faites	vous ferez	
ils font	ils feront	

Lire – *to read*

present	future	past
je lis	je lirai	j'ai lu, etc.
tu lis	tu liras	
il lit	il lira	
nous lisons	nous lirons	
vous lisez	vous lirez	
ils lisent	ils liront	

Mettre – *to put*

present	*future*	*past*
je mets	je mettrai	j'ai mis, etc.
tu mets	tu mettras	
il met	il mettra	
nous mettons	nous mettrons	
vous mettez	vous mettrez	
ils mettent	ils mettront	

Partir – *to leave*

present	*future*	*past*
je pars	je partirai	je suis parti(e), etc.
tu pars	tu partiras	
il part	il partira	
nous partons	nous partirons	
vous partez	vous partirez	
ils partent	ils partiront	

Pouvoir – *to be able, can*

present	*future*	*past*
je peux	je pourrai	j'ai pu, etc.
tu peux	tu pourras	
il peut	il pourra	
nous pouvons	nous pourrons	
vous pouvez	vous pourrez	
ils peuvent	ils pourront	

Prendre – *to take*

present	*future*	*past*
je prends	je prendrais	j'ai pris, etc.
tu prends	tu prendras	
il prend	il prendra	
nous prenons	nous prendrons	
vous prenez	vous prendrez	
ils prennent	ils prendront	

Savoir – *to know (something)*

present	*future*	*past*
je sais	je saurai	j'ai su, etc.
tu sais	tu sauras	
il sait	il saura	
nous savons	nous saurons	
vous savez	vous saurez	
ils savent	ils sauront	

Venir – *to come*

present	*future*	*past*
je viens	je viendrai	je suis venu(e), etc.
tu viens	tu viendras	
il vient	il viendra	
nous venons	nous viendrons	
vous venez	vous viendrez	
ils viennent	ils viendront	

Voir – *to see*

present	future	past
je vois	je verrai	j'ai vu, etc.
tu vois	tu verras	
il voit	il verra	
nous voyons	nous verrons	
vous voyez	vous verrez	
ils voient	ils verront	

Vouloir – *to want*

present	future	past
je veux	je voudrai	j'ai voulu, etc.
tu veux	tu voudras	
il veut	il voudra	
nous voulons	nous voudrons	
vous voulez	vous voudrez	
ils veulent	ils voudront	

Negative

The negative is formed by putting **ne** before the verb and **pas** after. **Ne** becomes **n'** before a vowel.

e.g.	Je ne suis pas français (I am not French)	Je n'ai pas d'argent (I've no money)

VOCABULARY

Various groups of specialized words are given elsewhere in this book and these words are not usually repeated in the vocabulary:

A

a, an	**un/une**	*e^n/u^e n*
abbey	**l'abbaye** *f*	*a-bay-ee*
able (to be)	**pouvoir**	*poo-vwar*
about	**autour (de)**	*oh-toor (de^r)*
above	**au-dessus (de)**	*oh de^r -su^e (de^r)*
abroad	**à l'étranger**	*alay-tra^n -zhay*
accept (to)	**accepter**	*ak-sep-tay*
accident	**l'accident** *m*	*ak-see-dah^n*
accommodation	**le logement**	*lozh-mah^n*
account	**le compte**	*ko^n t*

ache (to)	**avoir mal (à)**	*av-war mal (a)*
acquaintance	**la connaissance**	*ko-ne-sah^n s*
across	**à travers**	*a travair*
act (to)	**jouer**	*zhoo-ay*
add (to)	**ajouter**	*a-zhoo-tay*
address	**l'adresse** *f*	*a-dres*
admire (to)	**admirer**	*ad-mee-ray*
admission	**l'accès** *m*/**l'entrée** *f*	*ak-se/ah^n -tray*
adventure	**l'aventure** *f*	*a-vah^n -tu^e r*
advertisement	**la publicité**	*pu^e -blee-see-tay*
advice	**l'avis** *m*/**le(s) conseil(s)**	*a-vee/ko^n -se-y*
aeroplane	**l'avion** *m*	*av-yo^n*
afford (to)	**avoir les moyens (de)**	*av-war lay mwa-ya^n (de^r)*
afraid	**effrayé**	*ay-fre-yay*
afraid (to be)	**avoir peur**	*a-vwar pœr*
after	**après**	*a-pre*
afternoon	**l'après-midi** *m* or *f*	*a-pre-mee-dee*
again	**encore**	*ah^n -kor*
against	**contre**	*ko^n tr*
age	**l'âge** *m*	*azh*
...ago	**il y a...**	*eel-ya*
agree (to)	**consentir**	*ko^n -sah^n -teer*
ahead	**en avant**	*ah^n -navah^n*

air	l'air *m*	*air*
airbed	le matelas pneumatique	*ma-te' -la pne' -ma-teek*
air-conditioning	la climatisation	*klee-ma-tee-za-syo^n*
alarm clock	le réveil	*ray-ve-y*
alcoholic (drink)	alcoolisée (boisson)	*al-ko-lee-zay*
alike	semblable	*sah^n -blabl*
alive	vivant	*vee-vah^n*
all	tout/tous	*too/too*
all right	bien	*bya^n*
allow (to)	permettre	*pair-metr*
almost	presque	*pre-ske'*
alone	seul	*sœl*
along	le long de	*le' lo^n de'*
already	déjà	*day-zha*
also	aussi	*oh-see*
alter (to)	changer	*shah^n -zhay*
alternative	l'alternative *f*	*al-tair-na-teev*
although	quoique	*kwa-ke'*
always	toujours	*too-zhoor*
ambulance	l'ambulance *f*	*ah^n -bu^e -lah^n s*
America	l'Amérique *f*	*a-may-reek*
American	américain/ américaine	*a-may-ree-ka^n (-ken)*

among	**parmi**	*par-mee*
amuse (to)	**amuser**	*amuᵉ-zay*
amusement park	**le parc d'attractions**	*park da-trak-syoⁿ*
amusing	**amusant**	*amuᵉ-zahⁿ*
ancient	**ancien**	*ahⁿ-syaⁿ*
and	**et**	*ay*
angry	**fâché**	*fa-shay*
animal	**l'animal** *m*	*a-nee-mal*
anniversary	**l'anniversaire** *m*	*a-nee-vair-sair*
annoyed	**contrarié**	*koⁿ-trar-yay*
another	**un autre/une autre**	*eⁿ otr/uᵉ n otr*
answer	**la réponse**	*ray-poⁿ s*
answer (to)	**répondre**	*ray-poⁿ dr*
antiques	**les antiquités** *f*	*ahⁿ-tee-kee-tay*
anyone	**quelqu'un**	*kel-keⁿ*
anything	**quelque chose**	*kel-keʳ-shoz*
anyway	**de toute façon**	*deʳ toot fa-soⁿ*
anywhere	**quelque part**	*kel-keʳ-par*
apartment	**l'appartement** *m*	*a-par-teʳ-mahⁿ*
apologize (to)	**s'excuser**	*sek-skuᵉ-zay*
appetite	**l'appétit** *m*	*a-pay-tee*
appointment	**le rendez-vous**	*rahⁿ-day-voo*
architect	**l'architecte** *m, f*	*ar-shee-tekt*

architecture	l'architecture *f*	ar-shee-tek-tu^e r
area	la région/la zone	ray-zhyo^n/zon
arm	le bras	bra
armchair	le fauteuil	foh-tœ-y
army	l'armée *f*	ar-may
around	autour (de)	oh-toor (de^r)
arrange (to)	arranger	arah^n -zhay
arrival	l'arrivée *f*	a-ree-vay
arrive (to)	arriver	ar-ee-vay
art	l'art *m*	ar
art gallery	la galerie d'art	ga-le^r -ree dar
artificial	artificiel	ar-tee-fee-syel
artist	l'artiste *m,f*	ar-teest
as	comme	kom
as much as	autant que	oh-tah^n ke^r
as soon as	aussitôt que	oh-see-toh ke^r
as well/also	aussi	oh-see
ashtray	le cendrier	sah^n -dree-ay
ask (to)	demander	de^r -mah^n -day
asleep	endormi	ah^n -dor-mee
at	à	a
at last	enfin	ah^n -fa^n
at once	immédiatement	ee-may-dee-at-mah^n
atmosphere	l'atmosphère *f*	at-mos-fair

attention	l'attention *f*	*a-tah^n -syo^n*
attractive	beau/belle	*boh/bel*
auction	la vente aux enchères	*vah^n t oh-zah^n -shair*
audience	le public	*pu^e -bleek*
aunt	la tante	*tah^n t*
Australia	l'Australie *f*	*o-stra-lee*
Australian	australien/ australienne	*o-stra-lya^n (-lyen)*
author	l'auteur *m* (e) *f*	*o-tœr*
autumn	l'automne *m* or *f*	*o-ton*
available	disponible	*dees-po-neebl*
avalanche	l'avalanche *f*	*a-va-lah^n sh*
avenue	l'avenue *f*	*a-ve^r -nu^e*
average	moyen	*mwa-ye^n*
avoid (to)	éviter	*ay-vee-tay*
awake	(r)éveillé	*(r)ay-vay-yay*
away (to be)	absent (être)	*ab-sah^n (aytr)*
awful	affreux	*a-frœ*

B

B&B	la chambre d'hôtes	*shah^n m-br dot*
baby	le bébé	*bay-bay*
baby food	les aliments pour bébé	*a-lee-mah^n poor bay-bay*

babysitter	**le/la baby sitter**	*ba-bee see-tair*
bachelor	**le célibataire**	*say-lee-ba-tair*
back	**en arrière**	*ah^n -ar-yair*
back pack	**le sac à dos**	*sak a doh*
bad	**mauvais**	*mo-ve*
bag	**le sac**	*sak*
baggage	**les bagages** *m*	*ba-gazh*
baggage trolley	**le chariot à bagages**	*sha-ryo a ba-gazh*
bait	**l'appât** *m*	*a-pa*
balcony	**le balcon**	*bal-ko^n*
ball *sport*	**la balle/le ballon**	*bal/ba-lo^n*
ballet	**le ballet**	*ba-lay*
balloon	**le ballon**	*ba-lo^n*
band	**l'orchestre** *m*/**le groupe**	*or-kestr/groop*
bank	**la banque**	*bah^n k*
bank account	**le compte bancaire**	*ko^n t bah^n -kair*
bare	**nu**	*nu^e*
barn	**la grange**	*grah^n zh*
basket	**le panier**	*pan-yay*
bath	**la baignoire**	*ben-ywar*
bath essence	**le bain de mousse**	*ba^n de^r moos*
bathe (to)	**se baigner**	*se^r ben-yay*
bathing cap	**le bonnet (de bain)**	*bo-nay (de^r ba^n)*

bathing costume/ trunks	**le maillot (de bain)**	*ma-yo (de' ba^n)*
bathroom	**la salle de bain**	*sal de' ba^n*
battery	**la pile/la batterie** *car*	*peel/bat-ree*
bay	**la baie**	*be*
be (to)	**être**	*etr*
beach	**la plage**	*plazh*
beard	**la barbe**	*barb*
beautiful	**beau/belle**	*boh/bel*
because	**parce que**	*par-ske'*
become (to)	**devenir**	*de' -ve' -neer*
bed	**le lit**	*lee*
bedroom	**la chambre à coucher**	*shah^n -br a koo-shay*
before *in space*	**devant**	*de' -vah^n*
before *in time*	**avant**	*avah^n*
begin (to)	**commencer**	*kom-ah^n -say*
beginning	**le commencement**	*kom-ah^n -smah^n*
behind	**derrière**	*der-yer*
Belgian	**belge**	*belzh*
Belgium	**la Belgique**	*bel-zheek*
believe (to)	**croire**	*krwar*
bell	**la sonnette**	*so-net*
belong (to)	**appartenir**	*a-par-te' -neer*

below	**sous/au-dessous (de)**	*soo/oh-deʳ -soo (deʳ)*
belt	**la ceinture**	*saⁿ -tuᵉ r*
bench	**le banc**	*bahⁿ*
bend	**le tournant/le virage**	*toor-nahⁿ/vee-razh*
beneath	**sous/au dessous (de)**	*soo/oh deʳ -soo (deʳ)*
berth	**la couchette**	*koo-shet*
beside	**à côté (de)**	*a ko-tay (deʳ)*
best	**le meilleur/la meilleure**	*me-yœr/me-yœr*
bet	**le pari**	*pa-ree*
better	**mieux/meilleur**	*myeʳ/me-yœr*
between	**entre**	*ahⁿ tr*
bicycle	**la bicyclette/le vélo**	*bee-see-klet/vay-lo*
big	**grand**	*grahⁿ*
bill	**la note/l'addition** f	*not/a-dee-syoⁿ*
binoculars	**les jumelles** f	*zhuᵉ -mel*
bird	**l'oiseau** m	*wa-zoh*
birthday	**l'anniversaire** m	*a-nee-vair-sair*
bit	**le morceau**	*mor-soh*
bite (to) *animal*	**mordre**	*mordr*
bitter	**amer**	*a-mair*
blanket	**la couverture**	*koo-vair-tuᵉ r*
bleed (to)	**saigner**	*sen-yay*
blind	**aveugle**	*a-vœgl*

blister	l'ampoule *f*	*ah^n -pool*
blond	**blond**	*blo^n*
blood	**le sang**	*sah^n*
blouse	**le chemisier**	*she^r -mee-zyay*
blow	**le coup**	*koo*
blow (to)	**souffler**	*soo-flay*
(on) board	**à bord**	*a bor*
boat	**le bateau/la barque**	*ba-toh/bark*
body	**le corps**	*kor*
bolt	**le verrou**	*ve-roo*
bone (fish)	**l'os *m* (arête *f*)**	*os (a-ret)*
bonfire	**le feu (de joie)**	*fe^r (de^r zhwa)*
book	**le livre**	*leevr*
book (to)	**réserver/louer**	*ray-zair-vuy/loo-ay*
boot	**la botte/la chaussure montante**	*bot/sho-su^e r mo^n -tah^n t*
border	**la frontière**	*fro^n -tyair*
bored (to be)	**s'ennuyer**	*sah^n -nwee-yay*
boring	**ennuyeux**	*ah^n -nwee-ye^r*
borrow (to)	**emprunter**	*ah^n -pre^n -tay*
both	**(tous) les deux**	*too lay de^r*
bother (to) *annoy*	**ennuyer/embêter**	*ah^n -nwee-yay/ ah^n -bay-tay*
bottle	**la bouteille**	*boo-te-y*

bottle opener	le décapsuleur/ l'ouvre-bouteille *m*	*day-kap-su-lœr/ loovr-boo-te-y*
bottom	le fond	*fo^n*
bow-tie	le nœud papillon	*ne^r pa-pee-yo^n*
bowl	le bol	*bol*
box *container*	la boîte	*bwat*
box *theatre*	la loge	*lozh*
box office	le bureau de location	*bu^e -roh de^r lo-ka-syo^n*
boy	le garçon	*gar-soh^n*
bracelet	le bracelet	*bra-slay*
braces	les bretelles *f*	*bre^r -tel*
brain	le cerveau	*sair-vo*
branch *office*	la succursale	*su^e -ku^e r-sal*
branch *tree*	la branche	*brah^n sh*
brand	la marque	*mark*
brassiere	le soutien-gorge	*soo-tya^n gorzh*
break (to)	casser	*ka-say*
breakfast	le petit déjeuner	*pe^r -tee day-zhe^r -nay*
breathe (to)	respirer	*res-pre-ray*
brick	la brique	*breek*
bridge	le pont	*po^n*
bright *moon*	brillant	*bree-yah^n*
bright *colour*	vif/vive	*veef/veev*
bring (to)	apporter	*a-por-tay*

British	**britannique**	*bree-ta-neek*
broadband	**haut debit/ADSL**	*o-day-bee/a day es el*
broken	**cassé**	*ka-say*
brooch	**la broche**	*brosh*
brother	**le frère**	*frair*
bruise (to)	**contusionner**	*ko^n-tu^e-zyo-nay*
brush	**la brosse**	*bros*
brush (to)	**brosser**	*bro-say*
bucket	**le seau**	*soh*
buckle	**la boucle**	*bookl*
build (to)	**construire**	*ko^n-strweer*
building	**le bâtiment**	*ba-tee-mah^n*
bunch *flowers*	**le bouquet**	*boo-kay*
bunch *keys*	**le trousseau**	*troo-soh*
buoy	**la bouée**	*boo-ay*
burn (to)	**brûler**	*bru^e-lay*
burst (to)	**éclater/crever**	*ay-kla-tay/kre^r-vay*
bus	**l'autobus** *m*	*oh-toh-bu^e s*
bus stop	**l'arrêt** *m*	*a-re*
business	**l'affaire** *f*	*a-fair*
busy	**occupé**	*o-ku^e-pay*
but	**mais**	*me*
butterfly	**le papillon**	*pa-pee-yo^n*

button	**le bouton**	*boo-to^n*
buy (to)	**acheter**	*ash-tay*
by *near*	**près (de)**	*pre (de^r)*
by *via, means*	**par**	*par*

C

cab	**le taxi**	*tak-see*
cabin	**la cabine**	*ka-been*
calculator	**la calculatrice/la calculette**	*kal-ku^e-la-trees/ kal-ku^e-let*
calendar	**le calendrier**	*ka-lah^n-dree-yay*
call	**l'appel** *m*	*a-pel*
call *telephone*	**le coup de téléphone**	*koo de^r tay-lay-fon*
call *visit*	**la visite**	*vee-zeet*
call (to) *summon, name, telephone*	**appeler**	*a-pe^r-lay*
call (to) *telephone*	**téléphoner**	*tay-lay-fo-nay*
call on, at (to)	**rendre visite à**	*rah^n dr vee-zeet a*
calm	**calme**	*kalm*
camp (to)	**camper**	*kah^n-pay*
campsite	**le terrain de camping**	*te-ra^n de^r kah^n-ping*
can (to be able)	**pouvoir**	*poo-vwar*
can *tin*	**la boîte**	*bwat*

can opener	**l'ouvre-boîte** *m*	*oovr-bwat*
Canada	**le Canada**	*ka-na-da*
Canadian	**canadien/ canadienne**	*ka-na-dya^n (-dyen)*
cancel (to)	**annuler**	*a-nu^e-lay*
candle	**la bougie**	*boo-zhee*
canoe	**le canoë**	*ka-no-ay*
cap	**la casquette**	*kas-ket*
capable	**capable**	*ka-pabl*
capital city	**la capitale**	*ka-pee-tal*
car	**l'auto** *f*/**la voiture**	*oh-toh/vwa-tu^e r*
car park	**le parking/le parc de stationnement**	*par-king/park de^r sta-syon-mah^n*
carafe	**la carafe**	*ka-raf*
caravan	**la caravane**	*ka-ra-van*
card	**la carte**	*kart*
care	**le soin**	*swa^n*
careful	**soigneux/prudent**	*swan-ye^r/pru^e-dah^n*
careless	**négligent**	*nay-glee-zhah^n*
caretaker	**le concierge**	*ko^n-syairzh*
carpet	**le tapis**	*ta-pee*
carry (to)	**porter**	*por-tay*
cash	**l'argent** *m*	*ar-zhah^n*
cash (to)	**encaisser**	*ah^n-kay-say*

cashier	le caissier/ la caissière	kes-yay (-yair)
casino	le casino	ka-zee-no
castle	le château	sha-toh
cat	le chat	sha
catalogue	le catalogue	ka-ta-log
catch (to)	attraper	a-tra-pay
cathedral	la cathédrale	ka-tay-dral
Catholic	catholique	ka-toh-leek
cause	la cause	kohz
cave	la caverne/la grotte	ka-vairn/grot
cellar	la cave	kav
cement	le ciment	see-mah^n
central	central	sah^n-tral
centre	le centre	sah^n tr
century	le siècle	sy-ekl
ceremony	la cérémonie	say-ray-mo-nee
certain	certain	sair-ta^n
certainly	certainement	sair-ten-mah^n
chain *jewellery*	la chaîne	shen
chair	la chaise	shez
chambermaid	la femme de chambre	famde' shah^n -br
chance	le hasard/la chance	a-zar/shah^n s

(small) change	**la monnaie**	*mo-nay*
change (to)	**changer**	*shah{n} -zhay*
chapel	**la chapelle**	*sha-pel*
charge	**le prix**	*pree*
charge (to)	**faire payer/ demander (un prix)**	*fair pe-yay/de{r} -mah{n} -day (e{n} pree)*
cheap	**bon marché**	*bo{n} mar-shay*
check (to)	**vérifier**	*vay-ree-fyay*
chef	**le chef cuisinier**	*shef kwee-zee-nyay*
cheque	**le chèque**	*shek*
chess	**les échecs** *m*	*ay-shek*
chess set	**l'échiquier** *m*	*ay-shee-kyay*
child	**l'enfant** *m* or *f*	*ah{n} -fah{n}*
chill (to)	**faire rafraîchir**	*fair ra-fray-sheer*
china	**la porcelaine**	*por-se{r} -len*
choice	**le choix**	*shwa*
choose (to)	**choisir**	*shwa-zeer*
church	**l'église** *f*	*ay-gleez*
cigar	**le cigare**	*see-gar*
cigarette	**la cigarette**	*see-ga-ret*
cinema	**le cinéma**	*see-nay-ma*
circle *theatre*	**le balcon**	*bal-ko{n}*
circus	**le cirque**	*seerk*
city	**la grande ville**	*gra{n} d veel*

class	la classe	klas
clean	propre	propr
clean (to)	nettoyer	ne-twa-yay
cleansing cream	la crème démaquillante	krem day-ma-kee-yah^n t
clear	clair	klair
clerk	l'employé m or (e) f	ah^n -plwa-yay
cliff	la falaise	fa-lez
climb (to)	monter	mo^n -tay
cloakroom	le vestiaire	ves-tyair
clock	la pendule/ l'horloge f	pah^n -du^e l/or-lozh
close (to)	fermer	fair-may
closed	fermé	fair-may
cloth	l'étoffe f	ay-tof
clothes	les vêtements m	vet-mah^n
cloud	le nuage	nu^e -azh
coach	l'autocar m	oh-toh-kar
coast	la côte	kot
coat	le manteau	mah^n -toh
coat hanger	le cintre	sa^n tr
coin	la pièce de monnaie	pyes de^r mo-nay
cold	froid	frwa
collar	le col	kol

collect (to)	**collectionner**	*ko-lek-syo-nay*
colour	**la couleur**	*koo-lœr*
comb	**le peigne**	*pen-y*
come (to)	**venir**	*ve'-neer*
come in!	**entrez!**	*ahⁿ-tray*
comfortable	**confortable**	*koⁿ-for-tabl*
common	**ordinaire/commun**	*or-dee-nair/ko-meⁿ*
company	**la compagnie/ la société**	*koⁿ-pa-nee/so-syay-tay*
compartment	**le compartiment**	*koⁿ-par-tee-mahⁿ*
compass *on boat*	**la boussole/le compas**	*boo-sol/koⁿ-pa*
compensation	**le dédommagement**	*day-do-mazh-mahⁿ*
complain (to)	**se plaindre**	*se' plaⁿ dr*
complaint	**la plainte**	*plaⁿ t*
completely	**complètement**	*koⁿ-plet-mahⁿ*
computer	**l'ordinateur** *m*	*or-dee-na-tœr*
concert	**le concert**	*koⁿ-sair*
concert hall	**la salle de concert**	*sal de' koⁿ-sair*
concrete	**le béton**	*bay-toⁿ*
condition	**la condition**	*koⁿ-dee-syoⁿ*
condom	**le préservatif**	*pray-zayr-va-teef*
conductor *bus*	**le receveur**	*re'-se'-vœr*
conductor *orchestra*	**le/la chef d'orchestre**	*shef dor-kestr*

congratulations!	**félicitations!**	*fay-lee-see-ta-syo*[n]
connect (to)	**relier**	*re' -lee-ay*
connect (to) *train*	**faire la correspondance**	*fair la ko-res-po*[n] *-dah*[n] *s*
connected	**connecté**	*ko-nay-ktay*
connection *train*	**la correspondance**	*ko-res-po*[n] *-dah*[n] *s*
consul	**le consul**	*ko*[n] *-su*[e] *l*
consulate	**le consulat**	*ko*[n] *-su*[e] *-la*
contact lenses	**les verres de contact**	*vair de' ko*[n] *-takt*
contain (to)	**contenir**	*ko*[n] *-te' -neer*
contraceptive	**le préservatif**	*pray-zair-va-teef*
contrast	**le contraste**	*ko*[n] *-trast*
convenient	**commode**	*ko-mod*
conversation	**la conversation**	*ko*[n] *-vair-sa-syo*[n]
cook	**le cuisinier/ la cuisinière**	*kwee-zee-nyay (-nyair)*
cook (to)	**cuire**	*kweer*
cool	**frais**	*fre*
copper	**le cuivre**	*kweevr*
copy *book*	**l'exemplaire** *m*	*eg-zah*[n] *-plair*
copy *duplicate*	**la copie**	*ko-pee*
copy (to)	**copier**	*ko-pyay*
cork	**le bouchon**	*boo-sho*[n]
corkscrew	**le tire-bouchon**	*teer boo-sho*[n]

corner	**le coin**	*kwaⁿ*
correct	**exact**	*eg-za*
corridor	**le couloir**	*koo-lwar*
cosmetics	**les produits de beauté** *m*	*pro-dwee de^r buh-tay*
cost	**le prix**	*pree*
cost (to)	**coûter**	*koo-tay*
costume jewellery	**les bijoux de fantaisie**	*bee-zhoo de^r fahⁿ-tay-zee*
cot	**le petit lit**	*pe^r-tee lee*
cottage	**la villa**	*vee-la*
cotton wool	**le coton hydrophile**	*ko-toⁿ ee-dro-feel*
couchette	**la couchette**	*koo-shet*
count (to)	**compter**	*koⁿ-tay*
country *nation*	**le pays**	*pay-ee*
country *not town*	**la campagne**	*kahⁿ-pan-y*
couple	**le couple**	*koopl*
course *dish*	**le plat**	*pla*
courtyard	**la cour**	*koor*
cousin	**le cousin/la cousine**	*koo-zaⁿ (-zeen)*
cover	**la couverture**	*koo-vair-tu^e r*
cover (to)	**couvrir**	*koo-vreer*
cover charge	**le couvert**	*koo-vair*
cow	**la vache**	*vash*

crash *collision*	la collision	ko-lee-zyo^n
credit	le crédit	kray-dee
credit card	la carte de crédit	kart de^r kray-dee
crew	l'équipage *m*	ay-kee-pazh
cross	la croix	krwa
cross (to)	traverser	tra-vair-say
cross-country skiing	le ski de fond	skee de^r fo^n
crossroads	le croisement	krwaz-mah^n
crowd	la foule	fool
crowded	plein de monde	pla^n de^r mo^n d
cry (to) *shout*	crier	kree-ay
cry (to) *weep*	pleurer	plœ-ray
crystal	le cristal	kree-stal
cufflinks	les boutons de manchette	boo-to^n de^r mah^n -shet
cup	la tasse	tas
cupboard	le placard/ l'armoire *f*	pla-kar/ar-mwar
cure (to)	guérir	gay-reer
curious	curieux	ku^e -rye^r
curl	la boucle	bookl
current	le courant	koo-rah^n
curtain	le rideau	ree-doh
curve	la courbe	koorb

cushion	**le coussin**	*koo-sa^n*
customs	**la douane**	*dwan*
customs officer	**le douanier**	*dwan-yay*
cut	**la coupure**	*koo-pu^r*
cut (to)	**couper**	*koo-pay*
cycling	**le cyclisme**	*see-kleezm*
cyclist	**le cycliste**	*see-kleest*

D

daily	**tous les jours**	*too lay zhoor*
damaged	**endommagé**	*ah^n-do-ma-zhay*
damp	**humide**	*u^e-meed*
dance	**la danse/le bal**	*dah^n s/bal*
dance (to)	**danser**	*dah^n-say*
danger	**le danger**	*dah^n-zhay*
dangerous	**dangereux**	*dah^n-zhe^r-re^r*
dark	**noir/obscur**	*nwar/ob-sku^e r*
dark *colour*	**foncé**	*fo^n-say*
date *appointment*	**le rendez-vous**	*rah^n-day-voo*
date *time*	**la date**	*dat*
daughter	**la fille**	*fee-y*
day	**le jour/la journée**	*zhoor/zhoor-nay*
dead	**mort**	*mor*

deaf	**sourd**	*soor*
dealer	**le marchand**	*mar-shah^n*
dear	**cher**	*shair*
decanter	**la carafe**	*ka-raf*
decide (to)	**décider**	*day-see-day*
deck	**le pont**	*po^n*
deckchair	**la chaise longue**	*shez long*
declare (to)	**déclarer**	*day-kla-ray*
deep	**profond**	*pro-fo^n*
delay	**le retard**	*re^r-tar*
deliver (to)	**livrer**	*lee-vray*
delivery	**la livraison**	*lee-vrai-zo^n*
demi-pension	**la demi-pension**	*de^r-mee pah^n-syo^n*
dentures	**le dentier**	*dah^n-tyay*
deodorant	**le désodorisant/ déodorant**	*day-zo-do-ree-zah^n/ day-o-do-rah^n*
depart (to)	**partir**	*par-teer*
department	**le département**	*day-par-te^r-mah^n*
department store	**le grand magasin**	*grah^n ma-ga-za^n*
departure	**le départ**	*day-par*
dessert	**le dessert**	*de-ser*
detour	**le détour**	*day-toor*
dial (to)	**faire un numéro**	*fair e^n nu^e-may-ro*
dialling code	**l'indicatif (téléphonique)**	*a^n-dee-ka-teef (tay-lay-fo-neek)*

diamond	**le diamant**	*dya-mahⁿ*
dice	**les dés** *m*	*day*
dictionary	**le dictionnaire**	*deek-syo-nair*
diet	**le régime**	*ray-zheem*
diet (to)	**être au régime**	*etr oh ray-zheem*
different	**différent**	*dee-fay-rahⁿ*
difficult	**difficile**	*dee-fee-seel*
dine (to)	**dîner**	*dee-nay*
dining room	**la salle à manger**	*sal a mahⁿ -zhay*
dinner	**le dîner**	*dee-nay*
dinner jacket	**le smoking**	*smo-king*
direct	**direct**	*dee-rekt*
direction	**la direction**	*dee-rek-syoⁿ*
dirty	**sale**	*sal*
disappointed	**déçu**	*day-su^e*
discount	**la remise**	*re^r -meez*
dish	**le plat**	*pla*
disinfectant	**le désinfectant**	*day-zaⁿ -fek-tahⁿ*
distance	**la distance**	*dee-stahⁿ s*
disturb (to)	**déranger**	*day-rahⁿ -zhay*
ditch	**le fossé**	*fo-say*
dive (to)	**plonger**	*ploⁿ -zhay*
diving board	**le plongeoir**	*ploⁿ -zhwar*

divorced	**divorcé(e)**	*dee-vor-say*
do (to)	**faire**	*fair*
dock (to)	**accoster**	*a-kos-tay*
doctor	**le médecin**	*mayd-sa^n*
dog	**le chien**	*shya^n*
doll	**la poupée**	*poo-pay*
door	**la porte**	*port*
double	**double**	*doobl*
double bed	**le grand lit**	*grah^n lee*
double room	**la chambre pour deux**	*shah^n br poor de^r*
down (stairs)	**en bas**	*ah^n ba*
dozen	**la douzaine**	*doo-zen*
drawer	**le tiroir**	*teer-war*
dream	**le rêve**	*rev*
dress	**la robe**	*rob*
dressing gown	**la robe de chambre**	*rob de^r shah^n br*
dressmaker	**le couturier/ la couturière**	*koo-tu^e r-yay (-yair)*
drink (to)	**boire**	*bwar*
drinking water	**l'eau potable** *f*	*oh po-tabl*
drive (to)	**conduire**	*ko^n -dweer*
driver	**le chauffeur**	*sho-fœr*
driving licence	**le permis de conduire**	*pair-mee de^r ko^n -dweer*

drop (to)	**faire tomber**	*fair to^n -bay*
drunk	**ivre**	*eevr*
drunkard	**l'ivrogne**	*ee-vron-y*
dry *adj*	**sec** *m*/**sèche** *f*	*sek/sesh*
during	**pendant**	*pah^n -dah^n*
duvet	**le duvet**	*du^e -vay*
dye	**la teinture**	*ta^n -tu^e r*

E

each	**chaque**	*shak*
early	**tôt/de bonne heure**	*toh/de^r bon œr*
earrings	**les boucles d'oreilles** *f*	*bookl do-re-y*
east	**l'est** *m*	*est*
Easter	**Pâques**	*pak*
easy	**facile**	*fa-seel*
eat (to)	**manger**	*mah^n -zhay*
edge	**le bord**	*bor*
eiderdown	**l'édredon** *m*	*ay-dre^r -do^n*
elastic	**l'élastique** *m*	*ay-las-teek*
electric point	**la prise de courant**	*preez de^r koo-rah^n*
electricity	**l'électricité** *f*	*ay-lek-tree-see-tay*
elevator	**l'ascenseur** *m*	*a-sah^n -sœr*

embarrassed	**gêné**	*zhe-nay*
embassy	**l'ambassade** *f*	*ahⁿ -ba-sad*
emergency exit	**la sortie de secours**	*sor-tee de' se' -koor*
empty	**vide**	*veed*
end	**la fin**	*faⁿ*
engaged *people*	**fiancé(e)**	*fyahⁿ -say*
engaged *telephone*	**occupé**	*o-kuᵉ -pay*
engine	**le moteur**	*moh-tœr*
England	**l'Angleterre** *f*	*ahⁿ -gle' -tair*
English	**anglais/anglaise**	*ahⁿ -gle (-glez)*
enjoy (to)	**aimer**	*e-may*
enjoy oneself (to)	**s'amuser**	*sa-muᵉ -zay*
enough	**assez**	*a-say*
enquiries	**les renseignements** *m*	*rahⁿ -sen-ye' -mahⁿ*
enter (to)	**entrer**	*ahⁿ -tray*
entrance	**l'entrée** *f*	*ahⁿ -tray*
entrance fee	**le prix d'entrée**	*pree dahⁿ -tray*
envelope	**l'enveloppe** *f*	*ahⁿ -vlop*
equipment	**l'équipement** *m*	*ay-keep-mahⁿ*
escalator	**l'escalier roulant**	*es-ka-lyay roo-lahⁿ*
escape (to)	**s'échapper**	*say-sha-pay*
estate agent	**l'agent immobilier** *m*	*a-zhahⁿ ee-mo-bee-lyay*
even *opp. odd*	**pair**	*pair*

evening	**le soir**	*swar*
event	**l'événement** *m*	*ay-ven-mah^n*
every	**chaque**	*shak*
everybody	**tout le monde**	*too le' mo^n d*
everything	**tout**	*too*
everywhere	**partout**	*par-too*
example	**l'exemple** *m*	*eg-zah^n pl*
excellent	**excellent**	*ek-se-lah^n*
except	**sauf/excepté**	*sohf/ek-sep-tay*
excess	**l'excédent** *m*	*ek-say-dah^n*
exchange bureau	**le bureau de change**	*bu^e -roh de' shanzh*
exchange rate	**le taux du change**	*toh du^e shanzh*
excursion	**l'excursion** *f*	*ek-sku^e r-syo^n*
excuse	**l'excuse** *f*	*ek-sku^e z*
exhausted	**épuisé**	*ay-pwee-zay*
exhibition	**l'exposition** *f*	*ek-spo-zee-syo^n*
exit	**la sortie**	*sor-tee*
expect (to) *someone*	**attendre**	*a-tah^n dr*
expensive	**cher**	*shair*
explain (to)	**expliquer**	*ek-splee-kay*
express train	**l'express** *m*	*ek-spres*
extra	**supplémentaire**	*su^e -play-mah^n -tair*
eye-shadow	**l'ombre à paupières** *f*	*o^n br a poh-pyair*

F

fabric	le tissu	tee-su^e
face	le visage/la figure	vee-zazh/fee-gu^e r
face-cloth	le gant de toilette	gah^n de^r twa-let
face cream	la crème pour le visage	krem poor le^r vee-zazh
face powder	la poudre de riz	poodr de^r ree
fact	le fait	fe
factory	la fabrique/l'usine f	fa-breek/u^e -zeen
fade (to)	se faner	se^r fa-nay
faint (to)	s'évanouir	say-van-weer
fair	blond	blo^n
fair fête	la foire	fwar
fall (to)	tomber	to^n -bay
family	la famille	fa-mee-y
far	loin	lwa^n
fare	le prix du billet	pree du^e bee-yay
farm	la ferme	fairm
farmer	le fermier	fair-myay
farmhouse	la ferme	fairm
farther	plus loin	plu^e lwa^n
fashion	la mode	mod
fast	vite	veet

fat *food*	**gras**	*gra*
father	**le père**	*pair*
fault	**le défaut**	*day-fo*
fear	**la peur**	*pœr*
feed (to)	**nourrir**	*noo-reer*
feeding bottle	**le biberon**	*bee-bro^n*
feel (to)	**sentir**	*sah^n-teer*
felt-tip pen	**le crayon feutre**	*kre-yo^n fœtr*
female *adj*	**féminin**	*fay-mee-na^n*
ferry	**le ferry**	*fe-ree*
festival	**la fête/le festival**	*fet/fe-sti-val*
fetch (to) *person*	**amener**	*a-me^r-nay*
fetch (to) *thing*	**apporter**	*a-por-tay*
few	**peu**	*pe^r*
fiancé(e)	**le fiancé/la fiancée**	*fyah^n-say*
field	**le champ**	*shah^n*
fight (to)	**se battre**	*se^r batr*
fill/fill in (to)	**remplir**	*rah^n-pleer*
film	**le film**	*feelm*
find (to)	**trouver**	*troo-vay*
fine	**beau**	*boh*
finish (to)	**finir**	*fee-neer*
finished	**fini**	*fee-nee*

fire	le feu	*fe'*
fire escape	l'issue de secours *f*	*eesu^e de' se' -koor*
fire extinguisher	l'extincteur *m*	*eks-ta^n k-tœr*
fireworks *display*	le feu d'artifice	*fe' dar-tee-fees*
first	premier	*pre' -myay*
first aid	les premiers secours *m*	*pre' -myay se' -koor*
first class	première classe	*pre' -myair klas*
fish	le poisson	*pwa-so^n*
fish (to)	pêcher	*pe-shay*
fisherman	le pêcheur	*pe-shœr*
fit *adj*	en forme	*ah^n form*
fit (to)	aller bien	*a-lay bya^n*
flag	le drapeau	*dra-poh*
flat *adj*	plat	*pla*
flat *noun*	l'appartement *m*	*a-par-te' -mah^n*
flavour	le parfum	*par-fe^n*
flea market	le marché aux puces	*mar-shay oh pu^e s*
flight	le vol	*vol*
float (to)	flotter	*flo-tay*
flood	l'inondation *f*	*ee-no^n -da-syo^n*
floor	le plancher	*plah^n -shay*
floor *storey*	l'étage *m*	*ay-tazh*
floor show	le spectacle	*spek-takl*

flower	**la fleur**	*flœr*
fly	**la mouche**	*moosh*
fly (to)	**voler**	*vo-lay*
fly (to) *in plane*	**aller en avion**	*a-lay ahⁿ av-yoⁿ*
fog	**le brouillard**	*broo-yar*
fold (to)	**plier**	*plee-yay*
follow (to)	**suivre**	*sweevr*
food	**la nourriture**	*noo-ree-tuᵉr*
foot	**le pied**	*pyay*
football	**le football**	*foot-bol*
footpath	**le sentier**	*sahⁿ-tyay*
for	**pour**	*poor*
forbid (to)	**interdire**	*aⁿ-tair-deer*
foreign	**étranger**	*ay-trahⁿ-zhay*
forest	**la forêt**	*fo-re*
forget (to)	**oublier**	*oo-blee-ay*
fork	**la fourchette**	*foor-shet*
forward	**en avant**	*ahⁿ-na-vahⁿ*
forward (to)	**faire suivre**	*fair sweevr*
fountain	**la fontaine**	*foⁿ-ten*
fragile	**fragile**	*fra-zheel*
France	**la France**	*frahⁿs*

free	**libre**	*leebr*
freight	**le fret**	*fre*
French	**français/française**	*frah^n -say (-sez)*
fresh	**frais**	*fre*
fresh water	**l'eau douce** *f*	*oh doos*
friend	**l'ami** *m*/**l'amie** *f*	*a-mee*
friendly	**amical**	*a-mee-kal*
from	**de**	*de^r*
front	**le devant**	*de^r -vah^n*
frontier	**la frontière**	*fro^n -tyair*
frost	**le givre**	*zheevr*
frost *ground*	**le verglas**	*vair-gla*
frozen	**gelé**	*zhe^r -lay*
frozen *food*	**congelé/surgelé**	*ko^n -zhe^r -lay/ su^e r-zhe^r -lay*
fruit	**le fruit**	*frwee*
full	**plein**	*pla^n*
full board	**la pension complète**	*pah^n -syo^n kom-plet*
fun	**l'amusement** *m*	*a-mu^e z-mah^n*
funny	**drôle**	*drohl*
fur	**la fourrure**	*foo-ru^e r*
furniture	**les meubles** *m*	*mœbl*
further	**plus loin**	*plu^e lwa^n*

G

gallery	**la galerie**	*gal-ree*
gamble (to)	**jouer (de l'argent)**	*zhoo-ay (de^r lar-zhah^n)*
game	**la partie**	*par-tee*
garage	**le garage**	*ga-razh*
garbage	**les ordures** *f*	*or-du^e r*
garden	**le jardin**	*zhar-da^n*
gas	**le gaz**	*gaz*
gate	**la porte/le portail**	*port/por-ta-y*
gentleman	**monsieur**	*me^r -sye^r*
genuine	**authentique/ véritable**	*oh-tah^n -teek/vay-ree-tabl*
get (to)	**obtenir**	*ob-te^r -neer*
get off (to)	**descendre**	*de-sah^n dr*
get on (to)	**monter**	*mo^n -tay*
gift	**le cadeau**	*ka-doh*
gift-wrap (to)	**faire un paquet-cadeau**	*fair e^n pa-kay ka-doh*
girl	**la (jeune) fille**	*(zhœn) fee-y*
give (to)	**donner**	*do-nay*
glad	**heureux**	*œ-re^r*
glass	**le verre**	*vair*
glasses	**les lunettes** *f*	*lu^e -net*

gloomy	**sombre**	*son br*
glorious	**splendide**	*splahn -deed*
glove	**le gant**	*gahn*
go (to)	**aller**	*alay*
goal	**le but**	*buet*
God	**Dieu**	*dyer*
gold	**l'or** *m*	*or*
gold-plated	**plaqué or**	*pla-kay or*
golf course	**le (terrain de) golf**	*(tay-ran der) golf*
good	**bon**	*bon*
government	**le gouvernement**	*goo-vair-ner -mahn*
granddaughter	**la petite-fille**	*per -teet fee-y*
grandfather	**le grand-père**	*grahn pair*
grandmother	**la grand-mère**	*grahn mair*
grandson	**le petit-fils**	*per -tee fees*
grass	**l'herbe** *f*	*erb*
grateful	**reconnaissant**	*rer -ko-ne-sahn*
gravel	**le gravier**	*gra-vyay*
great	**grand**	*grahn*
Great Britain	**la Grande Bretagne**	*Grahn d-Brer -tan-y*
groceries	**les comestibles** *m*	*ko-mes-teebl*
ground	**le sol**	*sol*
grow (to)	**grandir**	*grahn -deer*

grow (to) *plants*	**pousser**	*poo-say*
guarantee	**la garantie**	*ga-rahⁿ -tee*
guard	**le garde**	*gard*
guard *on train*	**le chef de train**	*shef deʳ traⁿ*
guest	**l'invité**	*aⁿ -vee-tay*
guest house	**la pension**	*pahⁿ -syoⁿ*
guide *book/person*	**le guide**	*gheed*
guided tour	**la visite guidée**	*vee-zeet ghee-day*

H

hail	**la grêle**	*grel*
hair	**les cheveux** *m*	*sheʳ -veʳ*
hair brush	**la brosse à cheveux**	*bros a sheʳ ·veʳ*
hair spray	**la laque**	*lak*
hair spray can	**la bombe de laque**	*boⁿ b deʳ lak*
hair-dryer	**le sèche-cheveux**	*sesh sheʳ -veʳ*
hairgrip	**la barrette**	*ba-ret*
hairpin	**l'épingle à cheveux**	*ay-paⁿ gal a sheʳ -veʳ*
half	**demi**	*deʳ -mee*
half fare	**une place à demi-tarif**	*plas a deʳ -mee ta-reef*
half-board	**la demi-pension**	*deʳ -mee pahⁿ -syoⁿ*
hammer	**le marteau**	*mar-toh*

hand	la main	ma^n
handbag	le sac à main	sak a ma^n
handkerchief	le mouchoir	moo-shwar
handmade	fait à la main	fay a la ma^n
hang (to)	pendre	pah^n dr
hanger	le cintre	sa^n tr
happen (to)	arriver	a-ree-vay
happy	heureux	œ-re'
happy birthday	bon anniversaire	bon a-nee-vair-sair
harbour	le port	por
hard	dur/difficile	du^e r/dee-fee-seel
hardly	à peine	a pen
harmful	nocif *m*, nocive *f*; dangereux *m*, dangereuse *f*	no-seef (-seev); dah^n -zhe' -re' (-rœz)
harmless	sans danger, pas dangereux	sah^n dahn-zhay, pa dah^n -zhe' -re'
hat	le chapeau	sha-poh
have (to)	avoir	a-vwar
have to (to)	devoir	de' -vwar
he	il	eel
head	la tête	tet
headphones	les écouteurs *m*	ay-koo-tœr
health	la santé	sah^n -tay

hear (to)	**entendre**	*ah^n -tah^n -dr*
heart	**le cœur**	*kœr*
heat	**la chaleur**	*sha-lœr*
heating	**le chauffage**	*shoh-fazh*
heavy	**lourd**	*loor*
hedge	**la haie**	*eh*
heel *foot/shoe*	**le talon**	*ta-lo^n*
height	**la hauteur**	*oh-tœr*
helicopter	**l'hélicoptère** *m*	*ay-lee-kop-tair*
help	**l'aide** *f*	*ed*
help (to)	**aider**	*e-day*
hem	**l'ourlet** *m*	*oor-lay*
her/his	**son** *m*, **sa** *f*, **ses** *pl*	*so^n/sa/say*
here	**ici**	*ee-see*
hers/his	**la sienne** *pl*/**le sien**	*syen/sya^n*
high	**haut**	*oh*
hike (to)	**faire des excursions à pied**	*fair day zeks-ku^e r-syo^n a pyay*
hill	**la colline**	*ko-leen*
him	**lui/le**	*lwee/le^r*
hire (to)	**louer**	*loo-ay*
history	**l'histoire** *f*	*ees-twar*
hitch hike (to)	**faire de l'auto-stop**	*fair de^r loh-toh stop*

hobby	le passe-temps/ le hobby	*pas-tahⁿ/obee*
hold (to)	tenir	*te^r-neer*
hole	le trou	*troo*
holiday	le jour férié	*zhoor fay-ryay*
holidays	les vacances *f*	*va-kahⁿ s*
hollow	creux	*kre^r*
(at) home	chez soi/à la maison	*shay swa/a la me-zoⁿ*
honeymoon	la lune de miel	*lu^e n de^r myel*
hope	l'espoir *m*	*es-pwar*
hope (to)	espérer	*es-pay-ray*
horse	le cheval	*she^r -val*
horse race	la course de chevaux	*koors de she^r -vo*
horse riding	l'équitation	*ay-kee-ta-syoⁿ*
hose	le tuyau	*twee-yo*
hospital	l'hôpital *m*	*o-pee-tal*
host/hostess	l'hôte *m*/l'hôtesse *f*	*ot/otes*
hot	chaud	*shoh*
hot water bottle	la bouillotte	*boo-yot*
hotel	l'hôtel *m*	*o-tel*
hotel keeper	l'hôtelier *m*	*o-tel-yay*
hour	l'heure *f*	*œr*
house	la maison	*me-zoⁿ*

how?	**comment**	*ko-mah^n*
how much/many?	**combien?**	*ko^n -bya^n*
hungry (to be)	**(avoir) faim**	*a-vwar fa^n*
hunt (to)	**chasser**	*sha-say*
hurry (to)	**se dépêcher**	*se day-pe-shay*
hurt (to)	**faire mal**	*fair mal*
husband	**le mari**	*ma-ree*
hydrofoil	**l'hydrofoil** *m*	*ee-dro-foyl*

| I

I	**je**	*zhe^r*
ice	**la glace**	*glas*
ice cream	**la glace (à la crème)**	*glas (a la krem)*
ice lolly	**la sucette glacée**	*su^e -set gla-say*
identify (to)	**identifier**	*ee-dah^n -tee-fyay*
if	**si**	*see*
imagine (to)	**imaginer**	*ee-ma-zhee-nay*
immediately	**immédiatement**	*ee-may-dyat-mah^n*
important	**important**	*a^n -por-tah^n*
in	**dans**	*dah^n*
include (to)	**comprendre**	*ko^n -prah^n dr*
included	**compris**	*ko^n -pree*
inconvenient	**inopportun**	*ee-no-por-te^n*

incorrect	**inexact**	*ee-neg-za*
indeed	**vraiment**	*vre-mah^n*
independent	**indépendant**	*a^n -day-pah^n -dah^n*
indoors	**à l'intérieur**	*a la^n -tayr-yœr*
industry	**l'industrie** *f*	*a^n -du^e s-tree*
inexpensive	**peu cher/bon marché**	*pœ shair/bo^n mar-shay*
inflammable	**inflammable**	*a^n -fla-mabl*
inflatable	**gonflable**	*go^n -flabl*
inflate (to) *tyre etc.*	**gonfler**	*go^n -flay*
inflation	**l'inflation**	*a^n -fla-syo^n*
information	**les renseignements** *m*	*rah^n -sen-y-mah^n*
information bureau	**le bureau de renseignements**	*bu^e -roh de^r rah^n -sen-y-mah^n*
ink	**l'encre** *f*	*ah^n kr*
inn	**l'auberge** *f*	*o-bairzh*
insect	**l'insecte** *m*	*a^n -sekt*
insect sting	**la piqûre (d'insecte)**	*pee-ku^e r (da^n -selet)*
insect repellent	**le produit pour éloigner les insectes**	*pro-dwee poor ay-lwan-yay lay za^n -sekt*
inside	**à l'intérieur**	*a la^n -tayr-yœr*
instead (of)	**au lieu (de)**	*oh lye^r de^r*
instructor	**l'instructeur** *m*	*a^n -stru^e k-tœr*
insurance	**l'assurance** *f*	*a-su^e -rah^n s*

insure (to)	**assurer**	*a-su^e -ray*
insured	**assuré**	*a-su^e -ray*
interest	**l'intérêt** *m*	*a^n -tay-ray*
interested	**intéressé**	*a^n -tay-re-say*
interesting	**intéressant**	*a^n -tay-re-sah^n*
Internet	**l'Internet** *m* or *f*	*a^n -tair-nayt*
interpreter	**l'interprète** *m*	*a^n -tair-pret*
into	**dans**	*dah^n*
introduce (to)	**présenter**	*pray-zah^n -tay*
invitation	**l'invitation** *f*	*a^n -vee-ta-syo^n*
invite (to)	**inviter**	*a^n -vee-tay*
Ireland	**l'Irlande** *f*	*eer-lah^n d*
Irish	**irlandais/irlandaise**	*eer-lah^n -de (-dez)*
iron	**le fer**	*fair*
iron (to)	**repasser**	*re^r -pa-say*
island	**l'île** *f*	*eel*
it	**il/elle**	*eel/el*

J

jacket	**la veste**	*vest*
jar	**le pot**	*po*
jellyfish	**la méduse**	*may-du^e z*

jewellery	**la bijouterie**	*bee-zhoo-tree*
Jewish	**israélite, juif** *m*/ **juive** *f*	*ee-sra-ay-leet, zhweef/zhweev*
job	**l'emploi** *m*/**le travail**	*ah^n -plwa/tra-va-y*
journey	**le voyage**	*vwa-yazh*
jug	**le pichet**	*pee-shay*
jump (to)	**sauter**	*so-tay*
jumper	**le pull(over)**	*pu^e l (o-vair)*

K

keep (to)	**garder/tenir**	*gar-day/te^r -neer*
key	**la clé**	*klay*
kind	**l'espèce** *f*/**la sorte**	*es-pes/sort*
kind *adj*	**aimable, gentil** *m*, **gentille** *f*	*emabl, zhah^n -tee (-tee-y)*
king	**le roi**	*rwa*
kiss	**le baiser**	*be-zay*
kiss (to)	**embrasser**	*ah^n -bra-say*
kitchen	**la cuisine**	*kwee-zeen*
knife	**le couteau**	*koo-toh*
knock (to)	**frapper**	*fra-pay*
know (to) *fact*	**savoir**	*sa-vwar*
know (to) *person, place*	**connaître**	*ko-netr*

L

label	l'étiquette *f*	*ay-tee-ket*
lace	la dentelle	*dah^n -tel*
lady	la dame	*dam*
lake	le lac	*lak*
lake *ornamental*	le bassin	*ba-sa^n*
lamp	la lampe	*lah^n p*
land	la terre	*ter*
landing	le palier	*pa-lyay*
landlady/lord	la/le propriétaire	*pro-pree-ay-tair*
landmark	le point de repère	*pwa^n de^r re^r pair*
landscape	le paysage	*pay-ee-zazh*
lane	le chemin	*she^r -ma^n*
language	la langue	*lah^n g*
large	grand	*grah^n*
last	dernier	*dair-nyay*
late	tard/en retard	*tar/ah^n re^r -tar*
laugh (to)	rire	*reer*
launderette	la laverie automatique	*la-ve^r -ree oh-toh-ma-teek*
lavatory	les toilettes *f*	*twa-let*
lavatory paper	le papier hygiénique	*pap-yay ee-zhee-ay-neek*
law	la loi	*lwa*

lawn	**la pelouse**	*pe' -looz*
lawyer *general*	**l'homme de loi**	*om de' lwa*
lawyer *in court*	**l'avocat**	*a-vo-ka*
lawyer *for wills, sales etc.*	**le notaire**	*no-tair*
lead (to)	**conduire**	*ko^n -dweer*
leaf	**la feuille**	*fœ-y*
leak (to)	**perdre**	*pairdr*
learn (to)	**apprendre**	*a-prah^n dr*
least	**le moins**	*le' mwa^n*
at least	**au moins**	*oh mwa^n*
leather	**le cuir**	*kweer*
leave (to) *abandon*	**quitter**	*kee-tay*
leave (to) *go away*	**partir**	*par-teer*
left *opp. right*	**gauche**	*gosh*
left luggage	**la consigne**	*ko^n -seen-y*
leg	**la jambe**	*zhah^n b*
lend (to)	**prêter**	*pre-tay*
length	**la longueur**	*lo^n -gœr*
less	**moins**	*mwa^n*
lesson	**la leçon**	*le' -so^n*
let (to) *allow*	**laisser/permettre**	*le-say/pair-metr*
let (to) *rent*	**louer**	*loo-ay*
letter	**la lettre**	*letr*

level crossing	**le passage à niveau**	*pa-sazh a nee-voh*
library	**la bibliothèque**	*bee-blyo-tek*
licence	**le permis**	*pair-mee*
life	**la vie**	*vee*
lifebelt	**le gilet de sauvetage**	*zhee-lay de^r sov-tazh*
lifeboat	**le canot de sauvetage**	*ka-no de^r sov-tazh*
lifeguard	**le maître-nageur**	*metr-na-zhœr*
lift	**l'ascenseur** *m*	*a-sah^n-sœr*
light	**la lumière**	*lu^{e}m-yair*
light *colour*	**clair**	*klair*
light *weight*	**léger**	*lay-zhay*
light bulb	**l'ampoule** *f*	*ah^n-pool*
lighthouse	**le phare**	*far*
lightning bolt	**la foudre**	*foodr*
lightning flash	**l'éclair**	*ay-klair*
like (to)	**aimer**	*e-may*
line	**la ligne**	*leen-y*
linen	**le linge**	*la^n zh*
lingerie	**la lingerie**	*la^n zh-ree*
lipsalve	**la pommade pour les lèvres**	*po-mad poor lay levr*
lipstick	**le rouge à lèvres**	*roozh a levr*
liquid *adj*	**liquide**	*lee-keed*

liquid *noun*	**le liquide**	*lee-keed*
listen (to)	**écouter**	*ay-koo-tay*
little *amount*	**peu**	*pe'*
little *size*	**petit**	*pe'-tee*
live (to)	**vivre**	*veevr*
local	**local**	*lo-kal*
lock	**la serrure**	*se-ru'r*
lock (to)	**fermer à clé**	*fair-may a klay*
long	**long/longue**	*lon/lon g*
look (to) *at*	**regarder**	*re'-gar-day*
look (to) *for*	**chercher**	*shair-shay*
look (to) *like*	**ressembler**	*re'-sahn-blay*
loose	**lâche/desserré**	*lash/de-se-ray*
lorry	**le camion**	*ka-myon*
lose (to)	**perdre**	*pairdr*
lost property office	**les objets trouvés** *m*	*ob-zhay troo-vay*
(a) lot	**beaucoup**	*boh-koo*
loud	**bruyant**	*brwee-yahn*
love (to)	**aimer**	*e-may*
lovely	**beau/belle**	*boh/bel*
low	**bas**	*ba*
lucky (to be)	**avoir de la chance**	*a-vwar de' la shahn s*
luggage	**les bagages** *m*	*ba-gazh*
lunch	**le déjeuner**	*day-zhe'-nay*

M

mad	**fou/folle**	*foo/fol*
magazine	**la revue/le magazine**	*re' -vu^e/ma-ga-zeen*
maid	**la domestique**	*do-mes-teek*
mail	**le courrier**	*koor-yay*
main street	**la rue principale**	*ru^e pra^n -see-pal*
make (to)	**faire**	*fair*
make love (to)	**faire l'amour**	*fair la-moor*
make-up	**le maquillage**	*ma-kee-yazh*
male *adj*	**masculin**	*mas-ku^e -la^n*
man	**l'homme** *m*	*om*
manage (to)	**se débrouiller**	*se' day-broo-yay*
manager	**le directeur/le patron**	*dee-rek-tœr/pa-tro^n*
manicure	**le manucure**	*ma-nu^e -ku^e r*
man-made	**artificiel/synthétique**	*ar-tee-fee-syel/sa^n -tay-teek*
many	**beaucoup (de)**	*boh-koo (de')*
map *country*	**la carte**	*kart*
map *town*	**le plan**	*plah^n*
marble	**le marbre**	*marbr*
market	**le marché**	*mar-shay*
market place	**la place du marché**	*plas du^e mar-shay*

married	**marié(e)**	*mar-yay*
marsh	**le marais/** **le marécage**	*ma-re/ma-ray-kazh*
Mass	**la messe**	*mes*
massage	**le massage**	*ma-sazh*
match *light*	**l'allumette** *f*	*a-lu^e -met*
match *sport*	**le match**	*matsh*
material	**le tissue**	*tee-su^e*
matinée	**la matinée**	*ma-tee-nay*
mattress	**le matelas**	*mat-la*
maybe	**peut-être**	*pe^r -tetr*
me	**moi**	*mwa*
meal	**le repas**	*re^r -pa*
mean (to)	**signifier/vouloir dire**	*seen-yee-fyay/* *voo-lwar deer*
measurements	**les mesures** *f*	*me^r -zu^e r*
meet (to)	**rencontrer**	*rah^n -ko^n -tray*
memory stick	**la clé USB**	*klay u^e es bay*
mend (to)	**réparer**	*ray-pa-ray*
menstruation	**la menstruation/** **les règles**	*mah^n s-tru^e a-syo^n /regl*
mess	**le désordre**	*day-zordr*
message	**le message**	*me-sazh*
messenger	**le coursier/** **le commissionnaire**	*koor-syay/* *ko-mee-syo-nair*

metal	**le métal**	*may-tal*
midday	**midi**	*mee-dee*
middle	**le milieu**	*meel-yœ*
middle-aged	**d'âge mûr**	*dazh mu^e r*
middle class *noun*	**la classe moyenne**	*klas mwa-yen*
midnight	**minuit**	*mee-nwee*
mild	**doux**	*doo*
mill	**le moulin**	*moo-la^n*
mine *pronoun*	**le mien/la mienne**	*mya^n/myen*
minute	**la minute**	*mee-nu^e t*
mirror	**le miroir**	*meer-war*
Miss	**Mademoiselle (Mlle)**	*mad-mwa-zel*
miss (to)	**manquer**	*mah^n -kay*
mistake	**l'erreur** *f*	*e-rœr*
mix (to)	**mélanger**	*may-lah^n -zhay*
mixed	**mélangé**	*may-lah^n -zhay*
mobile phone	**le portable**	*por-tabl*
modern	**moderne**	*mo-dairn*
moisturizer	**la crème hydratante**	*krem ee-dra-tah^n t*
moment	**le moment**	*mo-mah^n*
monastery	**le monastère**	*mo-na-stair*
money	**l'argent** *m*	*ar-zhah^n*
monk	**le moine**	*mwan*

month	**le mois**	*mwa*
monument	**le monument**	*mo-nu^e-mah^n*
moon	**la lune**	*lu^{e}n*
moorland	**la lande**	*lah^n d*
moped	**le cyclomoteur**	*see-klo-mo-tœr*
more	**plus/davantage (de)**	*plu^e/dav-ah^n-tazh (de^e)*
morning	**le matin**	*ma-ta^n*
mortgage	**le prêt hypothécaire**	*pre ee-po-tay-kair*
mosque	**la mosquée**	*mos-kay*
mosquito	**le moustique**	*moo-steek*
most	**la plupart**	*plu^e-par*
mother	**la mère**	*mair*
motor bike	**la motocyclette**	*mo-to-see-klet*
motor boat	**le canot à moteur**	*ka-no a mo-tœr*
motor cycle	**la motocyclette**	*mo-to-see-klet*
motor racing	**la course automobile**	*koors oh-toh-moh-beel*
motorway	**l'autoroute** *f*	*oh-toh-root*
mountain	**la montagne**	*mo^n-tan-y*
mouse	**la souris**	*soo-ree*
mouth	**la bouche**	*boosh*
mouthwash	**l'eau dentifrice**	*oh dah^n-tee-frees*
move (to)	**bouger/remuer**	*boo-zhay/re^e-mu^e-ay*
Mr	**Monsieur (M.)**	*me^e-sye^e*

Mrs	**Madame (Mme)**	*ma-dam*
much	**beaucoup (de)**	*boh koo(de')*
museum	**le musée**	*mu^e -zay*
music	**la musique**	*mu^c -zeek*
muslim	**le musulman**	*mu^e -su^e l-mah^n*
must (to have to)	**devoir**	*de^r -vwar*
my	**mon** *m/***ma** *f/***mes** *pl*	*mo^n/ma/may*
myself	**moi-même**	*mwa-mem*

N

nail *carpentry*	**le clou**	*kloo*
nail polish	**le vernis à ongles**	*vair-nee a o^n gl*
nailbrush	**la brosse à ongles**	*bros a o^n gl*
nailfile	**la lime à ongles**	*leem a o^n gl*
name	**le nom**	*no^n*
napkin	**la serviette**	*sair-vyet*
nappy	**la couche**	*koosh*
narrow	**étroit**	*ay-trwa*
natural	**naturel** *m/* **naturelle** *f*	*na-tu^e -rel*
near	**près (de)**	*pre (de')*
nearly	**presque**	*presk*
necessary	**nécessaire**	*nay-se-sair*

necklace	**le collier**	*kol-yay*
need (to)	**avoir besoin (de)**	*a-vwar be' -zwaⁿ (de')*
needle	**l'aiguille** *f*	*eg-wee-y*
nephew	**le neveu**	*ne' -ve'*
net	**le filet**	*fee-lay*
never	**jamais**	*zha-me*
new *brand new*	**neuf/neuve**	*nœf/nœv*
new *fresh, latest*	**nouveau/nouvelle**	*noo-voh/noo-vel*
news	**les nouvelles** *f*	*noo-vel*
newspaper	**le journal**	*zhoor-nal*
New Zealand	**la Nouvelle Zélande**	*noo-vel zay-lahⁿ d*
New Zealander	**néo-zélandais/ néo-zélandaise**	*nay-o-zay-lahⁿ -day (-dez)*
next	**prochain/suivant**	*pro-shaⁿ/swee-vahⁿ*
nice	**gentil**	*zhahⁿ -tee*
niece	**la nièce**	*nyes*
nightclub	**la boîte de nuit**	*bwat de' nwee*
nightdress	**le chemise de nuit**	*she' -meez de' nwee*
no one	**personne**	*pair-son*
nobody	**personne**	*pair-son*
noisy	**bruyant**	*brwee-yahⁿ*
non-alcoholic	**non alcoolisé/sans alcool**	*noⁿ -nal-ko-lee-zay/ sahⁿ -zal-kol*
none	**aucun**	*oh-keⁿ*

normal	**normal**	*nor-mal*
north	**le nord**	*nor*
nosebleed	**le saignement de nez**	*sen-ye^r -mah^n de^r nay*
not	**ne … pas**	*ne^r … pa*
note *moncy*	**le billet**	*bee-vay*
notebook	**le carnet/le cahier**	*kar-nay/ka-yay*
nothing	**rien**	*rya^n*
notice	**l'avis** *m*	*a-vee*
notice (to)	**remarquer**	*re^r -mar-kay*
novel *book*	**le roman**	*ro-mah^n*
now	**maintenant**	*ma^n -te^r -nah^n*
number	**le numéro**	*nu^e -may-ro*
nylon	**le nylon**	*nee-lo^n*

O

obtain (to)	**obtenir**	*ob-te^r -neer*
occasion	**l'occasion** *f*	*o-ka-zyo^n*
occupation	**le métier/ la profession**	*may-tyay/pro-fe-syo^n*
occupied	**occupé**	*o-ku^e -pay*
ocean	**l'océan** *m*	*o-say-ah^n*
odd *opp. even*	**impair**	*a^n -pair*
odd *strange*	**singulier/bizarre**	*sa^n -gu^e -lyay/bee-zar*

of	de	de[r]
of course	naturellement/ bien sûr	na-tu[e] -rel-mah[n]/ bya[n] su[e] r
offer	l'offre f	ofr
offer (to)	offrir	o-freer
office	le bureau	bu[e] -roh
officer	l'officier m	o-fee-syay
official adj	officiel	o-fee-syel
official noun	l'employé/ le fonctionnaire	ah[n] -plwa-yay/ fo[n] k-syo-nair
often	souvent	soo-vah[n]
oily	gras	gra
ointment	la pommade	po-mad
OK	d'accord/entendu	da-kor/ah[n] -tah[n] -du[e]
old	vieuxm/vieille f	vye[r]/vye-y
on	sur	su[e] r
on foot	à pied	a pyay
on time	à l'heure	a lœr
once	une fois	fwa
online	en ligne	ah[n] leen-y
only adj/adv	seul/seulement	sœl/sœl-mah[n]
open (to)	ouvrir	oo-vreer
open air	de plein air	de[r] pla[n] nair
opening	l'ouverture f	oo-vair-tu[e] r

opera	l'opéra *m*	*o-pay-ra*
opportunity	l'occasion *f*	*o-ka-zyo^n*
opposite	en face (de)	*ah^n fas (de')*
optician	l'opticien *m*	*op-lee-sya^n*
or	ou	*oo*
orchard	le verger	*vair-zhay*
orchestra	l'orchestre *m*	*or-kestr*
order (to)	commander	*ko-mah^n -day*
ordinary	ordinaire	*or-dee-nair*
other	autre	*otr*
otherwise	autrement	*oh-tre' -mah^n*
ought	devoir	*de' -vwar*
our	notre sing/nos *pl*	*notr/no*
ours	le/la nôtre	*notr*
out of order	en panne/détraqué	*ah^n pan/day-tra-kay*
out of stock	épuisé	*ay-pwee-zay*
outside	dehors	*de' -or*
over	au-dessus (de)	*oh-de' -su^e (de')*
over *finished*	fini	*fee-nee*
over there	là-bas	*la-ba*
overcoat	le pardessus	*par-de' -su^e*
overnight	pour la nuit	*poor la nwee*
owe (to)	devoir	*de' -vwar*
owner	le/la propriétaire	*pro-pree-ay-tair*

P

pack (to) *luggage*	**faire les bagages**	*fair lay ba-gazh*
pack (to) *parcel*	**emballer**	*ah^n-ba-lay*
packet	**le paquet**	*pa-kay*
paddle	**la pagaie**	*pa-gay*
paddling pool	**la pataugeoire**	*pa-to-zhwar*
page	**la page**	*pazh*
pain	**la douleur**	*doo-lœr*
painkiller	**l'analgésique** *m*	*a-nal-zhay-zeek*
paint (to)	**peindre**	*pa^n dr*
painting	**la peinture**	*pa^n-tu^{e}r*
pair	**la paire**	*pair*
palace	**le palais**	*pa-lay*
pale	**pâle/blême**	*pal/blem*
panties	**le slip**	*sleep*
paper	**le papier**	*pap-yay*
parcel	**le colis/le paquet**	*ko-lee/pa-kay*
park	**le parc**	*park*
park (to)	**stationner**	*sta-syo-nay*
parking disc	**le disque de stationnement**	*deesk de^r sta-syo^n n-mah^n*
parking meter	**la parcomètre**	*parko-metr*

parking ticket	le P.V./la contravention	*pay-vay/ko^n -tra-vah^n -syo^n*
parliament	le parlement	*par-le^r -mah^n*
part	la partie	*par-tee*
party	la réception/ la soirée	*ray-sep-syo^n/swa-ray*
pass (to)	passer	*pa-say*
passenger *train*	le voyageur	*vwa-ya-zhœr*
passenger *sea, air*	le passager	*pa-sa-zhay*
passport	le passeport	*pas-por*
past	(le) passé	*pa-say*
path	le sentier	*sah^n -tyay*
patient	le/la malade	*ma-lad*
pavement	le trottoir	*trot-war*
pay (to)	payer	*pe-yay*
payment	le paiement	*pay-mah^n*
peace	la paix	*pe*
pearl	la perle	*pairl*
pebble	le galet	*ga-lay*
pedal	la pédale	*pay-dal*
pedestrian	le piéton	*pyay-to^n*
pedestrian-crossing	le passage clouté	*pa-sazh kloo-tay*
pedestrian precinct	la zone piétonnière	*zon pyay-to-nyair*
pen	le stylo	*stee-loh*

pencil	**le crayon**	*kre-yoⁿ*
penknife	**le canif**	*ka-neef*
pensioner	**le retraité/la retraitée**	*re^r-tray-tay*
people	**les gens** *m*	*zhahⁿ*
per person	**par personne**	*par pair-son*
perfect	**parfait**	*par-fe*
performance	**la représentation**	*re^r-pray-zahⁿ-ta-syoⁿ*
perfume	**le parfum**	*par-feⁿ*
perhaps	**peut-être**	*pe^r-tetr*
perishable	**périssable**	*pay-ree-sabl*
permit	**le permis**	*pair-mee*
permit (to)	**permettre**	*pair-metr*
person	**la personne**	*pair-son*
personal	**personnel**	*pair-so-nel*
petticoat	**la combinaison**	*koⁿ-bee-nay-zoⁿ*
photograph	**la photographie**	*fo-to-gra-fee*
photographer	**le/la photographe**	*fo-to-graf*
piano	**le piano**	*pya-no*
pick (to) *choose*	**choisir**	*shwa-zeer*
pick (to) *gather*	**cueillir**	*kœ-yeer*
picnic	**le pique-nique**	*peek-neek*
piece	**le morceau**	*mor-soh*
pier	**la jetée**	*zhe^r-tay*

pillow	**l'oreiller** *m*	*o-re-yay*
(safety) pin	**l'épingle** *f* **(de sûreté)**	*ay-pa^n gl (de' -su^e r-tay)*
pipe *to smoke*	**la pipe**	*peep*
pity	**la pitié**	*pee-tyay*
place	**l'endroit** *m*	*ah^n -drwa*
plain	**simple**	*sa^n pl*
plan	**le plan**	*plah^n*
plant	**la plante**	*plah^n t*
plastic	**le plastique**	*plas-teek*
plate	**l'assiette** *f*	*as-yet*
play	**la pièce (de théâtre)**	*pyes (de' tay-atr)*
play (to)	**jouer**	*zhoo-ay*
player	**le joueur**	*zhoo-œr*
please	**s'il vous plaît**	*seel-voo-ple*
pleased	**content**	*ko^n -tah^n*
plenty	**beaucoup (de)**	*boh-koo (de')*
pliers	**les pinces** *f*	*pa^n s*
plug *bath*	**la bonde**	*bo^{n}d*
plug electric	**la prise**	*preez*
pocket	**la poche**	*posh*
point	**le point**	*pwa^n*
poisonous *animal*	**venimeux**	*ve' -nee-mœ*
poisonous *plant*	**vénéneux**	*vay-nay-nœ*
police station	**le poste de police**	*post de' po-lees*

policeman	l'agent de police *m*	a-zhahⁿ de' po-lees
political	**politique**	po-lee-teek
politician	**l'homme/la femme politique** *m*	om/fam po-lee-teek
politics	**la politique**	po-lee-teek
pollution	**la pollution**	po-lu^e -syoⁿ
pond	**l'étang** *m*	ay-tahⁿ
poor	**pauvre**	povr
pope	**le pape**	pap
popular	**populaire**	po-pu^e -lair
porcelain	**la porcelaine**	por-se' -len
port	**le port**	por
possible	**possible**	po-seebl
post (to)	**mettre à la poste**	metr a la post
post box	**la boîte aux lettres**	bwat oh letr
post office	**le bureau de poste**	bu^e -roh de' post
postcard	**la carte postale**	kart pos-tal
postman	**le facteur**	fak-tœr
postpone (to)	**reporter/remettre**	re' -por-tay/re' -metr
pound	**la livre**	leevr
powder	**la poudre**	poodr
prefer (to)	**préférer**	pray-fay-ray
pregnant	**enceinte**	ahⁿ -sahⁿ t
prepare (to)	**préparer**	pray-pa-ray

present *gift*	**le cadeau**	*ka-doh*
president	**le président/ la présidente**	*pray-zee-dah^n (-dah^n t)*
press (to)	**repasser**	*re^r -pa-say*
pretty	**joli**	*zho-lee*
price	**le prix**	*pree*
priest	**le prêtre/le curé**	*pretr/ku^e -ray*
prime minister	**le premier ministre**	*pre^r -myay mee-neestr*
print	**l'estampe**	*es-tah^n p*
print *photo*	**l'épreuve**	*ay-prœv*
print (to)	**imprimer**	*a^n -pree-may*
print (to) *photo*	**tirer**	*tee-ray*
private	**privé**	*pree-vay*
problem	**le problème**	*pro-blem*
profession	**la profession**	*pro-fes-yo^n*
programme	**le programme**	*pro-gram*
promise	**la promesse**	*pro-mes*
promise (to)	**promettre**	*pro-metr*
prompt	**prompt**	*pro^n*
protestant	**protestant**	*pro-tes-tah^n*
provide (to)	**fournir**	*foor-neer*
public	**public**	*pu^e -bleek*
public holiday	**le jour férié**	*zhoor fay-ryay*
pull (to)	**tirer**	*tee-ray*

pump	la pompe	po^n p
pure	pur	pu^e r
purse	le porte-monnaie	port mo-nay
push (to)	pousser	poo-say
put (to)	mettre	metr
pyjamas	le pyjama	pee-zha-ma

Q

quality	la qualité	ka-lee-tay
quantity	la quantité	kah^n -tee-tay
quarter	la quart	kar
queen	la reine	ren
question	la question	$kes-tyo^n$
queue	la file/la queue	feel/ke^r
queue (to)	faire la queue	fair la ke^r
quick(ly)	rapide(ment)	ra-peed(-mah^n)
quiet	tranquille	$trah^n$ -keel
quite	tout à fait	too-ta-fe

R

racecourse	l'hippodrome m	ee-po-drom
races	les courses f	koors
radiator	le radiateur	ra-dya-tœr

radio	**la radio**	*ra-dyo*
railway	**le chemin de fer**	*she^r -maⁿ de^r fair*
rain	**la pluie**	*plwee*
rain (to)	**pleuvoir**	*plœ-vwar*
rainbow	**l'arc-en-ciel** *m*	*ark-ah-syel*
raincoat	**l'imperméable** *m*	*aⁿ -pair-may-abl*
rare	**rare**	*rar*
rate	**le taux**	*toh*
rather	**plutôt**	*plu^e -toh*
raw	**cru**	*cru^e*
razor	**le rasoir**	*ra-zwar*
razor blade	**la lame de rasoir**	*lam de^r ra-zwar*
reach (to)	**atteindre**	*a-taⁿ dr*
read (to)	**lire**	*leer*
ready	**prêt**	*pre*
real	**vrai**	*vre*
really	**vraiment**	*vre-mahⁿ*
reason	**la raison**	*re-zoⁿ*
receipt	**la reçu/la quittance**	*re^r -su^e/kee-tahⁿ s*
receive (to)	**recevoir**	*re^r -se^r -vwar*
recent	**récent**	*ray-sahⁿ*
recipe	**la recette**	*re^r -set*
recognize (to)	**reconnaître**	*re^r -ko-netr*

recommend (to)	**recommander**	*re′ -ko-mah^n -day*
record *sport*	**le record**	*re′ -kor*
refill	**la recharge**	*re′ -sharzh*
refrigerator	**le réfrigérateur**	*ray-free-zhay-ra-tœr*
refund	**le remboursement**	*rah^n -boor-se′ -mah^n*
regards	**les compliments** *m/* **les amitiés** *f*	*ko^n -plee-mah^n/ a-mee-tyay*
register (to)	**enregistrer**	*ah^n -re′ -zhees-tray*
register (to) *letter*	**recommander**	*re′ -ko-mah^n -day*
relatives	**les parents**	*pa-rah^n*
religion	**la religion**	*re′ -lee-zhyo^n*
remember (to)	**se souvenir (de)**	*se′ soov-neer (de′)*
rent	**le loyer**	*lwa-yay*
rent (to)	**louer**	*loo-ay*
repair (to)	**réparer**	*ray-pa-ray*
repeat (to)	**répéter**	*ray-pay-tay*
reply (to)	**répondre**	*ray-po^n dr*
reservation	**la réservation**	*ray-zair-va-syo^n*
reserve (to)	**réserver**	*ray-zair-vay*
restaurant	**le restaurant**	*res-to-rah^n*
return (to) *come back*	**revenir**	*re′ v-neer*
return (to) *give back*	**rendre**	*rah^n dr*
return (to) *go back*	**retourner**	*re′ -toor-nay*
reward	**la récompense**	*ray-ko^n -pah^n s*

ribbon	le ruban	ru ^{e} -bah^n
rich	riche	reesh
ride	la promenade	prom-nad
ride (to) *horse*	monter à cheval	mo^n -tay a she^r -val
right *opp. left*	droite	drwul
right *opp. wrong*	juste	zhu^e st
right (to be)	avoir raison	a-vwar re-zo^n
ring	la bague	bag
ripe	mûr	mu^{e}r
rise (to)	se lever	se^r le^r -vay
river	le fleuve/la rivière	flœv/reev-yair
road *between towns*	la route	root
road *within towns*	la rue	ru^e
road map	la carte routière	kart roo-tyair
road sign	le panneau de signalisation	pa-no hde^r seen-ya-lee-za-syo^n
road works	les travaux *m*	tra-vo
rock	le rocher	ro-shay
roll (to)	rouler	roo-lay
roof	le toit	twa
room	la chambre	shah^n br
rope	la corde	kord
rotten	pourri	poo-ree
rough *material, skin*	rêche	resh

round	**rond**	*ron*
rowing boat	**le bateau à rames**	*ba-toh a ram*
rubber	**caoutchouc**	*ka-oo-tshoo*
rubbish	**les ordures** *f*	*or-du[e] r*
rude	**grossier**	*groh-syay*
ruin	**la ruine**	*rween*
rule (to)	**gouverner**	*goo-vair-nay*
run (to)	**courir**	*koo-reer*

S

sad	**triste**	*treest*
saddle	**la selle**	*sel*
safe *secure*	**en sûreté**	*ah[n] su[e] r-tay*
safe *unharmed*	**sauf**	*sof*
sail	**la voile**	*vwal*
sailing boat	**le voilier**	*vwal-yay*
sailor	**le marin**	*ma-ra[n]*
sale *clearance*	**les soldes** *m*	*sold*
(for) sale	**à vendre**	*a vah[n] dr*
salesman/woman	**le vendeur/ la vendeuse**	*vah[n] -dœr/vah [n] -dœz*
salt	**le sel**	*sel*
salt water	**l'eau salée** *f*	*oh sa-lay*

same	le/la même	mem
sand	le sable	sabl
sandal	la sandale	sah^n -dal
sanitary towel	la serviette hygiénique	sair-vyet ee-zhyay-neek
satisfactory	satisfaisant	sa-tees-fe' -zah^n
saucer	la soucoupe	soo-koop
save (to)	économiser	ay-ko-no-mee-zay
save (to) *rescue*	sauver	so-vay
say (to)	dire	deer
scald oneself (to)	s'ébouillanter	say-boo-yah^n -tay
scarf	le foulard	foo-lar
scenery	le paysage	pay-ee-zazh
scent	le parfum	par-fe^n
school	l'école *f*	ay-kol
scissors	les ciseaux	see-zoh
Scotland	l'Écosse *f*	ay-kos
Scottish	écossais/écossaise	ay-ko-se (-sez)
scratch (to)	égratigner	ay-gra-teen-yay
screw	la vis	vees
sculpture	la sculpture	sku^e l-tu^e r
sea	la mer	mair
sea food	les fruits de mer *m*	frwee de' mair
seasickness	le mal de mer	mal de' mair

season	**la saison**	*se-zo^n*
seat	**la place**	*plas*
seat belt	**la ceinture de sécurité**	*sa^n -tu^e r de^e say-ku^e -ree-tay*
second	**deuxième**	*de^r -zyem*
second-hand	**d'occasion**	*do-ka-zyo^n*
see (to)	**voir**	*vwar*
seem (to)	**sembler**	*sah^n -blay*
self-contained (flat)	**indépendant**	*a^n -day-pay^n -dah^n*
sell (to)	**vendre**	*vah^n -dr*
send (to)	**envoyer**	*ah^n -vwa-yay*
separate(ly)	**séparé(ment)**	*say-pa-ray (-mah^n)*
serious	**sérieux**	*sayr-ye^r*
serve (to)	**servir**	*sair-veer*
served	**servi**	*sair-vee*
service (charge)	**le service**	*sair-vees*
service *church*	**l'office** *m*	*o-fees*
several	**plusieurs**	*plu^e -zyœr*
sew (to)	**coudre**	*koodr*
shade *colour*	**la teinte**	*ta^n t*
shade/shadow	**l'ombre** *f*	*o^n br*
shallow	**peu profond**	*pe^e pro-fo^n*
shampoo	**le shampooing**	*shah^n -pwa^n*
shape	**la forme**	*form*

share (to)	**partager**	*par-ta-zhay*
sharp	**aigu/pointu**	*egu^e/pwa^n -tu^e*
shave (to)	**se raser**	*se^r ra-zay*
shaving brush	**le blaireau**	*ble-roh*
shaving cream	**la crème à raser**	*krem a ra-zay*
shaving foam	**la mousse à raser**	*moos a ra-zay*
she	**elle**	*el*
sheet	**le drap**	*dra*
shelf	**l'étagère *f*/le rayon**	*ay-ta-zhair/ray-yo^n*
shell	**le coquillage**	*ko-kee-yazh*
shelter	**l'abri *m***	*a-bree*
shine (to)	**briller**	*bree-yay*
shingle	**le galet**	*ga-lay*
ship	**le bateau**	*ba-toh*
shipping line	**la compagnie de navigation**	*ko^n -pan-yee de^r na-vee-ga-syo^n*
shirt	**la chemise**	*she^r -meez*
shock	**le choc**	*shok*
shoe	**le soulier/la chaussure**	*soo-lyay/sho-su^e r*
shoe polish	**le cirage**	*see-razh*
shoelace	**le lacet (de soulier)**	*la-say (de^r soo-ly ay)*
shop	**le magasin**	*ma-ga-za^n*
shopping centre	**le centre commercial**	*sah^n tr ko-mair-syal*

shore	la côte/le rivage	*kot/ree-vazh*
short	**court**	*koor*
shortly	**bientôt**	*bya^n -toh*
shorts	**le short**	*short*
shoulder	**l'épaule** *f*	*ay-pol*
show *theatre*	**le spectacle**	*spek-takl*
show (to)	**montrer**	*mo^n -tray*
shower	**la douche**	*doosh*
shut (to)	**fermer**	*fair-may*
side	**le côté**	*ko-tay*
sights	**les monuments** *m*/ **les curiosités** *f*	*mo-nu^e -mah^n/ku^e r-yo-zee-tay*
sightseeing	**le tourisme**	*too-reesm*
sightseeing (to go)	**visiter les monuments**	*vee-zee-tay lay mo-nu^e -mah^n*
sign	**le signe**	*seen-y*
sign (to)	**signer**	*seen-yay*
signpost	**le panneau indicateur**	*pa-noh a^n -dee-ka-tœr*
silver	**l'argent** *m*	*ar-zhah^n*
simple	**simple**	*sa^n pl*
since	**depuis**	*de^r -pwee*
sing (to)	**chanter**	*shah^n -tay*
single	**seul**	*sœl*

single room	la chambre pour une personne	*shah[n] br poor u[e] n pair-son*
sister	la sœur	*sœr*
sit down (to)	s'asseoir	*sa-swar*
sitting	assis	*asee*
size	la grandeur/la taille	*grah[n]-dœr/ta-y*
skate (to)	patiner	*pa-tee-nay*
skating	le patinage	*pa-tee-nazh*
ski (to)	skier	*skee-ay*
skid (to)	déraper	*day-rap-ay*
skiing	le ski	*skee*
skirt	la jupe	*zhu[e] p*
sky	le ciel	*sy-el*
sleep (to)	dormir	*dor-meer*
sleeper	le wagon-lit	*va-go[n] lee*
sleeping bag	le sac de couchage	*sak de[r] koo-shazh*
sleeve	la manche	*mah[n] sh*
slice	la tranche	*trah[n] sh*
slip	la combinaison	*ko[n]-bee-ne-zo[n]*
slipper	la pantoufle	*pah[n]-toofl*
slow(ly)	lent(ement)	*lah[n] (-te[r]-mah[n])*
small	petit	*pe[r]-tee*
smart	chic	*sheek*
smell	l'odeur *f*	*o-dœr*

smell (to)	**sentir**	*sah^n -teer*
smile (to)	**sourire**	*soo-reer*
smoke (to)	**fumer**	*fu^e -may*
(no) smoking	**défense de fumer**	*day-fah^n s de' fu^e -may*
snack	**le casse-croûte**	*kas-kroot*
snorkel	**le tuba**	*tu^e -ba*
snow	**la neige**	*nezh*
snow (to)	**neiger**	*ne-zhay*
so	**si**	*see*
soap	**le savon**	*sa-vo^n*
soap flakes	**le savon en paillettes**	*sa-vo^n ah^n pa-yet*
soap powder	**la lessive**	*le-seev*
sober	**pas ivre**	*pa-zeevr*
sock	**la chaussette**	*sho-set*
socket *elec*	**la prise**	*preez*
soft	**mou** *m*/**molle** *f,* **dou** *m*/**douce** *f*	*moo/mol, doo/doos*
sold	**vendu**	*vah^n -du^e*
sold out	**épuisé**	*ay-pwee-zay*
sole *shoe*	**la semelle**	*se^r -mel*
solid	**solide**	*so-leed*
some	**quelque**	*kel-ke^r*
somebody	**quelqu'un**	*kel-ke^n*
something	**quelque chose**	*kel-ke^r -shoz*

sometimes	**quelquefois**	*kel-ke^r -fwa*
somewhere	**quelque part**	*kel-ke^r par*
son	**le fils**	*fees*
song	**la chanson**	*shah^n -so^n*
soon	**bientôt**	*bya^n -toh*
sort	**l'espèce** *f*	*es-pes*
sound	**le bruit/le son**	*brwee/so^n*
sound and light show	**le spectacle son et lumière**	*spek-takl so^n ay lu^e -myair*
sour	**aigre**	*egr*
south	**le sud**	*su^e d*
souvenir	**le souvenir**	*soov-neer*
space	**l'espace** *m*	*es-pas*
spanner	**la clé**	*klay*
spare	**de réserve/ de rechange**	*de^r ray-zairv/de^r re^r -shah^n zh*
speak (to)	**parler**	*par-lay*
speciality	**la spécialité**	*spay-sya-lee-tay*
spectacles	**les lunettes** *f*	*lu^e -net*
speed	**la vitesse**	*vee-tes*
speed limit	**la limitation de vitesse**	*lee-mee-ta-syo^n de^r vee-tes*
spend (to) *money*	**dépenser**	*day-pah^n -say*
spend (to) *time*	**passer**	*pa-say*

spice	l'épice f	ay-pees
spoon	la cuiller	kwee-yair
sport	le sport	spor
sprain (to)	se fouler	se' foo-lay
spring	le printemps	pra^n -tah^n
spring *water*	la source	soors
square *adj*	carré	ka-ray
square *in town*	la place	plas
stables	les écuries	ay-ku^e -ree
stage	la scène	sen
stain	la tache	tash
stained	taché	ta-shay
stairs	l'escalier *m*	es-ka-lyay
stalls	les fauteuils d'orchestre *m*	foh-tœ-y dor-kestr
stamp	le timbre	ta^n br
stand (to)	se tenir debout	se' te' -neer de' -boo
star	l'étoile f	ay-twal
start (to)	commencer	ko-mah^n -say
statue	la statue	sta-tu^e
stay (to)	rester	res-tay
step	le pas	pa
steward *airline*	le steward	styoo-ward

steward *ship*	le garçon de cabine	*gar-so^n de^r ka-been*
stewardess	l'hôtesse *f*	*o-tes*
stick	le bâton	*ba-to^n*
stiff	dur/raide	*du^e r/red*
still *not moving*	immobile	*ee-mo-beel*
still *time*	toujours/encore	*too-zhoor/ah^n -kor*
sting	la piqûre	*pee-ku^e r*
sting (to) *insect*	priquer	*pee-kay*
stolen	volé	*vo-lay*
stone	la pierre	*pyair*
stool	le tabouret	*ta-boo-ray*
stop (to)	s'arrêter	*sa-re-tay*
store	le magasin	*ma-ga-za^n*
storm	l'orage *m/* la tempête	*o-razh/tah^n -pet*
stove	le réchaud	*ray-shoh*
straight	droit	*drwa*
straight on	tout droit	*too drwa*
strange	étrange	*ay-trah^n zh*
strap	la courroie	*koor-wa*
stream	le ruisseau	*rwee-soh*
street	la rue	*ru^e*
street map	le plan des rues	*plah^n day ru^e*
stretch (to)	tendre/s'étendre	*tah^n dr/say-tah^n dr*

string	la ficelle	*fee-sel*
strong	fort	*for*
student	l'étudiant(e)	*ay-tu^e -dyah^n(t)*
stung (to be)	être piqué	*etr pee-kay*
style	le style	*steel*
subject	le sujet	*su^e -zhay*
suburb	la banlieue	*bah^n -lye^r*
subway	le passage souterrain	*pa-sazh soo-te-ra^n*
such	tel/pareil	*tel/pa-re-y*
suddenly	soudain/tout à coup	*soo-da^n/too-ta-koo*
suede	le daim	*da^n*
suggestion	la suggestion	*su^e -zhes-tyo^n*
suit *men*	le costume	*kos-tu^e m*
suit *women*	le tailleur	*ta-yœr*
suitcase	la valise	*va-leez*
summer	l'été *m*	*ay-tay*
sun	le soleil	*so-le-y*
sunbathe (to)	se bronzer/prendre un bain de soleil	*se^r broh^n -ay/prah^{n}dr e^n ba^n de^r so-le-y*
sunburn	le coup de soleil	*koo de^r so-le-y*
suncream	la crème solaire	*krem so-lair*
sunglasses	les lunettes de soleil *f*	*lu^e -net de^r so-le-y*
sunhat	le chapeau de soleil	*sha-poh de^e so-le-y*

sunny	**ensoleillé**	*ahⁿ-so-le-yay*
sunshade	**l'ombrelle** *f*	*om-brel*
supermarket	**le supermarché**	*suᵉ-pair-mar-shay*
supper	**le souper**	*soo-pay*
sure	**sûr**	*suᵉr*
surfboard	**la planche (de surf)**	*plahⁿsh (deᵉ surf)*
surgery/surgery hours	**le cabinet/ les heures de consultation**	*ka-bee-nay/ œr deᵉ koⁿ-suᵉ l-ta-syoⁿ*
surprise	**la surprise**	*suᵉr-preez*
surprise (to)	**surprendre**	*suᵉr-prahⁿdr*
surroundings	**les environs**	*ahⁿ-vee-roⁿ*
sweat	**la sueur**	*suᵉ-œr*
sweater	**le sweater**	*swe-tair*
sweet	**le bonbon**	*boⁿ-boⁿ*
sweet *adj*	**sucré**	*suᵉ-kray*
swell (to)	**enfler**	*ahⁿ-flay*
swim (to)	**nager**	*na-zhay*
swimming pool	**la piscine**	*pee-seen*
swings	**les balançoires** *f*	*ba-lahⁿ-swar*
Swiss	**suisse**	*swees*
switch *light*	**l'interrupteur** *m*	*aⁿ-tah-ruᵉp-tær*
Switzerland	**la Suisse**	*swees*
synagogue	**la synagogue**	*see-na-gog*

T

table	**la table**	*tabl*
tablecloth	**la nappe**	*nap*
tablet	**le comprimé**	*ko^n -pree-may*
tailor	**le tailleur**	*ta-yœr*
take (to)	**prendre**	*prah^n dr*
talk (to)	**parler**	*par-lav*
tall	**grand**	*grah^n*
tampon	**le tampon**	*tah^n -po^n*
tank	**le réservoir**	*ray-zair-vwar*
tanned	**bronzé**	*bro^n -zay*
tap	**le robinet**	*ro-bee-nay*
tapestry	**la tapisserie**	*ta-pees-ree*
taste	**le goût**	*goo*
taste (to)	**goûter**	*goo-tay*
tax	**la taxe/l'impôt** *m*	*taks/a^n -po*
taxi	**le taxi**	*tak-see*
taxi rank	**la station de taxis**	*sta-syo^n de^r tak-see*
teach (to)	**enseigner**	*ah^r -sen-yay*
tear	**la déchirure**	*day-shee-ru^{e}r*
tear (to)	**déchirer**	*day-shee-ray*
telephone	**le téléphone**	*tay-lay-fon*
telephone (to)	**le téléphoner**	*tay-lay-fo-nay*

telephone call	**le coup de téléphone**	*koo deʲ tay-lay-fon*
telephone directory	**l'annuaire** *m*	*a-nuᵉ -air*
telephone number	**le numéro de téléphone**	*nuᵉ -may-roh deʳ tay-lay-fon*
telephone operator	**le/la standardiste**	*stahⁿ -dar-deest*
television	**la télévision**	*tay-lay-vee-zyoⁿ*
tell (to)	**dire**	*deer*
temperature	**la température**	*tahⁿ -pay-ra-tuᵉ r*
temple	**le temple**	*tahⁿ pl*
temporary	**temporaire**	*tahⁿ -po-rair*
tennis	**le tennis**	*te-nees*
tent	**la tente**	*tahⁿ t*
tent peg	**le piquet (de tente)**	*pee-kay (deʳ tahⁿ t)*
tent pole	**le montant (de tente)**	*moⁿ -tahⁿ (deʳ tahⁿ t)*
terrace	**la terrasse**	*te-ras*
text message	**le texto**	*teks-toh*
than	**que**	*keʳ*
that	**cela**	*seʳ -la*
the	**le/la/les**	*leʳ /la/lay*
theatre	**le théâtre**	*tay-atr*
their(s)	**leur(s)**	*lær*
them	**les/leur/eux/elles**	*lay/lær/eʲ /el*
then	**alors**	*alor*

there	là	*la*
there is/are	il y a	*eel-ya*
thermometer	le thermomètre	*tair-mo-metr*
these	ces	*say*
they	ils/elles	*eel/el*
thick	épais	*ay-pe*
thief	le voleur	*vo-lœr*
thin	mince	*ma^{n}s*
thing	la chose	*shoz*
think (to)	penser	*pah^n-say*
thirsty (to be)	avoir soif	*a-vwar swaf*
this	ce/cet/cette	*se^r/set/set*
those	ces	*say*
though	quoique	*kwa-ke^r*
thread	le fil	*feel*
through	á travers/par	*a tra-vair/par*
throw (to)	lancer/jeter	*lah^n-say/zhe^r-tay*
thunder	le tonnerre	*to-nair*
thunderstorm	l'orage *m*	*o-razh*
ticket	le billet	*bee-yay*
ticket office	le bureau de vente des billets/le guichet	*bu^e-roh de^r vah^{n}t day bee-yay/ghee-shay*
tide	la marée	*ma-ray*
tie	la cravate	*kra-vat*

tie *sport*	le match nul	*matsh nu^e l*
tight	serré	*se-ray*
tights	les collants	*kò-lahⁿ*
time	le temps/l'heure *f*	*tahⁿ/œr*
timetable	l'horaire *m*	*o-rair*
tin	la boîte	*bwat*
tin opener	l'ouvre-boîte *m*	*oovr bwat*
tip	le pourboire	*poor-bwar*
tired (to be)	(être) fatigué	*(etr) fa-tee-gay*
to	à/pour	*a/poor*
tobacco	le tabac	*ta-ba*
together	ensemble	*ahⁿ -sahⁿ bl*
toilet	les toilettes	*twa-let*
toilet paper	le papier hygiénique	*pap-yay ee-zhyay-neek*
toll	le péage	*pay-azh*
tomorrow	demain	*de^r -maⁿ*
tongue	la langue	*lahⁿ g*
too also	aussi	*oh-see*
too much/many	trop (de)	*troh (de^r)*
toothbrush	la brosse à dents	*bros a dahⁿ*
toothpaste	le dentifrice	*dahⁿ -tee-frees*
toothpick	le cure-dents	*ku^e r-dahⁿ*
top	le sommet	*som-may*

torch	**la lampe (de poche)**	*lah^n p (de^r posh)*
torn	**déchiré**	*day-shee-ray*
touch (to)	**toucher**	*too-shay*
tough	**dur**	*de^e r*
tour	**le tour/la visite**	*toor/vee-zeet*
tourist	**le/la touriste**	*too-reest*
tourist office	**le syndicat d'initiative/ le bureau de tourisme**	*sa^n-dee-ka dee -nee -sya -teev/bu-roh de^r too-reezm*
towards	**vers**	*vair*
towel	**la serviette**	*sair-vyet*
tower	**la tour**	*toor*
town	**la ville**	*veel*
town hall	**l'hôtel de ville** *m*	*o-tel de^r veel*
toy	**le jouet**	*zhoo-ay*
traffic	**la circulation**	*seer-ku^e -la-syo^n*
traffic jam	**l'embouteillage** *m*	*ah^n -boo te-yazh*
traffic lights	**les feux** *m*	*fe^r*
trailer	**la remorque**	*re^r -mork*
train	**le train**	*tra^n*
trainers	**les baskets** *fpl*	*ba-sket*
tram	**le tram**	*tram*
transfer (to)	**changer**	*shah^n -zhay*

transit	**le transit**	*trah^n -zeet*
translate (to)	**traduire**	*tra-dweer*
travel (to)	**voyager**	*vwa-ya-zhay*
travel agency	**l'agence de voyages** *f*	*a-zhah^n s de^r vwa-yazh*
traveller's cheque	**le chèque de voyage**	*shek de^r vwa-yazh*
treat (to)	**traiter**	*tre-tay*
treatment	**le traitement**	*tret-mah^n*
tree	**l'arbre** *m*	*arbr*
trip	**l'excursion** *f*	*ek-sku^e r-syo^n*
trouble	**les ennuis** *m*	*ah^n -nwee*
trousers	**le pantalon**	*pah^n -ta-lo^n*
true	**vrai**	*vre*
trunk *luggage*	**la malle**	*mal*
trunks	**le caleçon**	*kal-so^n*
truth	**la vérité**	*vay-ree-tay*
try, try on (to)	**essayer**	*esay-yay*
tunnel	**le tunnel**	*tu^e -nel*
turn (to)	**tourner**	*toor-nay*
turning	**le tournant**	*toor-nah^n*
tweezers	**les pinces (à épiler)** *f*	*pa^n s (a ay-pee-lay)*
twin beds	**les lits jumeaux** *m*	*lee zhu^e -moh*
twisted	**tordu**	*tor-du^e*

U

ugly	**laid**	*le*
UK	**le Royaume-Uni**	*rwa-yom u^e-nee*
umbrella	**le parapluie**	*para-plwee*
(beach) umbrella	**le parasol**	*para-sol*
uncle	**l'oncle** *m*	*o^n kl*
uncomfortable	**mal à l'aise**	*mal a-lez*
unconscious	**sans connaissance**	*sah^n ko-ne-sah^{n}s*
under	**sous**	*soo*
underground	**le métro**	*may-tro*
underneath	**sous**	*soo*
underpants	**le slip**	*sleep*
understand	**comprendre**	*ko^n -prah^n dr*
underwater fishing	**la pêche sous-marine**	*pesh soo ma-reen*
underwear	**les sous-vêtements** *m*	*soo vet-mah^n*
university	**l'université** *f*	*u^e -nee-vair-see-tay*
unpack (to)	**défaire les bagages**	*day-fair lay ba-gazh*
until	**jusqu'à**	*zhu^e s-ka*
unusual	**peu commun**	*pe^r ko-me^n*
up (stairs)	**en haut**	*ah^n -oh*
urgent	**urgent**	*u^e r-zhah^n*
us	**nous**	*noo*
USA	**les États-Unis**	*ay-ta-zu^e -nee*

use (to)	**utiliser/se servir (de)**	*u^e -tee-lee-zay/*
		se^r sair-veer
useful	**utile**	*u^e -teel*
useless	**inutile**	*ee-nu^e -teel*
usual	**habituel/ordinaire**	*a-bee-tu^e -el/or-dee-nair*

V

vacancies	**chambres libres** *f*	*shahⁿ br leebr*
vacant	**libre**	*leebr*
vacation	**les vacances** *f*	*va-kahⁿ s*
valid	**valable**	*va-labl*
valley	**la vallée**	*va-lay*
valuable	**précieux**	*pray-sye^r*
value	**la valeur**	*va-lœr*
vase	**le vase**	*vaz*
VAT	**la TVA**	*tay-vay-a*
vegetable	**le légume**	*lay-gu^e m*
vegetarian	**végétarien**	*vay-zhay-ta-ryaⁿ*
vein	**la veine**	*ven*
ventilation	**l'aération**	*a-ay-ra-syoⁿ*
very	**très**	*tre*
very little	**très peu**	*tre pe^r*
very much	**beaucoup**	*bh-koo*

vest	**le maillot**	*ma-yo*
view	**la vue**	*vu^e*
villa	**la villa**	*vee-la*
village	**le village**	*vee-lazh*
vineyard	**la vigne/le vignoble**	*veen-y/veen-yobl*
violin	**le violon**	*vyo-lo^n*
visa	**le visa**	*vee-za*
visibility	**la visibilité**	*vee-zee-bee-lee-tay*
visit	**la visite**	*vee-zeet*
visit (to) *place*	**visiter**	*vee-zee-tay*
voice	**la voix**	*vwa*
voltage	**le voltage**	*vol-tazh*
voucher	**le bon**	*bo^n*

W

wait (to)	**attendre**	*a-tah^n dr*
waiter	**le garçon**	*gar-so^n*
waiting room	**la salle d'attente**	*sal da-tah^n t*
waitress	**la serveuse**	*sair-vœz*
wake (to)	**se réveiller**	*se^r ray-ve-yay*
Wales	**le Pays de Galles**	*pay-ee de^r gal*
walk	**la promenade**	*prom-nad*
walk (to)	**marcher/se promener**	*mar-shay/se^r prom-nay*

wall	**le mur**	*mu^e r*
wallet	**le portefeuille**	*port-fœ-y*
want (to)	**vouloir/avoir besoin (de)**	*voo-lwar/avwar be^r -zwa^n*
wardrobe	**l'armoire** *f*	*ar-mwar*
warm	**chaud**	*sho*
wash (to)	**laver**	*la-vay*
washbasin	**le lavabo**	*la-va-bo*
waste	**le gaspillage**	*gas-pee-yazh*
waste (to)	**gaspiller**	*gas-pee-yay*
watch	**la montre**	*mo^n tr*
water (fresh/salt)	**l'eau** *f* **(douce/salée)**	*oh (doos/sa-lay)*
water ski(-ing)	**le ski nautique**	*skee no-teek*
waterfall	**la chute d'eau**	*shu^e t doh*
waterproof	**imperméable**	*a^n -pair-may-abl*
wave *sea*	**la vague**	*vag*
way	**le chemin**	*she^r -ma^n*
we	**nous**	*noo*
wear (to)	**porter**	*por-tay*
weather	**le temps**	*tah^n*
weather forecast	**la météo, les prévisions météorologiques**	*may-tay-oh, pray-vee-zyo^n may-tay-o-ro-lo-zheek*
wedding ring	**l'alliance** *f*	*a-lyah^n s*

week	la semaine	*se'-men*
weigh (to)	peser	*pe'-say*
weight	le poids	*pwa*
welcome	bienvenu(e)(s)	*byaⁿ-ve'-nuᵉ*
well	bien	*byaⁿ*
well *water*	le puits	*pwee*
Welsh	gallois/galloise	*gal-wa (-waz)*
west	l'ouest *m*	*oo-est*
wet	mouillé	*moo-yay*
what?	quoi? quelle(s)/ quelle(s)?	*kwa/kel*
wheel	la roue	*roo*
wheelchair	le fauteuil roulant	*fo-tœ-y roo-lahⁿ*
when?	quand?	*kahⁿ*
where?	où?	*oo*
whether	si	*see*
which?	quel(s)/quelle(s)?	*kel*
while	pendant que	*pahⁿ-dahⁿ ke'*
who?	qui?	*kee*
(the) whole	le tout	*too*
whose?	à qui?	*a kee*
why?	pourquoi?	*poor-kwa*
wide	large	*larzh*
widow	la veuve	*vœv*

widower	**le veuf**	*vœf*
wife	**la femme**	*fam*
wild	**sauvage**	*so-vazh*
win (to)	**gagner**	*gan-yay*
wind	**le vent**	*vah^n*
window	**la fenêtre**	*fe' -netr*
wine merchant	**le marchand de vin**	*mar-shah^n de' va^n*
wing	**l'aile** *f*	*el*
winter	**l'hiver** *m*	*ee-vair*
winter sports	**les sports d'hiver**	*spor dee-vair*
wire	**le fil de fer**	*feel de' fer*
wish (to)	**souhaiter**	*swe-tay*
with	**avec**	*a-vek*
within	**dans/à l'intérieur**	*dah^n/a-la^n -tay-ryœr*
without	**sans**	*sah^n*
woman	**la femme**	*fam*
wonderful	**merveilleux** *m/* **merveilleuse** *f*	*mer-ve-ye' (-yœz)*
wood	**le bois**	*bwa*
word	**le mot**	*mo*
work	**le travail**	*tra-va-y*
work (to)	**travailler**	*tra-va-yay*
worry (to)	**s'inquiéter**	*sa^n -kye-tay*
worse	**pire**	*peer*

worth (to be)	**valoir**	*va-lwar*
wrap (to)	**envelopper**	*ah^n -vlo-pay*
write (to)	**écrire**	*ay-kreer*
writing paper	**le papier à lettre**	*pap-yay a letr*
wrong	**mauvais/incorrect**	*mo-ve/a^n -ko-rekt*
wrong (to be)	**avoir tort**	*a-vwar tor*

Y

yacht	**le yacht/le bateau à voile**	*yot/ba-toh a vwal*
year	**l'an** *m*/**l'année** *f*	*ah^n/a-nay*
yesterday	**hier**	*yair*
yet	**encore**	*ah^n -kor*
yet *nevertheless*	**pourtant**	*poor-tah^n*
you	**vous**	*voo*
young	**jeune**	*zhœn*
your	**votre** *sing*/**vos** *pl*	*votr/vo*
yours	**le/la/les vôtre(s)**	*vohtr*
youth hostel	**l'auberge de jeunesse** *f*	*o-bairzh de' zhœ-nes*

Z

zip	**la fermeture éclair**	*fair-me' -tu^e r ay-klair*
zoo	**le zoo**	*zo-oh*

INDEX